"An urgent call to Christian activism which also gives sound and
practical solutions to the pressing issues of the day. **Whether you agree
or disagree, this book is absolutely crucial reading.**"

*John W. Whitehead, author of THE STEALING
OF AMERICA*

"Franky Schaeffer is an author who holds his readers to the issues, even
when it might be more comfortable to be diverted. **Every Christian who
takes his faith seriously needs to face up to the issues raised in BAD
NEWS FOR MODERN MAN.**"

*Dr. Homer A. Kent, President, Grace Seminary and College
Winona Lake, Indiana*

"Franky Schaeffer has uncovered and identified a number of disturbing
trends within evangelical Protestantism. There are enough similarities
to the destructive movements which have plagued Catholicism for the
past 20 years that **all evangelical Christians should be alarmed.**"

James Hitchcock, Professor of History, St. Louis University

"[Franky Schaeffer attacks] the sorry and spineless state of affairs in
the boardrooms of some of the nation's most influential evangelical
Christian magazines, publishing houses and educational institutions."

The Chicago TRIBUNE, March 18, 1984

"Confrontation is never easy. But in this important book Franky
Schaeffer bravely deals with controversial weaknesses within the
church. BAD NEWS FOR MODERN MAN will be good news for
everyone if we heed Franky's appeal. **Those who are tired of an anemic
Christianty will applaud this book.**"

*Nelson Keener, Publisher, THE FUNDAMENTALIST
JOURNAL*

"If Franky Schaeffer and his father have their way, their evangelical
world will be revolutionized, the [New York] TIMES will have to
recognize that world's existence and strength, and evangelicals will
once again become imbued with the arts and humanities."

PUBLISHERS WEEKLY, March 9, 1984

"This is an excellent book exposing the crucial issues facing the church
today. A hard-hitting challenge to action and involvement. **No one
can read this book without being moved to doing something about
these issues.**"

*Marti Acevedo, President of Student Ministries, Gordon
College, Wenham, Massachusetts*

By Franky Schaeffer

Principal one-man shows (painting and/or graphics)

Frisch Gallery, New York, N.Y. (March 1970)
Garden Center, Tulsa, Oklahoma (February 1972)
Criteria Arts, London, U.K. (November 1972)
Galerie Chante-Pierre, Aubonne (Geneva), Switzerland (1974-75)

Films

Created/produced *How Should We Then Live?* 1974-75
Screenplay by and directed *Whatever Happened to the Human Race?* 1977-79
Hosted and directed *Reclaiming the World, Conversations with Francis and Edith Schaeffer* 1980
Screenplay by (with Harold Fickett) and directed *The Second American Revolution* 1981-82
Screenplay by (with Ray Cioni) and produced *The Great Evangelical Disaster* 1984

Books

Co-author of *Plan for Action* (Revell, 1980)
Addicted to Mediocrity (Crossway Books, 1981)
A Time for Anger (Crossway Books, 1982)

Franky Schaeffer

BAD NEWS
FOR
MODERN MAN

An Agenda for Christian Activism

CROSSWAY BOOKS • WESTCHESTER, ILLINOIS
A Division of Good News Publishers

Cover designed by Ray Cioni/The Cioni Artworks

First printing, 1984

Printed in the United States of America

Library of Congress Catalog Card Number 84-70082

ISBN 0-89107-311-6

The publisher would like to express appreciation for permission to quote from the following:

Loving God, by Charles Colson, copyright © 1983 by Charles W. Colson. Used by permission of Zondervan Publishing House, Grand Rapids, Michigan.
Having It All, by Helen Gurley Brown, copyright © 1982 by Helen Gurley Brown. Reprinted by permission of Linden Press, a division of Simon & Schuster, Inc.
The Spirit of Democratic Capitalism, by Michael Novak, copyright © 1982 by Michael Novak. Reprinted by permission of Simon & Schuster, Inc.
Humanhood, Essays in Biomedical Ethics, by Joseph Fletcher, copyright © 1979. Used by permission of Prometheus Books.
Lost in the Cosmos, by Walker Percy, copyright © 1983 by Walker Percy. Reprinted by permission of Farrar, Straus and Giroux, Inc.
The Economy in Mind, by Warren T. Brookes, copyright © by Warren T. Brookes. Used by permission of Universe Books.
Psychological Seduction, by William Kirk Kilpatrick, copyright © 1983 by William Kirk Kilpatrick. Used by permission of Thomas Nelson Publishers.
Idols for Destruction, by Herbert Scholossberg, copyright © 1983 by Herbert Schlossberg. Used by permission of Thomas Nelson Publishers.
"When Nice People Burn books," by Nat Hentoff. Reprinted by permission from *The Progressive* (February 1983), 409 East Main Street, Madison, Wisconsin 53703. Copyright © 1983 The Progressive, Inc.
"Letter to the Editor," by William Vandersteel, copyright © 1983 by Dow Jones & Company, Inc., from December 7, 1983 *Wall Street Journal.*
"If Abortion Becomes Murder," copyright © 1983 by *Chicago Tribune,* from October 10, 1983 issue.
"Unilateral Disarmers Prepare to Meet Their Doom," by Gerald Frost, copyright © 1983 by Dow Jones & Company, Inc., from October 26, 1983 *Wall Street Journal.*
"Three Key Moments in Modern Japanese History," by Alexander Solzhenitsyn, copyright © 1983 by *National Review,* from December 9, 1983 issue.
"Catholic Scholars Veer Towards Pacificism," by Professor Finn, copyright © 1983 by Dow Jones & Company, Inc., from December 27, 1983 *Wall Street Journal.*
"Forced Famine in the Ukraine: A Holocaust the West Forgot," by Adrian Karatnycky, copyright © 1983 by Dow Jones & Company, Inc., from July 7, 1983 *Wall Street Journal.*
Article on AIDS from *Time* magazine, July 4, 1983, used by permission.
"Passe in the Big City, Playboy's Ailing Club's Search for Profits in America's Hinterlands," copyright © 1983 by Dow Jones & Company, Inc., from September 28, 1983 *Wall Street Journal.*
"First Church of Christ, Socialist," by Lloyd Billingsley, copyright © 1983 by *National Review,* from October 28, 1983 issue.
" 'Right on' on the Campus," by Phillip Marcus, copyright © 1983 by *National Review,* from September 1983 issue.
"The Lonely Voice of Alexander Solzhenitsyn, by John Train, copyright © 1983 by Dow Jones & Company, Inc., from June 23, 1983 *Wall Street Journal.*

CONTENTS

To Jim Buchfuehrer, who as my film producer and friend, has provided the kind of friendship and support that makes life rich and pleasant and permits me to work very hard on projects such as this book and the many films we have made together. Merci cher ami

ACKNOWLEDGMENTS

First let me thank my wife, Genie, and my three children, Jessica, Francis, and John Lewis. We all ask ourselves occasionally, "What's the use of it all?" Being surrounded by a loving family gives meaning to a great deal that would otherwise seem rather pointless. Thank you to my father, Francis Schaeffer, for fighting for and defending ideas with courage, and above all, teaching me that ideas do have consequences. Thanks are due to him, too, for the courage with which he has recently not only defended ideas but fought his illness, and the inspiring example that this has been to me. Many thanks to my mother, Edith Schaeffer, for the love and support she gives her whole family, and for her dedication to her own outstanding work as represented by L'Abri Fellowship and her many books. Thank you, John Whitehead, for your friendship and stimulating ideas. Thank you to my friends and co-laborers for their ideas, stimulation, and friendship. In this regard, I would particularly like to thank Jim Buchfuehrer, already mentioned in the dedication, Ray Cioni for his outstanding design of this book, Lane and Jan Dennis, my very supportive publishers and editors, and Peg and Ruth and the Swift Office Services for their typing and retyping. Also Susie Skillen, for all her hard work on the final typing of this manuscript. Thank you all.

Woe to us, for the day goes away, For the shadows of evening are lengthening. . . . Everyone deals falsely . . . Saying, "Peace, peace!" when there is no peace.

(Jeremiah 6:4, 14)

At least Judas got the money. Instead we're being sold down the river for the price of fashion.

Franky Schaeffer
1984

Part I

BAD NEWS FOR SECULAR MAN

1 THE MAD DAYS OF JUNE

The *Wall Street Journal* (Thursday, June 16, 1983) reported that, by a six to three vote, the Supreme Court had struck down as "unconstitutional" a number of local and state ordinances which had sought to regulate or curb access to abortion.

After having listed the laws which had been overturned, the *Journal* went on to report: "The Justices did uphold several provisions of the Missouri law. The high court upheld a requirement that two doctors be present when an abortion is performed after the fetus is capable of living outside the mother. One doctor would be there to attend to the mother and the other to save the life of the fetus, if possible."

I have never read a paragraph which, to my mind, more clearly illustrates the meaning of the word *schizophrenic*. Like some passenger caught with one foot on the dock and one foot on a slowly departing ship, the Supreme Court now finds itself doing an excruciating mental split. The increasing number of late-term abortions resulting in live births, and the increasing publicity surrounding these births, has prompted the ideological gymnastics of the proabortion Court. While the Court can legalize killing the unborn child moments before *in utero,* it nevertheless must add a sentimental cosmetic touch by requiring a second medical team "in case the fetus survives."

Picture the scene in your mind's eye. In one room the abortionist and his team busy themselves with the task of injecting poisonous saline solutions, preparing buckets to receive the fetal garbage, arranging suction apparatuses and curettes, and whispering soft words about six-month-old "nonviable fertilized eggs." At the same time, the life team turns on the heating pad in an isolette, prepares eye drops, no doubt procures the appropriate chart on which to mark birth weight, fingerprints, and other

3

physical characteristics, and alerts the Infant Intensive Care Unit to a possible new arrival.

In the parlance of medical etiquette, I wonder what the "professional" attitude of the life doctor and the life team should be toward the death team. Should they hover to one side of the operating room, delicately averting their eyes? Should they feign disinterest in the whole procedure? Does the life doctor secretly hope that the death doctor is injecting a faulty batch of saline solution so that, in fact, the life doctor is more likely to get a "living fetus" than a "salted out" one? As the death doctor works with studied professional casualness, will he discuss topics of mutual interest with the life doctor? What will they talk about? Golf? The weather? Blood types? World population statistics? The Super Bowl? Will the life team's nurses gossip about their boyfriends with the death team's nurses?

Doctor Kenerai, a pioneer in abortion techniques, has called the live delivery of an aborted child "the ultimate complication." Will the death doctor be embarrassed if he produces "the ultimate complication" and the life team must take over? Moreover, what will the mother-to-be, or in the case of a successful procedure, the mother-to-was, secretly be hoping for? When the second medical team comes in, will she be told why they are there? Will the room be too crowded to work in comfortably? As the isolette, with its warm, womblike interior beckoning, its row of monitors winking, is rolled to one side of the operating table, and a garbage bucket with a plastic liner is placed on the other, what will the woman be thinking?

If the nine Justices of the Supreme Court were standing there watching, whose side would they be on? They have defined abortion as "legal." Would Justice Blackmun be mildly curious as to the outcome of the procedure? Would he perhaps make a gentleman's wager for a few dollars with Justice Brennan as to the "viability" of the fetus, or infant, in question? Would the six prodeath Justices cheer the death team? Would the three prolife Justices cheer the life team?

If the ultimate complication occurred and a "viable fetus" was delivered, crying lustily into the room, would the death doctor ask for just a couple more minutes to try to make his procedure succeed? Would the life doctor wrestle the infant-viable-fetus away from the death doctor? Would the life doctor place the infant-viable-fetus on the breast of the now mother-to-is?

Who would sue whom? Would the mother-to-be/was/is sue the life doctor for fouling up the smooth medical procedure that she had been "constitutionally" entitled to?

Will the death team, watched by the life team, work doubly hard to make sure they produce a nonviable fetus, as a point of professional pride? Or will they feel sorry for the life team, that month after month has to stand there with nothing to do, while the garbage can wins? Might the death team occasionally throw the life team a sop, as it were, by deliberately bungling the application of the saline solution?

And after the procedure is complete, will the death team and the life team have lunch together? Will the life doctor congratulate the death doctor on a procedure well done? Will the death doctor congratulate the life doctor on managing to resuscitate the heretofore nonviable fetus and the now viable infant, even after he has done his best to make that infant nonviable? And later still, will the death doctor, as a friend of the family, come to the infant's christening? And later still, will the infant, when grown, seek reparation from the death doctor for any mutilation, blindness, missing limbs, and other medical problems he may have incurred? Or will he regard him as a sort of uncle?

At a midlife crisis, when both doctors turn forty-three, will they each have a change of conscience? Will the life doctor abandon pediatric surgery and retrain as an obstetrician and head up the death team? Will the death doctor decide that viable fetuses are more interesting after all, and retrain as a pediatrician? If both the life doctor and death doctor have degrees in pediatric surgery and gynecology, will they trade off, one heading the life team for one procedure, and then the death team the next time, and so forth? If the death doctor is a woman and the life doctor a man, or vice versa, will they become friends, lovers, husband and wife, perhaps go into a medical partnership?

Has the Supreme Court defined clearly when the fetus/infant/ child/egg (take your pick) has really been "born"? When does the life team take over from the death team? When the baby's head just crowns? When the head has fully emerged? Only after head and shoulders are out? Or must the whole umbilical cord and placenta also be out? If some part of the baby is still "unborn," can the death doctor finish him off? If the head emerges crying, can he "take suitable action" before the rest is born? Or when any part of the baby is delivered "alive," does the life doctor take over? Who gets to cut the umbilical cord? Who gets to sign the birth/death certificate?

From the woman's point of view, will she be billed once, twice, three times? If the life team merely stands by and does nothing, will they bill her for their time? If the "procedure" fails and the infant is born alive, will the death team still send a bill? Will the woman be billed for both the abortion procedure and the resuscitation?

If the child is born severely damaged by the failed abortion procedure—eyes gouged out, missing a limb or two—will the life team discontinue treatment? Discontinue feeding? Call back the death team? If a Supreme Court Justice is childless and wishes to adopt an infant, does he/she get automatic first refusal on all children the life team resuscitates? Does the Supreme Court own all such infants?

Who will adjudicate disputes between the life team and the death team? In an instance in which the life doctor testily claims that the death team doctor reached into his isolette and finished off the "product of conception" after signs of life were in evidence (as in the trial for murder of Dr. Waddill), whose word is to be believed? Does the mother-to-be/was/is decide? In certain cases, where the death team claims success but the life team obstinately claims definite signs of life, who decides on what course is to be taken? If the infant/fetus/child is still twitching, is this life or just the muscle spasms of death? Is this choice to be made by vote, coin toss, a quick call to Justice Blackmun at the Supreme Court? How?

What will be the customary signal between the life team and the death team for the changeover of procedure? Will it be a gladiatorial thumbs-up or thumbs-down signal? A new medical-ethical, linguistic term such as, "The infant is becoming a via-tron"? Will the mother-to-be/was/is have the right to call in a second opinion on the child's viability/unviability?

And what of twins? Do the twins count as one or as separate viable/ unviable fetuses? Does the mother-to-be/was/is have a right to change her mind during the procedure? Can the death team's and life team's order of work be reversed? For instance, can the life team deliver a healthy, bouncing baby and then turn it over to the death team if the mother decides her privacy is being violated after all?

Can the whole procedure be televised to run as a daytime legal soap opera, à la "People's Court"? In cities with a call-in response to cable stations by viewers, can the viewers be polled as to a thumbs-up or -down? Will Medicaid pay for both the abortion and the life support efforts? Is the Supreme Court mad, demoniac, taking LSD? Is there a Court there at all, or just some damnable computer that is malfunctioning? Could you explain the logic of the Court's ruling to a bright eight-year-old?

The Right to Know

One of the state regulations the Supreme Court struck down was an Akron, Ohio, law that sought to require doctors to describe the physical character-istics of the fetus which the woman was asking them to abort, *before* performing the abortion. The law, in one form or another, had also been implemented in a dozen other states.

This particular ruling, aside from the actual abortion controversy, gives new meaning to the word "hypocrisy." This is the same liberal activist Court that for fifty years has regulated and forced businesses to disclose everything from the chemical contents of products to the amount of dust in the air that workers are breathing, that now strikes down a state ordinance based on the idea of informed consent.

It seems that our right to know about everything from the intimate details of homosexual copulation to the contents of a pain-killer is a God-given constitutional right. But the right to know the precise nature of the abortion "operation" is something that the Court is not about to encourage. So much for rational "choice." Surely, the notion of choice, even to a proabortionist, must imply a choice between tangible alternatives. Needless to say, the abortionist who earns his living through this dreadful trade in human flesh has more than a slight vested interest in the woman making the "right choice." He is not a neutral observer. It therefore seems reasonable to require him to inform his patient of the details of the "operation."

The proabortion forces tell us that abortion is just "another operation" and "the removal of unwanted tissue," much like an appendectomy, let's say, or the excision of a benign tumor. Yet, one can hardly imagine the Supreme Court of the United States going to the trouble of striking down a state ordinance that requires doctors to inform patients of what an appendectomy entails, in the way the Court has struck down the Akron requirement for abortion information. Why is this?

It is simply because abortion is *not* just another operation. Nor was the concentration camp Terrazin just a holiday camp for wealthy Jews, as the Nazis claimed. It was an annex to Auschwitz. The Nazis invited the Red Cross for limited and periodic inspections for propaganda purposes. With similar deception, the Supreme Court may talk of "choice," but when it comes to suppressing information about abortion, the picture seems to change. The words the proabortion forces use—"choice," "informed consent," "mature decisions"—are purely symbolic.

The *Wall Street Journal* tells us, "The American Civil Liberties Union says the ruling also will invalidate the laws of 17 other states." We can be sure the ACLU will be there to assist the Court in such an "invalidating" process. Is it not ironic that the ACLU, which has fought many times on the side of the conservationists/consumers/Naderists lobby, finds itself ardently expostulating *deregulation* of the medical industry? For years the regulators have been calling for more regulation, including total state control through a national health system.

But enough of pretense. The Court is certainly not promoting choice. What they *are* promoting is abortion. Justice Powell says women should not be given information about their child's fetal development because: "Much of the information is designed not to inform the woman's consent but to persuade her to withhold it altogether." And that would never do! Ordinary women might prove to be more compassionate and sensitive than Powell and his colleagues. Once women understood what they were about to kill, they might fear to tread where Powell and his friends have so eagerly rushed in.

Later in the same article, the *Journal* reported:

The Justices also upheld part of the Missouri law that requires parental consent of court approval for abortions on women who are under the age of 18. Relying on past decisions, the high court said that the state law is valid because it permits a judge, if parents refuse consent, to decide that the minor is mature enough to make her own decision.

There is a wonderful, godlike logic in this. Parents may, according to the Court, help their daughter decide *to* have an abortion. But if the parents decide *against* abortion, a judge may step in and override the parents' discretion. In other words, advocating "choice" is, once again, merely a ploy to persuade people, in this case "parents," to choose (or be coerced) in the direction the Supreme Court favors.

The parent/child relationship is sacred to the Court only in instances where the parents have enough wisdom and perception to choose what the Court deems "best" for their daughter. In political terms we call this one-party politics or demagoguery. In the Soviet Union one is allowed to vote for, and indeed encouraged to choose to one's heart's content, the *official* candidate of the Communist Party. In China one is free to choose to agree with the local party Secretary on one's chosen profession. In the United States the Court, in its munificent bounty, has now ruled that the State of Missouri may allow parents to make choices for their daughters who are minors, as long as those choices coincide with those that the Court has made regarding its proabortion policy.

Notice that the Court has allowed this parental "discretion" because "it permits a judge, if parents refuse consent," to intervene. Notice that it is a *judge*, not a doctor or, God forbid, a minister, let alone a priest. Even in making this purely symbolic gesture, a nod toward the ancient tradition of parental authority, the Court was not unanimous. Diehard proabortion Justices Harry Blackmun, William Brennan, Thurgood Marshall, and John Stevens voted against letting even this ordinance stand. They could not find it in their shriveled hearts to allow even a symbolic ordinance that would require parents to be notified and consulted, notwithstanding the fact that a judge could then remove their daughter against her parents' wishes and allow her to have the abortion anyway!

Perhaps we should bring the Court's game to an end with a national referendum. We could declare the Supreme Court to be, in fact, God. Indeed, with the secularization of our culture nearly complete, there seem to be some in our midst who, perfectly seriously, are proposing that the Court expand its already godlike powers to almost infinite extremes. Consider a Letter to the Editor in the *Wall Street Journal,* (December 7, 1983) from one Mr. William Vandersteel in response to a *Journal* article on the Baby Jane Doe infanticide case:

The dilemma posed by the Baby Jane Doe case will remain unresolved until the Supreme Court defines what is meant by the term "life" as it appears in our Declaration of Independence and the Constitution . . . . The Declaration speaks of our unalienable rights to life, liberty and the pursuit of happiness. The life referred to is clearly that of an independently thinking human being capable of enjoying liberty and the pursuit of his or her happiness and it does not include a newborn infant whose very life depends upon its parents or guardians. A clear distinction must be drawn between the term "life" used in a political sense and "life" in a biological sense, which is purely a medical question.

. . . Clearly what is needed to resolve this dilemma is to have the Supreme Court set an age at which a person achieves "political" life. Before that age the infant is the sole responsibility of its parents or guardians and the government may not intervene. [That is, to save the baby's life.]

This question can best be resolved by the United States Supreme Court as, in the end, it is an arbitrary judgment in much the same way as eighteen was deemed to be the age at which a person becomes competent to vote.

Until there is a legal definition of "political" age, the Baby Jane arguments will continue ad nauseum.

As the firstborn were presented to the Temple in Israel, so now each child could be symbolically laid upon the courthouse steps within eight days of its birth and "presented" to the Chief Justice, or at least to a good picture of him, surrounded by flowers, candles, and incense.

The court, like Napoleon crowning himself Emperor, is practicing a kind of moral imperialism, giving itself authority at the expense of all other traditional authority figures—fathers, teachers, doctors, ministers, Congress. God has been described in the Bible as "a jealous God." Similarly, the Supreme Court cannot tolerate anyone but a Justice sitting on the bench coming between it and its subjects. This is especially true when the Court is dispensing life and death favors or status, personhood, or nonpersonhood to whole classes of people. Even proabortion *Newsweek* (July 18, 1983) was moved to note recently: "The Burger court has become America's life-and-death tribunal. No other Supreme Court in history has been as preoccupied with—or bedeviled by—the questions of when life begins and when a state may snuff one out. The Justices, of course, took their burden upon themselves a decade ago [*Roe v. Wade*]. . . ."

America is ruled by the Constitution, and the Constitution seems to depend for its content on what our new Olympian gods, Harry Blackmun & Co., arbitrarily decide at any given moment. Bless me, Harry, for I have sinned.

Theatre of the Absurd

Meanwhile, such organizations as the American Civil Liberties Union, which claim to stand between omnipotent state fiat and the rest of us, resemble Saul at the stoning of Stephen. Namely, they officiate, approve, and "hold the cloaks" of the Justices while they do their divine dirty dictating to the rest of us. Those who are pragmatic should begin formulating suitable prayers addressed to Supreme Court Justices: "Dear Heavenly Blackmun, give us this day our daily rights . . ."

Those of us who are principled might prayerfully consider buying an airplane ticket to Outer Mongolia. But perhaps, as God, the Court can see you wherever you are and there is no escape: "Even though I descend unto hell, Thou art there."

George F. Will, in a *Washington Post* column (June 19, 1983) titled "Abortion: The Court's Intellectual Scandal," wrote:

> Concerning abortion, the Justices use words and categories the way babies use forks and spoons: with gusto, but sloppily. In 1973, the court made much—or thought it did—of "trimesters." But regarding pregnancy a trimester is a demarcation without moral or medical significance, and without much legal significance, in spite of the Court's attempt to give it such. . . .
>
> In Maryland, a fetus has a right to inherit property if the fetus is conceived before the death of the person from whom the property will be inherited. Prenatal medicine can perform wonders for fetuses that can be aborted at any stage. Malpractice cases are establishing that a child born injured as a result of negligent prenatal medicine can claim violation of rights it had as a fetus.
>
> Fetuses, it seems, have various rights—but no right to life. Cut adrift by its 1973 decision from constitutional and biomedical realism, the Court manufactures ever finer distinctions from never relevant categories.

The Court's hair-splitting, inconsistencies, schizophrenic attitude, and simple illogic will continue as long as it refuses to reconsider its basic antilife persuppositions. If the foundation of a large office building tilts only half an inch to one side or the other, it may not be noticeable on the first two or three floors, but by the time you get to 120 stories, the building will look like the Leaning Tower of Pisa. Just so, the Court's original folly is now mirrored and exemplified to the point of making it a laughingstock as it sweats and scurries around the base of the crooked building it has built, doing all it can to prop up this precariously listing edifice, which is obviously too heavy for it to move. If there is any justice in this world, the proabortion members of the Court will eventually be keelhauled, or at least tarred and feathered and run out of town on a rail. After that, perhaps we can find a way to have a Supreme Court that is satisfied with dispensing justice rather than conjuring up whimsical and dubious constitutional "legislation."

If the Court's actions sound like the theatre of the absurd, they are. The Court plays not, however, on an off-Broadway stage, but it directs the life (and death) of the nation. Not as some playwright's fantasy, but as a reality of ludicrous deathliness perpetrated by the six horribly sane madmen occupying the Court prodeath majority. These six "wrongful lives" seem to be vying to be first among equals in that chamber of hell reserved for twentieth-century genocidal dictators. Consider the logic of their folly as revealed in this quote from a *Chicago Tribune* article titled, "If Abortion Becomes Murder" (October 10, 1983):

> Surely when the Supreme Court decided more than a decade ago that women had an almost unrestricted right to abortion, the justices never foresaw the kind of tragedy that led, last week, to a physician being convicted of murder in connection with the termination of a pregnancy.
>
> Dr. Raymond Showery was sentenced to 15 years in prison on charges that he drowned an infant in a bucket of water and dropped the body in a plastic bag after the baby survived a hysterotomy abortion. Although the mother was reported to be 24 weeks pregnant, witnesses described the newborn as weighing 3 to 5 pounds. The bag was apparently thrown away; the infant's body was not subsequently found.
>
> Dozens of other infants have been born alive as the result of abortions. Most are too small and too damaged by the abortion process to survive for more than a few minutes or a few hours. Most states have laws requiring that such infants be treated as other premature babies and every effort made to keep them alive.
>
> There have been other instances in which physicians have been tried on charges of killing a baby who survived abortion. Dr. William Waddill, accused of choking to death a 2 pound, 14 ounce girl following a saline abortion, went through two long trials, but charges were finally dismissed when neither jury could reach a verdict. Dr. Kenneth Edelin, who allegedly stalled in completing a hysterotomy abortion to make sure the baby was dead, was found guilty of manslaughter, but the Massachusetts Supreme Court reversed the decision.
>
> It is a tragic irony that physicians can be charged—and in Dr. Showery's case, convicted—for murder in killing a baby outside his mother's womb just minutes after it is perfectly legal to kill the same infant inside his mother's body. It is even more ironic that the infant who can be killed legally is probably healthy and normal; the abortion survivor who must be kept alive no matter what is almost certainly damaged by the abortion process, may suffer serious, lifelong handicaps as a result of being born so prematurely and has parents who tried to end his life because they so intensely didn't want him.
>
> The Supreme Court's 1973 decision legalizing abortion rested on assumptions about scientific facts that may have been dubious even at the time. Since then, new medical technology and new neonatal intensive care centers have made it possible for babies to survive after much

shorter pregnancies than envisioned a decade ago. The inevitable result will be that more infants are going to survive abortion, although the odds are high that they will have serious handicaps as a result and taxpayers and health insurers will not only have to pay for expensive neonatal care for them, but perhaps lifelong institutionalization as well.

The Supreme Court isn't likely to reverse the basic thrust of *Roe v. Wade,* the case that made abortion legal. The court has already overturned many state and federal laws that sought to put restrictions on the access to abortion. . . .

The *Tribune,* while clearly seeing the absurdity of doing everything possible to kill babies in the womb at one moment and then at the next moment turning around and doing everything possible to save those same babies when the "abortion procedures" don't work, fails to make the simple, logical connection—that maybe we shouldn't be killing babies in the womb in the first place.

We can be sure of one thing, secularist pride being what it is: the present proabortion majority of the Court will never reconsider the fundamental logic of its decisions. Change if change comes will be forced on these supremely arrogant beings. Where is the liberal heritage of all things being open to question and change, let alone civil rights or a humanitarian concern for the aborted baby? Liberals have told us there are certain principles worth defending. The trouble is, they do not know what those principles might be.

2 LOGIC

Someday in the near future, I fully expect to open a newspaper, perhaps the *New York Times,* and see the well-known, hungry child in a starving world advertisement facing me, but with a slight difference.

THIS IS TANYA. Tanya is five years old. She has never known a home, a father or mother. [Tanya stares out soulfully—big, liquid-brown eyes, slightly distended belly, pleading expression.] Tanya has no hope. Will you give her your love? Fifteen dollars is all it takes. Perform the choice of compassion today . . . ONLY $15.00 AND WE'LL SEE THAT TANYA NEVER EATS AGAIN. (This appeal is brought to you by the World Planned Population Federation.)

3 PEACE NOW!

George Orwell, in an essay entitled "Inside the Whale" (New York: Harvest Books, 1953, p. 238), notes the following: "So much of the left wing's thought is a kind of playing with fire by people who don't even know that fire is hot."

Solzhenitsyn has said,

It is normal to be afraid of nuclear weapons. I would condemn no one for that. But the generation now coming out of Western schools is unable to distinguish good from bad. Even those words are unacceptable. This results in impaired thinking ability. Isaac Newton, for example, would never have been taken in by Communism! These young people will soon look back on photographs of their own demonstrations and cry. But it will be too late. I say to them: You are protesting nuclear arms, but are you prepared to try to defend your homeland with non-nuclear arms? No. These young people are unprepared for *any* kind of struggle. (See Appendix 1 for the complete text of "The Lonely Voice of Alexander Solzhenitsyn.")

The *Wall Street Journal* (October 26, 1983) carried an article by Gerald Frost, Director of the Institute for European Defense and Strategic Studies in London. Here are his comments:

UNILATERAL DISARMERS PREPARE TO MEET THEIR DOOM
LONDON—As could be seen from last weekend's "peace protests," the unilateral disarmament movement has many of the aspects of a secular religion. Those who belong to it display the convert's passionate zeal and intensity, as well as a mission to "save" humanity. They behave as if they enjoyed both a monopoly of virtue and unique access to the truth. . . .

The central article of faith is, of course, the belief that if the West disarmed unilaterally the Soviet Union would follow suit. No amount of argument to the effect that the Soviet Union failed to respond to the lowering of the Western nuclear guard in the 1960s and '70s can shake this conviction. Nor, indeed, does the observation that the Soviet Union has not in any way been influenced by the West's reluctance to develop and deploy chemical weapons. . . .

But the main thrust of the argument is that if its own panacea—one-sided disarmament—is not quickly adopted, the apocalypse will be upon us. Indeed, many of the slogans still seen on sandwich boards paraded by religious fundamentalists in front of Saturday night cinema queues—"Prepare to Meet Thy Doom," "Renounce the Devil," "Repent for the End Is Nigh"—would not be out of place in an anti-nuclear demonstration. . . .

For those who are stricken by such fears the peace credo offers a simple, non-rational solution to a range of complex, frightening and mysterious problems, just as pagan religion provided an explanation to the baffling natural phenomena of thunder, lightning and earthquakes, as well as a purpose for living. It also offers hope of salvation: "Protest and Survive" is, after all, the title of the best-selling and most influential unilateralist tract. . . .

Finally, since leaps of faith should not be the sole prerogative of the unilateralist, it is to be hoped that the churches will rediscover their traditional role of administering to spiritual needs rather than providing ersatz religion and abandoning Christian insights for secular views. For while it is true that the peace movement resembles a secular religion, churches have come to resemble the peace movement. Indeed, the two are sometimes indistinguishable. So it is that unilateralist tracts are peddled to shoppers from the forecourts of Quaker Houses of Friends and that a Roman Catholic priest, holding aloft a unilateralist symbol—that skewed and inverted version of the cross—is to be found at the head of the British unilateralist movement.

It is interesting to note that this secular observer has seen the full-scale rush towards fashion by the *church* and an abandonment of its previous principles, the willingness to resist unjust aggression by force in favor of being in tune with a pacifist solution to the world's problems. But of that, more later.

Vladimir Bukovsky, in *Commentary* magazine (May 1982), in an article called "The Peace Movement and the Soviet Union," writes,

The purpose of all this peace pandemonium was well calculated in the Kremlin. First, the threat of nuclear war (of which the Soviets periodically created a reminder by fomenting an international crisis), combined with the scope of the peace movement, should both frighten the bourgeoisie and make it more tractable. Second, the recent subjugation of central European countries should be accepted with more serenity by Western public opinion and quickly forgotten. Third, the movement should help to stir up anti-American sentiment among Europeans, along with a mistrust of their own governments, thus moving the political spectrum to the left. Fourth, it should make military expenditures and the placement of strategic nuclear weapons so unpopular, so politically embarrassing, that in the end the process of strengthening Western defenses would be considerably slowed, giving the Soviets crucial time to catch up. Fifth, since the odd mixture of fools and knaves described above is usually drawn from the most socially active element in the population, its activism should be given the right direction.

Newsweek magazine (June 6, 1983) in their "Periscope" section, reported:

The Soviet Union is surreptitiously pumping thirty million annually into the West German peace movement, including the Green Party, which holds 27 seats in Parliament, according to a secret investigation by the Bundesnachrichtendienst, West Germany's equivalent of the Central intelligence Agency. The funds are channeled into the country through front groups used mostly to buy routine supplies such as megaphones, posters and office equipment. The findings of the investigation have not been released, possibly because Chancellor Helmut Kohl wants to avoid controversy before his July visit to Moscow.

In the same "Periscope" section, *Newsweek* reported,

Capitol Hill and U.S. intelligence sources charge that the Soviet Union has 50% more nuclear warheads aimed at western Europe than the number commonly accepted. The Soviets are known to have deployed two SS20's armed with three warheads at each of its 240 launch sites in the European part of the USSR. But according to several official Washington sources, intelligence photos and other evidence suggests that there is a third 3-warhead missile hidden in the vicinity of each launch site. These sources also say that some of the hidden missiles were placed for as long as three years before they were discovered, raising serious questions about the U.S.'s ability to verify Soviet claims.

In *Commentary* magazine (June 1983) in an article by Leopold Tyrmand entitled, "What Do the Poles Want?" the author notes,

The crux of Communism's superiority over us is that it has both a scenario for how to do us in and the faith that it can be done. Why bother to wage war if we can be brought to our knees by a combination of hard core, strategic harassment and subtle self-doubt implanted into the very fabric of our civilization and culture? No one in the West has given serious thought to destroying Communism since 1918, while the

Communists, ever since the October revolution, have been thinking both methodically and strenuously about how to liquidate Democratic Capitalism.

Genuine Insanity

But few in the West are listening, including Christians, people that supposedly understand evil and who should know better. (See Appendix 2 on "Yellow Rain.")

For example, take an article in *Christianity Today* (July 15, 1983) covering a conference sponsored by Fuller Seminary, the National Association of Evangelicals, and thirty-nine other evangelical organizations, in Pasadena, California. The conference theme was "The Church and Peacemaking in the Nuclear Age," and the article presented the views of Ronald J. Sider, author and lecturer. *Christianity Today* characterizes Sider as someone who presents a "constant emphasis on evangelism, . . . commitment to scripture . . . and [has a] humble willingness to consider others' views. . . . He is highly respected by those with whom he disagrees."

Christianity Today notes, "Sider opts for what he calls 'the way of the cross.'" To Sider, according to *Christianity Today* (and confirmed by Sider's own book), the way of the cross is the following: "He believes the U.S. should embark on a fundamentally different path. That new path is civilian based defense. He proposes that the U.S. channel money now being spent on nuclear arms into a massive program to educate its citizens in the methods of non-violent, non-cooperative self defense—principles espoused by Gandhi. . . ."

Sider, who identifies Soviet totalitarianism as a "ghastly evil," believes that if the U.S. would disarm, *the Soviets would almost surely invade and thousands would likely be tortured and killed. But, he says, "If hundreds of thousands of committed, praying Christians died in a [non-violent campaign], I predict we would see the most rapid expansion of the Christian faith the world has ever known"* [emphasis mine].

I would merely add that I have heard some Christians "lovingly" propose support for legalized abortion on the grounds that aborted babies go straight to heaven. Evangelism also no doubt justified the Crusades. By the same logic, slavery then must have been a good thing, giving the poor black the opportunity to hear the gospel! That forty-one *evangelical* organizations would hold a conference to provide a forum for airing views such as Sider's in the context of allegedly serious debate says a great deal about the state of evangelical clear-mindedness, or lack thereof.

Ron Sider, who is calling for the emulation of Gandhi, does in fact reflect his views rather accurately. One little-known fact about Gandhi, propaganda films notwithstanding, is that he naively wrote to Hitler, fully expecting that his pleasant letter asking Hitler to be "peaceful" would be welcomed and followed. He was disappointed. In addition to that, Gandhi stated publicly that the Jews should be willing to die cheerfully *without resisting* the Nazis in a sort of pacifist mass suicide that would redound to their credit. (Richard Grenier in his book *The Gandhi Nobody Knows* has detailed these points very well.)

In the old left of the 1960s, one would link such pacifist utopian comments to hallucinogenic drugs. However, in the "new" Christian left today, one is at a loss to explain such wrongheadedness.

Those like Sider who espouse such views live in the fantasy world of American evangelicalism, which is itself one step removed from reality in its *own* nation, let alone the rest of the world. Alexander Solzhenitsyn, by way of contrast, has not only lived in the world, but has also lived in the Soviet Union. In addition, he has not only lived in the Soviet Union, but has also been persecuted as an orthodox believer for the very reasons Mr. Sider *advocates* we should all volunteer to be persecuted. In addition, Solzhenitsyn withstood the persecution, was not bowed or broken, and came away from it with *a very different set of ideas about resisting persecution than those put forth by Mr. Sider.* Solzhenitsyn believes that evil must be forcefully resisted. Solzhenitsyn understands what would have happened to Gandhi's nonviolence in the face of Soviet tanks in Hungary, Czechoslovakia, Poland, or Afghanistan. Solzhenitsyn is anxious that the West defend itself against the horror of eternal totalitarian evil, while Ronald Sider wants to *volunteer all of us, including our children, for a great experiment in passive resistance and suffering.*

Solzhenitsyn, writing in the *National Review* (December 9, 1983), in an article entitled "Three Key Moments in Modern Japanese History," had this to say:

Rather than betraying allies and neighbors, however small, we should be giving our support to everyone who offers resistance to the pestilence of world communism. Each fresh victim surrendered into the maw of communism only whets its appetite for aggression. Any compromise with any form of communism spells disaster. The Communists are no ordinary political negotiating partners, and the only ones to benefit from any such negotiations are they themselves. To expect that the Communists will ever show any sign of mercy is to delude oneself; they have given no quarter in the past, and will not in the future. Moreover, when analyzing events in the world today we can no longer rely on our former concept of the nation state as one in which the government serves the interests of the people. One third of the world states already have Communist regimes, and this is something we have to grasp. There is only one shield against Communism—iron resolution. . . .

It is a vain hope that communism in the USSR or any other country will collapse of itself or will be regenerated for the better.

Thanks to the incessant capitulation of the outside world and the commercial and economic aid it provides . . . thanks to all this, communism is advancing unchecked. It is a fatal illusion to suppose that communism can be restrained by gentle treatment or elegantly phrased concessions. It cannot. Only by spelling out its vices for all the world to see can you have any prospect at all of holding it in check. The Communists themselves have not the slightest compunction about waging their "ideological war" of destruction, whatever phony detente may happen to be in force.

It is worth noting, in passing, that there are many who argue that people such as Ron Sider are not in any way "leftist" but are just carrying on the tradition of the Anabaptists. While this may be true in the hairsplitting sense of finding correct theological labels, it is not true in terms of the overall reality of the present situation and *results*. What do I mean by this? Simply that *we are responsible for how our positions fit in with the day and age around us*. For instance, if there had been some Lutheran minister in Nazi Germany who believed that Jews were inferior for "scriptural reasons," citing as historical antecedence church anti-Semitism all the way back to the thirteenth century and quoting Martin Luther, he himself might not actually be a "Nazi." However, because of his anti-Semitism, he would be contributing to the Nazi cause, and for all intents and purposes be a Nazi, whatever he called himself. Similarly, today's pacifists, liberation theologians, and others can attempt to hide behind labels such as Anabaptists, Mennonites, or members of other long church "traditions," but the reality of the situation is that they must take responsibility for how they fit in and affect the present age around them. In the same way, we now hold Voltaire and Rousseau responsible for their philosophy making way for the reality of the terror of the French Revolution. Theory must be judged by reality and results.

Weakness, pacifism, and appeasement have always produced war not peace when used to counter totalitarian evil. To propose these as solutions to communist aggression is *true warmongering,* however well intentioned. Those who advocate such "solutions" must be held responsible for the holocaust their views lead to—all in the name of "peace" and "love."

The forces of the left today are dominant in the world at large; and those who fit in conveniently with them may as well be on the same side. They are mutually supportive. If you do not believe this, ask yourself the following question. Whom do you think the Communist officials who rule the Soviet Union would rather have dominating the thinking of America, or even the thinking of the evangelical world—Alexander Solzhenitsyn or Ron Sider?

Milton Friedman refers to sincerity as the most overrated virtue in America today. Simply being a nice guy, even one who "listens to his opponents' views seriously," is not enough. *Truth demands a commitment to the real world over and beyond wishful thinking.* Truth demands a submission to *facts,* not reliance on irrational hopes, even if presented "lovingly." To abandon Western democracy in the name of "compassion" or even "the cross" (a code name for bastardized Marxism baptized as Christianity, it now seems) to totalitarian rule, whether it is done nonviolently or not, is not loving, nor is it even evangelistic, let alone sensible. To suggest that we voluntarily exchange a potential nuclear war for certain torture is demented. What kind of a bargain is that?

It is interesting to note that the myth of neutrality (which is a strong leftward bias in the media masquerading as pluralism) has so permeated the evangelical world that, like the secular world, we will quietly accept any extremism from the left. At the same time we are made nervous by conservative views, let alone the extreme right. Imagine the reaction in the evangelical press if a statement comparably extreme as Sider's were presented from the right.

Let's say Jerry Falwell stood up and called for an immediate build-up of superior nuclear force in the United States to be used within a year for a first-strike against all civilian targets in the Soviet Union, Eastern Europe, and China, with the aim of not only destroying them militarily, but also annihilating their entire population. Suppose this was presented as the *only* Christian moral alternative to the Soviet nuclear arms build-up and that Falwell called for worldwide bloodshed, holocaust, and terrible oppression of people by unleashing total nuclear war on a first-strike basis, saying this would be a "good price to pay in view of the fact that the few who were left would turn back to God in a massive revival and that all of this apocalyptic upheaval would hasten the return of Christ." Suppose Falwell also called for the government to use its funds to train American Christians to model their faith on King Richard the Lion-Hearted, looking to a series of new banner-waving military crusades to "spread the gospel," predicting that through the saved there would come the "greatest revival the world has ever known." This is certainly no more ridiculous than the virtues of torture chambers that Sider is proposing from the left, and yet his views are accorded respect, with time being taken to point out that he's a nice fellow, after all. I do not believe that an extreme statement of folly from the right would be reported with the same respect given to Sider's folly. Fashion seems to dictate, and the left is fashionable, even when it chooses to be crazy.

When serious evangelical publishers print books espousing such views by Ron Sider (as they have), when serious Christian magazines report such ideas without derision and the raspberry which they so richly deserve, and when evangelical organizations give forums to such thoughts, one not only wonders about the sanity of the individual espousing such mumbo-jumbo but also about that of the evangelical establishment. If this is not a suicidal death wish, a total self-hatred in the worst sense, what is?

Most unfortunately, this same abandonment of the traditional and orthodox view is also taking place within the Roman Catholic Church. (For a complete account of this, see Appendix 6 by James Hitchcock.) Consider the Catholic primary school movement to push parochial schools toward total pacificism. In the *Wall Street Journal,* (December 27, 1983), in an article entitled "Catholic Schools Veer Towards Pacifism" by Professor Finn (Vanderbilt University), the following was reported:

> If you thought that creeping pacifism in the classroom affected only those public schools in the thrall of the National Education Association, think again. The largest group of private schools in the U.S., the Roman Catholic parochial schools, is running up the white flag, too, and urging teachers to turn students into "peacemakers."
>
> . . . This is plainly shown in the extended interpretation of the "Peace Pastoral" contained in the December issue of *Momentum,* the major journal of the National Catholic Educational Association. ("Peace" will also be a major theme of the NCEA's coming annual convention.) . . . Its message is unmistakable. "Peacemaking," the bishops say, "is not an optional commitment but a requirement of our faith." Accordingly, the obligation of Catholic schools is not just to introduce issues of war and peace into the curriculum but, rather, to impart to children the beliefs, attitudes and assumptions about the international order that were enshrined in the bishops' pastoral letter. The overriding objective, in the astonishing phrase used by San Francisco Archbishop John Quinn, is "to disarm the spirit."
>
> How, exactly, are Catholic educators advised to achieve this dubious end? The NCEA authors are certainly inventive.
>
> The principal of Hale's Franciscan High School in Chicago recommends asking Daniel Berrigan to address the students. The Director of the Center for Education for Justice and Peace suggests teaching non-violence via "Gandhian philosophy" and "global thinking about conflict." The Director of the Office for World Justice and Peace celebrates "the infusion method," which consists primarily of replacing familiar notions of nationalism and patriotism with UNESCO-style ideas about "interdependence," "world order," "multi-cultural understanding" and a more equitable distribution of "the world's resources."
>
> . . . One thing is clear, but it's sadly ironic. On such fundamental questions of curriculum and pedagogy as what and how to teach children about their country and their world, the leaders of American Catholic education have now adopted the ideological coloration of those—such as the NEA and other advocates of pedagogical statism—who over the years have also been the bitterest critics of non-governmental education and the most relentless foes of all public aid for children attending private schools.

Sadly, the evangelical world is also being penetrated willy-nilly by those of similar views who wish to reorganize evangelicalism in their own liberal image—that is, the image of leftist utopianism, the same guiding spirit of appeasement and compromise which led directly to World War II by its nonconfrontational policies against Hitler. Evangelicals can perhaps take comfort from the fact that Catholics are being similarly infiltrated by liberal attitudes; this shows we are no more stupid than anyone else. But is any of this necessary? Again, even as the world hungers after tradition the church, instead of standing fast, seems to lust after media acceptance.

Michael Novak, in his book *The Spirit of Democratic Capitalism* (p. 343), notes:

> The single greatest temptation for Christians is to imagine that the salvation won by Jesus has altered the human condition. Many attempt to judge the present world by the standards of the gospels, as though the world were ready to live according to them. Sin is not so easily overcome.

Richard Grenier, writing in *Chronicles of Culture* (January 1984), in an article on George Orwell, had this to say:

> . . . But the quintessence of irresponsibility in thought is . . . calmly, complacently, smugly, to hold two totally contradictory thoughts in one's head at the same time. To know that they are contradictory, and yet not to know. To say things one does not believe, and yet hypnotize one's self into thinking that one does believe them. To know that the weak must yield to the strong, and yet by self-hypnosis to convince oneself that the Kingdom of God is somehow come, and that righteousness rules the earth.

Sider and other leftist evangelicals seem to have found creative interpretations for the "turn the other cheek" verse when taken out of context. Just think what could be done with the one about "plucking out your eye lest it offend you." Forceps, anyone?

Because the left is fashionable and conservatism is not, we accept verses taken out of context to support a leftist position totally at variance with the main thrust of the Bible. It seems natural to take a verse that endorses turning the other cheek and parlay it into the nuclear freeze movement. But to accept this thinly disguised ideology in the form of "theology" is just as silly as it would be to take a verse which says something such as, "To him to whom much has been given more will be added, and to him to whom little has been given what little he hath shall be taken away," and parlay that statement, out of context, into a "theological" foundation for the most rapacious capitalism of the industrial revolution. If an idea of social concern cannot be argued on the basis of logic and common sense, which presumably, as Christians, we believe God gave us along with the Scriptures, it is doubtful that it will be assisted by the addition of a few Bible verses. The Bible, in a certain context, may call us to be "foolish for Christ," but I have not yet found the verse that extols the virtues of voluntarily being blind in one's outlook!

Death Wish

Erik von Kuehnelt-Leddihn, writing in the *National Review* (September 30, 1983), in an article entitled "Death Wish," points out the seeming desire for self-destruction of the European "peace" movement. His analysis (though unintended) describes perfectly the irrationalism and lack of direction that has also taken over the "new" evangelicals and their sympathasizers.

> James Burnham wrote a remarkable book, *The Suicide of the West,* and Malcolm Muggeridge, a remarkable article, "The Great Liberal Death Wish," about the tendency towards self-destruction in modern civilization. . . .
>
> Those afflicted with it are on the moderate Left (which in America arrogates the name "Liberal"). Perhaps out of a feeling of inferiority, these half-hearted representatives of the Marxist ideology that dominates the East behave as if they expect and desire their own annihilation. While the Soviets can openly embrace a coherent system of political thought, these western Liberals must pay their respects publicly, at least, to a hodgepodge faith that gets its value from everywhere—the French Revolution, the Enlightenment, diluted Christianity, humanism, behaviorism, and social welfarism. They stand for everything and nothing. They feel weak, lacking in conviction, compared to the vigorous, young, unspoiled and enthusiastic East. It matters little that their perception has no basis in reality.

If you are not ready to throw your lot in with idiocy, pragmatism, the *New York Times,* Ronald Sider, *et al,* you might be interested in the following. In the *Wall Street Journal* (Thursday, July 7, 1983), an article appeared entitled "Forced Famine in the Ukraine: A Holocaust the West Forgot." The article was written by Adrian Karatnycky, Research Director of the A. Philip Randolph Institute and editor of the quarterly journal, *Workers Under Communism.* This piece is interesting on two counts: (1) it reveals more about the way the Soviet Union works than you will learn from a lifetime of reading most newspapers or Christian magazines and ten lifetimes of watching network news; and (2) it reveals a great deal about the way the liberal media function—here represented by the *New York Times*—both past and present.

Fifty years ago this past spring, the normally bountiful fields of the Ukraine were filled with the odor of death. Crows flew over the steppe, awaiting their feast of human carrion. Corpses littered the streets and roadways. . . . In the June 6, 1933, issue of the *London Morning Post,* Malcolm Muggeridge depicted the following scene:

"If you go now to the Ukraine or the North Caucasus, exceedingly beautiful countries and formerly amongst the most fertile in the world, you will find them like a desert; fields choked with weeds and neglected; no livestock or horses; villages deserted; peasants famished, often their bodies swollen, unutterably wretched.

"You will discover if you question them that they have had no bread at all for three months past; only potatoes and some millet, and they are now counting potatoes one by one. . . . They will tell you that many have already died of famine and that many are dying every day; that thousands have been shot by the government and hundreds of thousands exiled."

The devastation Mr. Muggeridge described wasn't caused by any natural catastrophe. It was an entirely new phenomenon—history's first artificial famine: a consequence of Stalin's effort to collectivize agriculture and crush the nationally conscious Ukrainian peasantry.

With the exception of Mr. Muggeridge's reports, William Henry Changerlin's in the *Christian Science Monitor,* and the publication of several stories and a number of shocking photographs of starving children in the Hearst newspapers, the Western press was largely silent about the genocide that was occurring in the Soviet Ukraine. Europe and the U.S. were in the throes of the Great Depression. Violence in the streets was common. Fascism was on the march. The forced famine of 1933 had regrettably come at an inopportune time.

Some reporters from the West concealed the truth because of an ideological commitment to Soviet communism. Others, like *New York Times* correspondent Walter Duranty, were seduced by official favors and access to high government circles into deliberately and shamelessly attempting to suppress the story of the famine, while writing fawning articles on Stalin's rule. For this Mr. Duranty was rewarded with Pulitzer prizes and the Order of Lenin.

None of the day's newspaper reports was able to grasp the enormity of the cataclysm. Today, reliable academic estimates place the number of Ukrainian victims of starvation at 4.5 million to 7 million. This dark event, which rivals in its magnitude the Jewish Holocaust and the massacre of the Cambodians by the Khmer Rouge, is still largely unknown outside the private memories of some survivors. . . .

Yet despite the pivotal importance of the forced famine, for 50 years its full story has remained untold. Not one serious book on this tragedy is available in English.

Today—at a time when some would recast Soviet communism in a friendlier mold, the better to negotiate arms reductions with—may once again be an inopportune time to bring up the terrible loss of life and the painful trauma of the brutally scarred Ukrainian nation. Yet 50 years seems too long to remain silent about one of the greatest crimes in mankind's history.

The Ukrainian holocaust notwithstanding, the *New York Times* is still winning Pulitzer Prizes (and Orders of Lenin, for all I know) in spite of its leftist propagandizing which it does from its comfortable seat in capitalistic New York City, and the Soviet Union continues to treat its people in much the same way now as it did then. Perhaps it's not wise to dwell on these things, for one's faith in Sider's great revival through volunteering for torture might be a little hard to sell. After all, it is one thing to *talk* Christian pacifism and another to have to starve and count one's dwindling potato supply "one by one."

Lastly, before we hand ourselves over to communist torturers, as Mr. Sider advocates, let us consider the sort of people we would be dealing with. In an article from *Commentary* magazine (October 1983) titled "Yellow Rain: The Conspiracy of Closed Mouths," by well-known Italian journalist Lucio Lami, we find:

Two years back rumors were heard in Bangkok to the effect that the Vietnamese were producing new gas mixtures that were capable of deceiving investigators as to their toxic content and their origin. These new substances—it was said—were the result of experiments in a laboratory conducted by a "new Doctor Mengele" who operated on human subjects. No one accepted these rumors, which were so clearly "defamatory" to Vietnam. But in April 1982, Adelia Bernard, of COER, was secretly taken to Phnom Penh where, thanks to a person who worked at the Hôpital Sovietique, she was informed of the incredible truth. The experiments were taking place, in that very same hospital as well as elsewhere, and were being conducted on healthy children ranging from two to ten years of age. The children were kept in special homes and during the experiments were placed in transparent plastic spheres equipped with two valves, one for oxygen, the other for the gas that was being tested. There were approximately one hundred child guinea pigs in the area of the hospital alone, while many others lived in laboratory camps built on the tiny islands of the Mekong. The latter were injected with toxic substances.

Incredulous, Mrs. Bernard asked for proof and after negotiating the payment of $300, her interlocutor entered the hospital and returned with a plastic sphere, with valves and tubes, inside of which lay the dead body of a three-year-old baby. Adelia Bernard put the sphere in a sack and carried it back to Bangkok, where she deposited it on the desk of Mark Brown, a representative of the UN High Commission for Refugees. Brown did nothing, and no "case" was opened.

Brown has gone, perhaps prudently transferred or removed. But not a word is to be heard of that terrible episode, which takes us back to the days of Treblinka, and which makes us all guilty of a shameful silence.

Christians have not cried out nor stood up courageously against the authorities in the United States who allow such things as the starving of Infant Doe and abortion-on-demand. Is there any reason to suppose, as Mr. Sider does, that the American church would unite in courageous "passive evangelistic resistance" against such masters? If we have been so apathetic in the green season, does anyone really expect courage in the dry?

4 BRUTALIZATION FOR FUN AND PROFIT

The Killing of Infant Doe

Jesus died for your sins, Field Marshall Rommel agreed to commit suicide to save his family from going to a concentration camp, President Kennedy died because Lee Harvey Oswald was a better than average shot, Leonid Brezhnev expired because he was an elderly man and even his psychic healer could not help him, and Infant Doe of Bloomington, Indiana, died because he had the misfortune to be born into a brutal nation of activist barbarians and passive Christians.

As with the Unknown Soldier, Infant Doe never had the dignity of a real name, even to put on his grave. Unlike Gandhi, Infant Doe was never considered trendy enough to be given a cover story by *Christianity Today*. Born with Down's syndrome and esophagel atresia, he was a helpless infant ripe for the taking—taking by judges, doctors, lawyers, and parents infected with the acrid and ungenerous spirit of late-twentieth-century America. Like the eye-watering fumes from a smashed bottle of ammonia, the stench of the killing of Infant Doe caused even a nation, surfeited with the blood of the innocent, to gasp, if only for a short moment, with horror.

Surgery to repair the atresia, which prevents normal feeding, is almost always completely successful, with a very acceptable level of risk for the child. However, Infant Doe's parents, following the logical conclusion of the *Roe* v. *Wade* proabortion mentality of the Supreme Court, decided to exercise their "constitutional right to privacy" by "choosing" on behalf of their infant, refusing to allow the attending physician to perform this simple surgery. A nurse, no doubt under the impression that she had qualified to practice medicine and not attend a latter-day Auschwitz, notified a local prosecutor that the baby was being deliberately starved to death. The prosecutor brought the hospital and parents before a juvenile judge. The local publicity at that point brought forth many childless couples and others ready and willing to adopt Infant Doe into a loving family where he *was* wanted. However, the Juvenile Court judge sustained the parents' refusal of surgery and allowed the killing by starvation to continue. The State Supreme Court allowed the juvenile judge's ruling to stand, declining to hear an appeal on behalf of truly the most helpless and innocent victim to come before the Indiana Supreme Court since its founding. After six days of being denied food, water, and care, Infant Doe died of starvation.

Later, in December 1983, the U.S. Supreme Court allowed a lower New York Court ruling to stand which had upheld the "right" of the parent of a little girl known as Baby Jane Doe to refuse surgery to correct the baby's spinal bifida. Thus the Court confirmed the terrible precedent of infanticide as a "treatment" for the handicapped. Welcome to Auschwitz. Christians, seduced by the spirit of Lady Macbeth, looked the other way.

"Even the jackals present their breasts to nurse their young; but the daughter of my people has become cruel, . . . The tongue of the infant clings to the roof of its mouth for thirst; the young children ask for bread, but no one breaks it for them. . . . Their skin clings to their bones, it has become as dry as wood. Those slain by the sword are better off than those who die of hunger; for these pine away, stricken for lack of the fruits of the field" (Lamentations 4:3-9).

Four decades ago, the United States judicial system participated in the prosecution of war criminals at Nuremberg, Germany. Doctors who had permitted or assisted experimentation on live human beings at the concentration camps, justices and Nazi SS officers who had meted out punishment by starvation, and high officials who said they were "only obeying orders" were executed by the allied powers and the U.S. government for crimes of brutality.

As with the rich man calling to Lazarus from the bowels of hell, one can imagine the Nazi SS doctors accusing America before the living God of justice: "Why, O Living God, are we here in eternal suffering for our crimes against the innocent while you prosper the wicked in the very nation who condemned us?"

The black of the justice's robe in America today often seems to be cut from the same black material as the old SS uniforms of Nazi Germany. If you think this is mere rhetoric, you are guilty of gross complacency. No language is strong enough to sufficiently capture the horror of deliberately starving to death a newborn baby or the dismemberment of an unborn child. Yet these barbarities are committed with legal sanction in these United States, supposedly our "free country."

Dante's inscription over hell, "Abandon all hope, ye who enter here," is grimly appropriate in reference to some late twentieth-century children's hospitals. For those curious to meet genuine barbarians, they need look no further than America's liberal, proabortion and proinfanticide elite. To complete the picture we should present graduating medical students with clubs and poison darts and other tools of carnage and dismemberment suited to the practice of modern-day gynecology and pediatrics. Troglodyte gynecologists of the world, unite!

Modern "Ethics"

The starving of Infant Doe was not a temporary aberration of modern ethics. Indeed, it was consistent with the position of many leading "ethicists" teaching in major institutions today. To give you an idea of the pervasiveness of the proinfanticide thinking among modern "ethicists," consider the flippancy with which Joseph Fletcher addresses the problem. In his book *Humanhood, Essays in Biomedical Ethics* (Prometheus Books, 1979), on page 141 we read, concerning infanticide:

> My premise will be that induced death, as such, may not be condemned categorically, and that truly rational ethical issues only arise when responsible moral agents set about determining answers to operational questions—who, why, what, when, and how. It is unreasonable ethically to say that all acts of euthanasia are wrong. . . .

Fletcher deals with the concern of religious people opposed to euthanasia in the form of infanticide in these terms:

> Loving concern (agape) is a standard of good and evil which could be validated in either a theistic or humanistic belief system. A theist might, of course, believe that God forbids infanticide by a rule, perhaps along with other things such as adultery or baking bread on Sundays. (p. 147)

To Fletcher, then, "loving concern" is the basis on which infanticide is to be practiced. To those backward religionists who oppose such an idea, their aversion to the starving of an Infant Doe can be likened to a belief that God forbids such things as "baking bread on Sundays." The fact that Fletcher can deal in such a cavalier manner with the serious anti-infanticide arguments raised by those such as Dr. Paul Ramsey, Melinda Delahoyde, and others illustrates how totally he presupposes his audience to be in his favor. And indeed, unfortunately the biomedical elite in the United States today follows Fletcher all too closely in its pattern of thinking. People such as Daniel Maguire of Marquette University, Peter Singer, and others are virtually carbon copies of Joseph Fletcher. Not only that, the press is often swayed by proinfanticide rhetoric. In the case of Baby Jane Doe there was, like the Gadarene swine, a headlong stampede to condone, explain, and legitimize as moral the removal of care from the baby. Even the normally conservative *Wall Street Journal* could not avoid dipping its hand in this noxious dish. The media, having championed abortion, has naturally found it impossible to draw the line at infanticide. Indeed, what was once unthinkable is now defended as "a reasonable alternative to costly health care."

To those who doubt that infanticide is the natural and logical consequence of the acceptance of abortion, let them hear Joseph Fletcher once again.

> Obviously the ethics of abortion runs close to the ethics of infanticide. . . . If fetuscide is licit, why not infanticide? (p. 140)

Fletcher (p. 156 in his chapter on euthanasia) also gives us an idea of how all this killing is to work practically, vis-a-vis the law.

> Acts of deliberate omission [read "starvation"] are morally not different from acts of commission [read "poisoning, drowning, smothering, etc."]. But in the Anglo-American law, it is a crime to push a blind man off a cliff. It is not, however, a crime to deliberately not lift a finger to prevent his walking over the edge [read "neglecting to feed"]. . . .
> Occasionally I hear a physician say that he could not bring himself to resort to direct euthanasia [read "kill, murder, execute, etc."]. That may be so. What anybody would do in such tragic situations *is a problem in psychology, however, not ethics* [emphasis mine].

And there you have it. All this boils down to our psychological mind-set and is not a problem of "ethics," let alone absolutes. Like Lady Macbeth who was sentimentally squeamish about stabbing the King herself because he looked like her father, Fletcher reduces ethics to mere sentimentality. But also like Lady Macbeth, he approves the killing and seems to say, as Macbeth did, "If it were done when 'tis done, then 'twere well it were done quickly." If doctors have second thoughts, they can find a stern injunction to carry on their killing either from Fletcher who gives them subtle encouragement, or from his apparent mentor, Lady Macbeth, the original feminist, for more robust advice: "I have given suck, and know how tender 'tis to love the babe that milks me: I would, while it was smiling in my face, Have pluck'd my nipple from his boneless gums, And dash'd the brains out, had I so sworn as you: Have done to this" (*Macbeth*, Act I, Scene II).

It all comes down to *how you feel about it psychologically* rather than the actual facts of the case. This is underlined by the fact that, to Fletcher, active euthanasia is permissible on behalf of people who are in "hopeless misery." But who is to judge what "hopeless misery" consists of, particularly for inarticulate infants? If we were dealing with true ethics and a question of right and wrong, the fact that such questions *cannot* always be resolved would be reason enough to let such infants live and to care for them. But today it all boils down to a matter of "psychology" rather than "ethics," how we *feel* about it rather than right and wrong. If you *feel* someone is living in "hopeless misery," or is in the way of your being King, or, like John Hinkley, *feel* animosity toward the President, and you can tolerate the feeling psychologically of ending their life, then it is O.K. to do away with them.

Milton Friedman, as noted before, has said that sincerity is the most overrated virtue in America today. When the media deals with cases of infanticide, it often speaks of the "agony" the parents underwent in making their "heart-rending" decision. In other words, if they are willing to pay the psychological dues and appear sincere enough in their "agonizing," their "feeling," then society will allow them to starve their infant rather than care for him. They believe that to go through the psychological dues-paying process legitimizes their action. We need look no further than Joseph Fletcher and his crusading posse to find the philosophical argument responsible for Infant Doe's starvation. In Infant Doe's death Richard Weaver's concept, expressed in his book *Ideas Have Consequences* (a Midway reprint, Chicago, Illinois), finds a horrible vindication in a negative sense. In *Pediatrics* (Vol. 72, No. 1, July 1983, p. 138), the *Journal of the American Academy of Pediatrics*' biomedical ethicist (whatever that is) Peter Singer defends infanticide:

> Once the religious mumbo-jumbo surrounding the term "human" has been stripped away, we may continue to see normal members of our species as possessing greater capacities of rationality, self-consciousness, communication, and so on, than members of any other species; but we will not regard as sacrosanct the life of each and every member of our species, no matter how limited its capacity for intelligent or even conscious life may be. If we compare a severely defective human infant with a nonhuman animal, a dog or a pig, for example, we will often find the nonhuman to have superior capacities, both actual and potential for rationality, self-consciousness, communication, and anything else that can plausibly be considered morally significant. Only the fact that the defective infant is a member of the species *Homo sapiens* leads it to be treated differently from the dog or pig. Species membership alone, however, is not morally relevant. Humans who bestow superior value on the lives of all human beings, solely because they are members of our own species, are judging along lines strikingly similar to those used by white racists who bestow superior value on the lives of other whites, merely because they are members of their own race. (See Appendix 3 for full text.)

(The editors of *Pediatrics,* a respected journal supposedly dedicated to the well-being of children, and the writer of the above seem to be unaware of or I suspect no longer care for what Christ had to say about the comparative value of human life in Matthew 12:11, 12. He said, "If any of you has a sheep and it falls into a pit on the Sabbath, will you not take hold of it and lift it out? How much more valuable is a man than a sheep!")

We are a nation peopled by ghosts.

If Joseph Fletcher, Peter Singer, and company had written *A Christmas Carol,* the last scene would have Scrooge and Bob Cratchett beating Tiny Tim to death with his little crutch, as the Ghost of Christmas Present wiped a tear from his eye, moved by their compassion for the little fellow.

Fun in the Bushes

Let us sample what "the good life" consists of today. When the AIDS epidemic claimed its thousandth victim, homosexual organizations, instead of questioning their own "values," blamed the United States government for not spending enough on research. They want to enjoy their "gay lifestyle" and at the same time be protected from health consequences by government-funded research. *Time* magazine (July 4, 1983) reported the following on the AIDS epidemic:

> In Manhattan last week a WABC-TV crew refused to enter the Gay Men's Health Crisis Office to cover a story on AIDS. Two backup crews also balked at going in. Said one of the technicians, "Look, nobody knows anything about AIDS. What makes them so cocksure I'm not going to get it from a sweaty palm?" . . . Three nurses at a hospital in San Jose, California, quit rather than deal with AIDS cases; some staff members at San Francisco General Hospital refused to carry trays to such patients. . . .
>
> AIDS has clearly changed the rules of the sexual game for homosexuals. Anonymous and casual sex can be fatal. Says Mel Rosen of the Gay Men's Health Crisis Office, "People are saying, 'If I only want to go to bed with someone once, then I won't go to bed with them at all.' " Says Craig Roland, 34, of Manhattan: "You're always looking at a potential partner and thinking, 'Is this the one who will kill me?' " Roland screens out men who look run down, or have suspicious strawberry marks associated with some forms of AIDS. "Then I get his health history. I say, 'I'm concerned about my health and I'd like to know about yours.' " . . .
>
> Some foot-loose gays are turning to monogamy. Peter Schiffman, 30, a Manhattan ad salesman, says he was encouraged to fidelity by his terrified boy friend, who is "totally freaked out by AIDS." For many homosexuals accustomed to having many partners, staying faithful to one lover is not an option. New York psychiatrist Norman Levy says he sees more gay patients in therapy these days "because they have become aware that they had become addicted to anonymous sex as a way of coping with stress and tension." For some, the allure of the unknown

stranger is too strong, or the idea of social life without instant sex is unthinkable. Says Altanta gay activist Frank Scheuren, *"The tradition in the gay community is that you have sex first, then talk"* [emphasis mine].

Still, Scheuren sees a trend towards calmer and more cautious sex lives. "There is even an effort to start courtships again," he says. At gay bars and parties, there is far more hand holding and the sort of coy romance usually associated with heterosexuality. . . . The gay culture is awash with rumors of unnamed victims who are purposely trying to infect as many others as possible. And some homosexuals have become increasingly reckless in response to the crisis. Three San Francisco therapists distributed questionnaires to about 1,000 gays last March. . . . Ten percent said they had increased high risk sexual behavior since learning of AIDS.

(The above did not stop a Broadway prohomosexual propaganda musical, *Les Cages aux Folles,* from opening to rave reviews by the prohomosexual media in New York.)

Children

As another example of "the good life" consider this: I received the following newsletter, which will be of particular interest to these who are fond of children.

Dear Friend,

As this day ends and another begins, I take these brief moments to write this letter. *Please,* read what I have to tell you.

Children are being bought and sold! Their bodies and spirits are being corrupted. They are being abused and degraded almost beyond comprehension.

Where?

Right here—at home—in our cities!

Thirteen years ago, I didn't know there were thousands of runaway and abandoned children in this country, or that so many of them—just to survive—are forced into prostitution and pornography.

I learned the hard way.

One night, in the winter of 1969, six teenage runaways knocked on the door of my tenement apartment where I was living to serve the poor of New York's Lower East Side. They asked if they could sleep on my floor and I took them in. I didn't have the guts to turn them away. The next day, four more came—and kids have been coming ever since. That, in essence, is how Covenant House was born.

Today, its UNDER 21 crisis centers help tens of thousands of homeless and runaway kids from all over the country. Not knowing where to turn, these youngsters often gravitate to the sordid streets of New York's infamous Minnesota Strip and similar red light zones in other cities. Too often the only place they can call "home" is a stretch of city blocks filled with porno parlors, strip joints, cheap bars, fleabag motels, and thousands of drifters, hookers, and pimps.

It is no place for a child.

Yet these areas act as magnets for the estimated *one million* children who run away from home each year in our country.

Whose children are these? Whose sons? Whose daughters? Nieces? Nephews? They are ours! Yours and mine!

What fate awaits these children? Too often they become commodities in the multi-billion-dollar sex industry that festers in our inner cities. Their young bodies are bought and sold like so much merchandise. These kids are subjected to every perversion that man can create. They are beaten, raped, and shot full of drugs. Some are tortured; others are killed—all are victims.

Take Veronica, for example. She was *only eleven* when I met her. She had already been arrested eight times for prostitution. The authorities never bothered to check her age, so she was never referred to Family Court to receive care. Each time she was taken to the Adult Criminal Court. Each time the judge fined her $100. And each time her pimp paid it and put her back on the street.

Veronica didn't make it much past her twelfth birthday. She was thrown from a tenth-story window. Maybe by a pimp. Maybe by a customer. No one has been held responsible.

Those children who survive become hardened by life on the streets. They become prematurely old, prematurely wise—and more cynical with each degrading sexual transaction. Even so, they are good kids.

Some come from warm, loving homes; but most of them are from broken, troubled homes. But what happens to them on the street simply should not be allowed to happen.

There was a time when I turned kids away because there simply was no room. I can't do that any more. I know only too well what the streets have in store for a kid all alone.

The work of Covenant House/UNDER 21 has grown with the increasing numbers of children coming to us for food, for shelter, for medical attention, and for *the most important thing of all*—hope. Hope for the future and a belief in themselves.

In the last few months, we have received requests from a dozen other cities to come help their kids. The number of homeless and runaway kids is growing at a frightening rate.

Father Bruce Ritter

It's fun to grow up in America today. With all the old restrictive fundamentalist taboos gone, there's so much more to experience! Children with mothers working away from the home, children of divorced parents, children conceived by lesbian mothers via sperm banks—all enjoy so much more *freedom*.

Entertainment
If you're interested in the psychology and philosophy of entertainment as seen from Hollywood and New York, you will enjoy the following article from *Variety* (Wednesday, May 25, 1983). This article does not concern itself with moral issues or pros and cons of what it is discussing. It is discussing the marketability of decadence in much the same way that a sump pump salesman will discuss the various merits of different kinds of pumps, tubing, and piping. Its dispassionate tone is all the more horrendous because of the complete abandonment of traditional values by the entertainment industry. The producers in Hollywood and the pimps who sell children portrayed in the letter quoted above would understand each other very well.

OLDER WOMEN, YOUNGER MEN

Seduction-Themed Pix Woo Filmgoers
by Lawrence Cohn

New York, May 24—The "older woman" seducing a young boy, a film topic dating back to many popular films such as "The Graduate" (Anne Bancroft, Dustin Hoffman), is shaping up as the next commercial film trend. Current releases "My Tutor" and "Private School" exploit the theme, with several major pictures to follow.

Popularity of the subgenre was demonstrated by two low-budget hits filmed in 1980 (released in 1981 and 1982), Jensen Farley Pictures' acquisitions "Private Lessons" and "Homework."

Both featured European leading ladies, Sylvia Kristel and Joan Collins, and stressed the sexual initiation of a youth by an experienced older woman as both major plot cog and marketing tool. "Lessons" posted $12,500,000 in domestic rentals while "Homework" amassed $3,400,000.

Since their success, Universal picked up the distribution rights to "Lesson's" followup film, "Private School," from its producer, R. Ben Efraim, after U parent MCA had handled cable, homevid and other ancillary uses of "Lessons."

"School," set in a private school for girls is closer to the youth comedy vein of "Porky's," but features Kristel as a sex education teacher in a reprise of her older woman role. Nearly all of the "Porky's" genre of raunchy comedies including Embassy's recent "Losin' It," have a sexual initiation subplot involving the young male protagonists with an older female prostitute.

In the case of Cannon's "The Last American Virgin," Louisa Moritz portrayed a housewife who accommodated the trio of teenage male leads.

Crown's current hit "My Tutor" toplines Caren Kaye in the first all-American leading lady casting within the cycle. Upcoming from the majors this year are two more pictures in the genre, Orion's "Class," starring Jacqueline Bisset (who beds her son's classmate), and 20th Century Fox' "Heaven," with Lesley Ann Warren romantically linked with teen Christopher Atkins.

Reprise For Bisset

For Bisset (allowing it is hard to think of the glamorous actress as "an older woman"), "Class" represents a return to this type of film. In her last picture, which she coproduced with William Allyn, the late George Cukor's "Rich and Famous," Bisset was paired with younger men including a sex scene with a teen actor.

Early in her career in 1969, she made two pictures in the genre: Allan Carr and Roger Smith's "The First Time," concerning the sexual initiation of a trio of boys, and the French picture "Secret World," in which a young boy became obsessed with Bisset, his English governess.

The older-women pictures have been commercially successful low-budgeters up until now (the Bisset and Warren opuses are larger-scale projects), but overshadowed by the more spectacularly grossing teen comedies. . . .

The older woman-young boy plot device has already replaced its much-publicized forerunner of the late 1970's, in which Brooke Shields, Jodie Foster, Tatum O'Neal and Kristy McNichol were featured as nymphettes involved with older men in such films as "Pretty Baby," "Taxi Driver" and "Little Darlings."

By inverting the sexes in the May-December pairings, the new films have largely defused the "kiddie porn" controversy that surrounded the pictures involving underage girls, particularly since the sex objects in the recent films are undeniably the mature women rather than the youthful male protagonists.

In her discussion of this trend (regarding mother-son incest pictures such as "Luna" and "Flesh And Blood") in the 1980 book "The Best Kept Secret: Sexual Abuse of Children," author Florence Rush noted that such films counter the unsavory male image by utilizing the time-proven strategy of blaming females for what men do.

European Prototypes

The prototype for "Private Lessons" and its offspring is the European governess genre, particularly Italian films popular a decade ago such as Salvatore Samperi's hits starring Laura Antonelli, "Malizia" and "Venial Sin."

Closely related to these pictures generically in Europe are the hundreds of incest-themed films that have proliferated since censorship was relaxed in the 1960's.

However, in the U.S. only incest pictures within the porno film industry have been commercially successful. Mainstream releases such as Louis Malle's "Murmur Of The Heart" and Bernardo Bertolucci's

"Luna" have generated considerable critical coverage but prominent releases such as "Cat People" and "Five Days One Summer" have been b.o. failures.

The porno field has recently seen the emergence of older women as leading stars, often paired with young men in a traditionally youth-oriented industry, notably Georgina Spelvin, Juliet Anderson (known popularly as her screen persona "Aunt Peg") and British actress Kay Parker.

Parker's 1980 incest film "Taboo" (plus its recent sequel) was a significant success, tapping an audience in a limited market that no mainstream picture has found to date.

Except for Suzanne Pleshette in Pete Hamill's "Flesh And Blood," television treatments of the incest genre have emphasized the highly relevant social problem of father-daughter relations. Lamont Johnson's "Off The Minnesota Strip" was a trailblazer in this regard, using the Hal Holbrook-Mare Winningham relationship as a key subplot to its story of teen prostitution.

(See Appendix 4 for a brilliant article by producer Ben Stein on Hollywood vs. Jerry Falwell.)

Walker Percy, in his magnificent book *Lost in the Cosmos,* (Farrar, Straus & Giroux, 1983), has a chapter called "The Promiscuous Self." Here is an excerpt.

A recent survey in a large city reported that 95 percent of all video tapes purchased for home consumption were *Insatiable,* a pornographic film starring Marilyn Chambers.

Of all sexual encounters on soap opera, only 6 percent occur between husband and wife.

In some cities of the United States, which now has the highest divorce rate in the world, the incidence of divorce now approaches 60 percent of married couples.

A recent survey showed that the frequency of sexual intercourse in married couples declined 90 percent after three years of marriage.

"A female sexologist reported . . ." that a favorite fantasy of American women, second only to oral sex, was having sex with two strange men at once.

According to the president of the North American Swing Club Association, only 3 percent of married couples who are swingers get divorces, as compared with over 50 percent of non-swinging couples.

In large American cities, lunch-break liaisons between business men and women have become commonplace.

Sexual activity and pregnancy in teenagers have increased dramatically in the last twenty years, in both those who have received sex education in schools and those who have not. In some cities, more babies are born to single women than to married women.

A radio psychotherapist reported that nowadays many young people who disdain marriage, preferring "relationships" and "commitments," speak of entering into simultaneous relationships with a second or third person as a growth experience.

In San Francisco's Buena Vista Park, to the outrage of local middle-class residents, homosexuals cruise and upon encountering a sexual prospect, always a stranger, exchange a word or a sign and disappear into the bushes. In a series of interviews, Buena Vista homosexuals admitted to sexual encounters with an average of more than 500 strangers.

A survey by a popular magazine reported that the incidence of homosexuality in the United States had surpassed that of the Weimar Republic. . . .

> A letter to Dear Abby:
> I am a twenty-three-year-old liberated woman who has been on the pill for two years. It's getting pretty expensive and I think my boyfriend should share half the cost, but I don't know him well enough to discuss money with him. [Abigail Van Buren, *The Best of Dear Abby* (New York: Andrews and McMeel, 1981), p. 242.]

How to Do It

At the opposite end of the spectrum there is Helen Gurley Brown and her book *Having It All* (Simon & Schuster, 1983). Helen Gurley Brown is editor of *Cosmopolitan* magazine, whose "self-help credo is the touchstone for its countless readers in the United States and the 17 countries where *Cosmo* appears in foreign language editions." According to the front and back flap copy on the book, "Reading *Having It All* is like having Helen Gurley Brown as your 24-hour-a-day advisor, sharing with you the wisdom of a lifetime, helping, scolding, inspiring—a warm, supportive and unshockable friend who's been through it all herself and is *convinced* that you too can have the success and fulfillment *you* deserve." Johnny Carson gave Helen Gurley Brown major air time. Barbara Walters interviewed her. The *New York Times* praised her book. (They said, however, that they "did not understand" Walker Percy's book.) And the *Washington Post* loved it. If you'd like to find out what all these people love so much and what this leader of women thinks, let's dip into the book at a couple of places.

On page 238, Helen Gurley Brown tells us: "Heaven in *this* life is desiring someone so much that you must *claw* your way off to the nearest bed." (Then, no doubt, off to the nearest doctor or vet.)

On page 247 we find:

> It's almost a shame sex is so acceptable, clean and friendly now, like eating Granola with skimmed milk—not that it doesn't still feel very nice. Whatever you do to keep sex naughty in your life, I hope you are

doing. . . . Reading pornography (I love erotic Indian and Chinese art), seeing naughty movies, having fantasies, either in your head or talked out with him.

On pages 366, 367, and 368 we find:

Well, in *case* you're one of the ones who doesn't want to stay home and stay faithful—and you *know* I want for you whatever you feel will complete your life—here are some ground rules gleaned from some women I know who also don't stay home and stay faithful and have strayed more or less "successfully" for years. . . .
    Let's just get on with the rules. (1) The most equitable affairs for the married occur between two married partners. . . . Be *insanely* careful not to have your husband find *out*. This means not taking phone calls from your lover at home, not cuddling in public even if nobody you know is around . . . tell virtually no one . . . don't escalate . . . don't confess . . . be prepared eventually to be found out no matter how careful you are. . . . A few [affairs] may last as long as 12, 20, 30 years, but that's rare.

(It had better last *forever,* since once you get herpes, no one else will want you.)
    In case you're interested in other amusement besides extramarital affairs, here's some other advice, on page 231: "One night stands have a bad name. They shouldn't." On page 227 we read:

Sleeping with more than one man on the same day or in the same week could be considered promiscuous, I suppose, yet I think you can do quite a lot of that and *not* be promiscuous. Maybe liking sex is comparable to the way James Beard feels about food; he cooks and eats a lot, but his attitude is never *casual.* People who have a lot of sex are not necessarily casual about it *either.* . . . When I was single (me again—I hope this isn't tacky) it never occurred to me not to have plenty of this pleasurable thing. If, in one week, two of one's dearest friends happen to be visiting (in my case, Los Angeles) from another city, why would one not fit them both in? There are, after all, twenty-one breakfasts, lunches, and dinners in a 168-hour week. It seems to me you can *certainly* accommodate more than one love if neither is classifiable as the man in your life.

(Why not try having sex with James Beard's food and cooking your friends from L.A.?)
    If you would like to hear her economic philosophy, we find on page 441:

Life is pricey. You can have nearly everything *from* it if you want and you're a fool if you don't take your share, because hardship and grizzlies happen to people who *don't* take, so you might as well compensate for them with *success*.

(The possibility of this line of reasoning being mistaken for the Beatitudes seems remote. A lot of women can forget their alimony checks forever if their ex-hubbies ever adopt this piece of philosophy. This is also a good argument in favor of rape—take! take! take!)

And on page 16, more of her economic plan for life:

The plan to get all the things you want—is, yes, your job. That's where the money, success and clout come from. Also, the kind of job you have can seriously affect what kind of men you meet. . . . Despite every gain of the Women's Liberation Movement, lots of women still prefer their man to have the important job, while they nurture and support him emotionally and occasionally dip into the professional world to stave off ennui. . . . Oh, my poor benighted darlings, even Jackie, at age 46, found that being a rich, beautiful adored person was not necessarily the answer. . . . I've already mentioned (I'm very big on this point!) that a smashing job puts you in touch with the kind of man you couldn't get to as a drone or non-worker.

(Drones are the *male* bees. Strange that the Eastern media elite, who find capitalism so distasteful, should so readily embrace Helen Gurley Brown's crass materialism, which is light years beyond anything the Robber Barons ever practiced. But the feminist label works wonders of alchemy, transmuting base desires into the gold of exalted action. Now, if Adam Smith's name had only been Gloria Steinem . . .)

It occurs to me that many women who raise their families, stay with one man, do not have affairs, or follow most of Helen Gurley Brown's advice might resent being referred to as "a drone" or a "non-worker." However, never mind all that. The *New York Times* approves of Helen Gurley Brown and that's all that counts. After all, we must keep our priorities straight. (In our new pantheon of the gods, if the Supreme Court has replaced the Supreme Being, then the *Times* can be its prophet, minus sackcloth and ashes of course, and Joan Rivers and Helen Gurley Brown its vestal "virgins!")

After 462 nauseating, endless pages of this nonsense, Helen Gurley Brown ends her book:

Oh, darlings, I could go on and on, [God forbid!] but I've *got* to stop so you can get to your mouse-burgering! And I can get back to *mine*. I am wishing you all the happiness I can possibly wish you—and this is something to think about—though I don't know who said it: "Do not follow where the path may lead. Go, instead, where there is no path and leave a trail." I'll bet that's what *you'd* do.

The Bunnies' Last Stand
In the *Wall Street Journal* (September 28, 1983), in an article entitled "Passé in the Big City, Playboy's Ailing Club's Search for Profits in America's Hinterlands," we read the following:

> Playboy Clubs have been hurt by, . . . in no small measure, a changing society. When the Club started in 1960, the . . . bunnies who socialized with the customers were the height of raciness. When the San Francisco Club closed in 1976, it was because nearby topless bars stole the business. "Playboy was as wild as it knew how to be," says a company consultant.
>
> That still may be good enough for more modest markets, however, and that's what Playboy is banking on. Its name continues to be a bit naughty in the heartland and that's a good customer draw.

Oh, wonderful irony! Playboy Enterprises, the brainchild of philosopher Hugh Hefner, is now reduced to pursuing a shrinking sea of decency and virtue across the American Midwestern wastes, while having to abandon the more citified gentry which it has done so much to render so entirely decadent that its services are no longer required! Playboy seems to have fulfilled its own prophecies too well. Having opened the door to the "Playboy philosophy" (Caligula actually started all this, not Hefner), Playboy now finds itself reaping its own whirlwind: it must now compete with child pornography, pedophilia, and other aspects of our "liberated" society, for a dwindling group of customers who can still be titillated by just good old-fashioned cheesecake! There is justice in this world after all. (Hugh would do well to make personal contributions to the Moral Majority and Jerry Falwell to attempt to maintain some level of decency in the country. After all, as he has now seen, if decadence becomes too commonplace, you can't even sell it!)

The State of the Union
If this chapter is descriptive of the country in which you want to live, raise your children, and try to be a human being, you should be satisfied. Like the "new passive moderate evangelicals," you are moving with the powers that be, with the trends of the time. On the other hand, if this makes you a bit queasy, or makes you want to emigrate to Ireland, perhaps you ought to consider what you can do to stem the tide. If this is not the America you want, you had better do something about it (unless you're too busy going to church and hearing sermons on "love," discussing the Third World,

reading inspiring articles in *Christianity Today* about Gandhi, or buying Christian exercise records, etc., ad nauseum).

Across the country, in gay bars and other homosexual "recreational facilities," the following notice has recently been posted: "*AIDS* is everyone's problem. Protect yourself and those you love. Use condoms. Avoid any exchange of body fluids. Limit your use of recreational drugs. Enjoy more time with fewer partners." Welcome to secular America.

The Dead and Dying

Yet all of the above notwithstanding, the evangelical establishment sleeps on, ironically finding more and more reasons to do less and less about a deteriorating situation. Like stewards rearranging deck chairs on the *Titanic* and telling people, "be calm," they believe they are on an "unsinkable" ship.

I always think it's rather pitiful to read, "He died in his sleep." This seems to be the epitaph the evangelical and Christian community is after, however. I hope this chapter hasn't *disturbed you*. Back to our conferences on church growth, our editorials on redaction criticism, our fellowshipping, sharing, discipling, and potluck dinners. One of these days, should you decide to sneak off to watch a pornographic movie (perhaps to prove to yourself that you are *not* a fundamentalist), the star on the screen may just turn out to be your child. But then again, if we cared about our children we would never have allowed the decline of morality in America to go this far in the first place. Thanks goes to all the *nice, nice* "dialoguing," "loving," "nonconfrontational," "spiritual," "moderate" people who have made compromise so very *nice:* a profitable and quiet way of life for the evangelical establishment. But of all this, more in the next chapter.

If you're still upset, join a major evangelical organization, or better yet go to seminary and study redaction criticism, and learn to call evil good and good evil, or at least to mumble, "I don't know, it's just *so* complicated." All of which will help you still that unseemly passion, calm those fears, quell that desire for action. Sleep tight. And pleasant dreams.

Part II

BAD NEWS FOR RELIGIOUS MAN

5 HOW TO BECOME A JELLYFISH

E vangelicals are a lot like jellyfish. They float with the tides. They do not direct their own course. Sometimes the currents of the sea beach them. Then they melt in the sun on the sand. Later they disappear altogether. The jelly dries and no trace is left. The tide goes out, the wind moans softly, and no one notices.

Many Christian leaders, as well as some Christian magazines, periodicals, radio shows, seem much more interested in finding excuses for *not* involving themselves in the society around them than for looking for ways *to* involve themselves. The idea of actually changing the country for the better and bringing it into alignment with Judeo-Christian principles horrifies them. Being accepted and fashionably uncontroversial, or at least choosing fashionable controversies to talk about (peace, Third World, "social justice," etc.), seems more important than the judgment of God. Persuaded by the deceiving faces of this acquiescence and compliance, they compromise in the name of "spirituality," or "Christian living," or most usually "love." The clear, loud call for accommodation comes wrapped in the name of the Gospel of Niceness. Sin as the source of *all* human problems is banished and a call for repentance is rarely made. As examples of ths dismal trend, this drifting on the tide, this pitiful scampering to conform, consider the following.

Our Man in Washington

In *Christianity Today* (November 12, 1982), there was an interview with Senate Chaplain Richard Halverson. I have heard people say they are grateful that there is a "genuine evangelical" as Senate Chaplain to provide "guidance" to our decision-makers. If the following is an example of such "guidance," there is little mystery that so many Christians in the Senate, when the time comes for principled confrontation, have acted spinelessly.

The *Christianity Today* interviewer asked Senate Chaplain Halverson about such issues as abortion and active involvement by Christians. Here is the answer he gave as to why Christians do not all see eye to eye on a number of issues *including* abortion.

> It's just very difficult: I don't really know the answers. Perhaps part of the explanation is that all of us hear God's truth a little differently. We hear it in terms of the way we are made, our backgrounds, our genes. The result is that the body of Christ is very diverse. And I suppose there is a sense in which we have to honor individualism within the church.

As nice a statement of relativism and situational ethics as one could hope for. Eat your heart out, Joseph Fletcher. Halverson's ambivalence was reconfirmed in a *Washington Post* interview (August 3, 1983), in which he said, "I would say right away that I oppose abortion, but I also believe very strongly that God endowed us with free will and the responsibility for free choice." The *Post* also noted that Halverson said he had "no desire to influence legislation." So much for the evangelical man on the spot! In other words, "I personally believe, but . . ." The ultimate cop-out.

Honoring individualism is fine concerning disagreements such as how many angels can dance on the head of a pin, or which was written first, Mark or Luke. When it comes to critical issues of human life as expressed in the abortion debate, however, *to not have a clear call for prolife action from the "evangelical" Christian placed in the position of Senate Chaplain is disastrous*. Only blocks away from where this interview was given is an abortion clinic which routinely performs hundreds of abortions unopposed. Halverson's comments seem to contradict Christian conscience, in light of the feeble cries of a dying baby gurgling in a stainless steel tray not a mile away. At last count Washington, D.C., has more abortions every year than live births.

Perhaps Halverson noticed that Mother Teresa fell from fashion because she committed the *faux pas* of calling for action against abortion in her Nobel Peace Prize acceptance speech. Perhaps he learned the lesson: Always mumble, never speak plainly, and certainly do not say anything that could possibly offend the media elite or, God forbid, change society for the better.

What an unfortunate contrast the remarks by this "evangelical" Senate Chaplain make with the moving and robust defense of the traditional orthodox Christian position made by Terence Cardinal Cooke of New York. From his deathbed, terminally ill with leukemia, he continued to condemn "mercy killing," and as his last act on earth prepared a letter to be read in the New York Diocese after his death. He said,

It is a tragedy that in our times concepts which are disastrous for the human family of God, such as abortion, euthanasia and infanticide, are falsely presented as easy and even respectable solutions to human and social problems. . . . From the most profound depths of my being I implore you to reject this concept that is contrary to life, contrary to children, contrary to humanity. . . . Life is no less beautiful when it is accompanied by illness or weakness, hunger or poverty, physical or mental diseases, loneliness or old age. . . . Oppose with all your strength the deadly technology that results daily in the death of innocent and helpless beings. [As quoted from the *Chicago Tribune,* October 3, 1983.]

Cardinal Cooke ended his moving plea by saying that even in his exceedingly painful and failing condition he would continue his "apostolate in defense of life." What a disgrace that evangelical leaders in similar positions of prominence have failed so uniformly to speak with conviction on these issues. Where are our leaders?

The *Reformed Journal*

The *Reformed Journal,* in their May 1983 issue, printed an article by Ronald A. Wells, a professor of history at Calvin College. The article, titled "Whatever Happened to Francis Schaeffer?" was a thinly veiled attempt to categorize, debunk, and undo the work of Francis A. Schaeffer, who is thought to pose a threat to those sponsoring liberal causes from the base of "evangelical scholarship." The article also attempted to lay down a *new* set of criteria for the "new" evangelical leftist agenda. Wells wrote:

Schaeffer was not interested in meaningful social change. . . . He seemed disinterested in such issues as war and peace and *structural injustices of industrial capitalism* [emphasis mine].

In other words, Francis Schaeffer has failed to fall into line behind Ron Sider and company. A serious crime, indeed! Especially when one considers how *unfashionable* this makes him, and on the other hand how *fashionable* it makes those who attack his insensitivity to the "structural injustices of industrial capitalism." Wells then goes on to point out that the difference between his position and that of Schaeffer is Wells's "willingness to accept the reality of ambiguity." In other words, the willingness to *not* see issues clearly, to *not* take clear stands, and to tolerate a Christianity so fuzzy around the edges that it can accommodate all comers (except conservative orthodox thinkers), and *not* require one to be singled out as somehow different.

Lest anyone think that this is not what Wells and others of his stripe believe, let them consider that in offering his alternative to Francis

Schaeffer's view of history, he suggests as one of his main three concluding points that what Christians must do is to engage in "definitive repentance from the evangelical ethos. If the gospel is to be a witness to North American culture [notice he presumes it hasn't been so far], it must *not* be seen as a force which withdraws from mainline institutions and churches to form its own para-church institutions and endlessly fragmenting mini-denominations." In other words, Christians are not to stand on the basis of their individual conscience for what they believe against the tide around them within their denominations. This eliminates believing Catholics such as James Hitchcock (a founder of the "para-church" Fellowship of Catholic Scholars), who would stand up and speak against his own bishops in the name of biblical absolutes. It also eliminates those such as Francis Schaeffer (founder of "para-church" L'Abri), who would plead for a purity of the visible church. (It also is a strange statement to make from a historian, of all people, since *all* Protestant denominations were formed by withdrawing, "fragmenting," from Rome anyway, as were most Catholic orders such as the Franciscans who formed a living alternative to the corruption of some in the medieval church.)

But let us examine a little more closely what Wells and others like him are proposing in terms of whom we should not take a stand against, or whom we should not be "fragmented" from. Take, for instance, the policy statement adopted by the 195th General Assembly 1983 of the Presbyterian Church USA. (A "mainline" church indeed!) Their policy statement is called "Theological Reflections on Contraception and Abortion." In glowing endorsement of abortion, this "mainline" Presbyterian Church affirms the 1973 *Roe* v. *Wade* decision and

> opposes attempts to limit access to abortion by: (a) denial of funding for abortions to women who receive federal funding for their medical care; (b) restriction of covering by insurance companies for abortion procedure; (c) the passage of federal, state and local legislation which has the effect of harassing women contemplating abortion; (d) restriction of federal funding to medical centers and teaching institutions where abortions are performed; (e) passage of a constitutional amendment or other legislation which would return control over abortion to individual states or prohibit it as a national policy; (f) restriction of the jurisdiction of federal and supreme courts in the area of abortion.

The "mainline" statement then goes on to urge,

> (a) opposing adoption of all measures which would serve to restrict full and equal access to contraception and abortion services to all women regardless of race, age and economic standing; (b) working *actively* to restore public funding by federal, state and local governments for the

availability of a full range of reproductive health services for the medically indigent . . . (d) challenging Presbyterian doctors in institutions to provide contraception and abortion services at cost or free-of-charge to those who no longer have access to public funding . . . (g) opposing efforts to use zoning regulations to preclude the establishment of abortion clinics [emphasis mine].

This "mainline" statement is based on the following "theological and scholarly" reasoning:

The legal right to have an abortion is a necessary prerequisite to the exercise of conscience in abortion decisions. Legally speaking, abortion should be a woman's right because, theologically speaking, making a decision about abortion is, above all, her responsibility. (For a full reproduction of "Covenant and Creation: Theological Reflections on Contraception and Abortion," Presbyterian Church USA, see Appendix 5.)

To emphasize the depravity of this "mainline" theological reasoning, let's rephrase the above statement as follows:

The legal right to own slaves is a necessary prerequisite to the exercise of conscience in slave-owning decisions. Legally speaking, slavery should be a white man's right because, theologically speaking, making a decision about Negroes is, above all, the white race's responsibility.

The Presbyterian Church USA is one of those "mainline institutions and churches" from which, according to Mr. Wells, it is *paramount* that evangelicals *not* withdraw. Thus we must accept all this. To use his own words, Wells has shown a great "willingness to accept the reality of ambiguity." No wonder those who, like Mr. Wells, accept such a level of ambiguity in their thinking are at odds with those who are talking about, God forbid, "taking a stand"! No wonder they attempt to debunk those whose purity of vision remains clear as they muddy their own spiritual insight in a move to the left.

The *Reformed Journal,* like Ronald Wells, has a sad history of deliberately equivocating instead of taking a clear Christian stand. As long ago as September 1974 the *Reformed Journal* printed an article entitled "Abortion and the Definition of a Person" by William Haskell. It is interesting to note that in 1974, with the ink hardly dry on the 1973 *Roe v. Wade* ruling, the *Reformed Journal* was already scrambling to translate and make palatable the unpalatable decision of the Supreme Court to evangelicals.

It seems undesirable to treat the fetus in the very early stages of pregnancy as already a human person. . . . The fetus is to be regarded and treated as a human person when it reaches the stage of development at which it is capable of independent existence as a human organism, supported by the care which is normally given to newborn children.

. . . It follows, of course, that in certain circumstances abortion may be contemplated as a morally acceptable course of action. . . . In the present imperfect state of the world penicillin has its work to do, and so, sometimes, does abortion. . . . It will allow us to make decisions of compassion which meet ineluctable needs of the already living persons without carrying in our hearts the guilt of murder. [What is an "already living" person, for heaven's sake? Does this mean there are "as yet unliving" persons?]

Professor Haskell at the time was teaching at Huntington College. Though as a professor of philosophy he should have known better, he seems to have escaped any close study of fetology, and the state of the fetuses to be aborted seems to have been omitted in preparing his rather sweeping statements about what is or is not a human being.

What is intriguing, however, is that the *Reformed Journal* would be so quick in affirming the Supreme Court ruling, using almost their own wording as to "viability." Since the *Reformed Journal* was not crusading for the legalization of abortion before 1973, this can be seen only as one more example of evangelicals pathetically lagging behind the parade, yet scrambling with a great deal of unseemliness to jump on board whatever secular bandwagon happens to be passing. And all too often, this bandwagon turns out to be a garbage truck.

His Magazine
In February 1979 *His* magazine, the official publication of the evangelical organization Inter-Varsity Christian Fellowship, not to be outdone by the *Reformed Journal*'s scramble to be fashionable, had its own issue on abortion. In it they printed an interview with Dr. C. Everett Koop presenting the prolife position and a Dr. Gary Strokosh presenting a "Christian prochoice" position. The fact that these positions were presented on equal footing, with no editorial comment beyond one that could be summed up as saying, "Now you've seen both Christian alternatives, choose which one you like better," is almost as scandalous as the behavior of the *Reformed Journal*.

It is interesting to note that of the fifteen letters commenting on the Koop-Strokosh interview *His* subsequently printed, twelve were strongly prolife and many of these were appalled that *His* would allow a prochoice position to be presented in its pages without comment. *His*'s response: "It was not the purpose of the abortion article to present *His*'s official stand on the issue. Rather, it was supposed to stimulate your thinking." They cutely add, "Now you know even *more* why you think abortion is unbiblical." Yes, but at that time we still didn't know what *His* thought.

The situation at *His* has greatly improved since the February 1979 fiasco and its sorry followup. Since then the magazine has published two strongly prolife articles and three generally sound—but rather too personalistic—prolife editorials. And through *His* has yet to print an editorial that comes right out and states that the only possible Christian position on abortion is one that affirms the sanctity of all human life from the time of conception onward, we can be grateful that this evangelical magazine has apparently done an about-face on abortion.

Christianity Yesterday

Unfortunately, even as one evangelical magazine moves in a more hopeful direction another one appears to be badly drifting. Over the past year *Christianity Today* has subtly shifted from its previously solid evangelical base. A series of articles clearly reflect this shift—especially if they are read in relation to liberal secular coverage of the same events. Take for example *Christianity Today*'s coverage of the National Council of Churches' release of its "Inclusive Language Lectionary" which attempts to replace traditional biblical language with "non-sexist" language. While this abomination was being exposed and ridiculed in the secular press for what it was, *Christianity Today* chose to cover it only in their news section and took a wishy-washy, "let's hear from all sides" approach. Why was there no editorial outcry from our leading evangelical publication against the NCC's feminist Bible? (Three months after the event, once the editors at *Christianity Today* had no doubt confirmed which way the wind was blowing, and therefore found the courage to do so, they did print an editorial against the Inclusive Language Lectionary. But as usual with a magazine whose editorial policy is dictated by fashion and marketing concerns, it was too little too late.)

We have a similar situation with respect to *Christianity Today*'s coverage (September 16, 1983) of the World Council of Churches' Sixth Assembly. About eight months earlier a number of articles appeared in the secular press exposing the WCC as a leftist organization. Then, while *Time* magazine was blasting the World Council for ignoring Soviet aggression, financing leftist revolutionaries, and being extremely anti-Western, *Christianity Today* printed a very positive article on the WCC. In a long and prominently placed essay, the author argued that the WCC was becoming more "evangelical." He urged evangelicals to join it despite the Council's proabortion, pro-Marxist, profeminist theology, and its disastrous involvement in an ecumenism of unbelief.

The same compromising note was sounded by the magazine in relation to a number of other events. While the leftist *Village Voice* was printing a strong condemnation of the Baby Jane Doe infanticide ruling (by Nat Hentoff, an atheist and jazz critic), *Christianity Today* remained silent.

While Christianity Today was eulogizing Gandhi, Jewish agnostic editor Norman Podhoretz, in his magazine *Commentary*, exposed Gandhi in all his dayglow inconsistencies. The message to evangelicals is, "We can all get along just fine, thank you; never mind about the details." Virtue through wishy-washiness.

Evangelicals must decide what sort of "evangelicals" they wish to be. Are they going to be part of the vast co-opted evangelical establishment which engulfs many magazines, institutions, and Christian colleges? Take, for example, evangelical colleges, which "open-mindedly" tolerate proabortion professors, totally unbalanced political science and economics courses where Ron Sider and other ideological leftists are required reading, and highly secularized social sciences. Perhaps unwittingly, a recent Wheaton College advertisement extolling the virtues of obtaining a master's degree at that school revealed more than was intended. "An M.A. from Wheaton College uniquely blends God's Word with the latest thinking in your field of study. Dream a little. With an education like that, what could God do with you?" (Advertisement for Wheaton College in *Christianity Today*, November 11, 1983.) To which we must respond that if the "blending" has been successful, perhaps God can do *nothing* with you.

On the other hand, are believing evangelicals going to align themselves with other orthodox Christians—Roman Catholics, fundamentalists, charismatics, and others *who hold to an orthodoxy of belief in both doctrine and a view of the world?* The choice must be made and the lines drawn lest we slip into a new mire of cultural liberalism comparable to the old theological liberalism which overtook the Protestant denominations at the beginning of this century in America. Do we really want to be burned twice in the same century? From the call to repentance we have gone to the sociological "gospel" of dialogue.

The tortuous mental Rubic's Cubes that some evangelicals construct to avoid confronting the issues clearly are amazing for their ingenuity, if not their logic. Consider the evangelical magazine editor who told me the following: "These issues of medical ethics are really very complicated. For instance, have you ever considered the fact that heart pacemakers are too expensive to be available to Third World patients? Really these questions of abortion are so complex and these sanctity-of-life decisions so agonizing, there are no simple solutions." This was his "answer" as to why he was not taking a stand through his writing on the issue of abortion. To such people any red herring is preferable to being pinned down to specifics and being held accountable. This tactic is accurately described by Brian F. Griffin in his book *Panic Among the Philistines* (Regnery/Gateway) as "the anguish of a nervous intellectual imposter who is determined to keep the conversation hovering around one minor observation because he knows he would have little to say about any of the major implications" (p. 146).

Typical of this attitude among evangelical leaders are the strangely ambivalent remarks concerning abortion by several Gordon College professors quoted in the January 16, 1984, issue of the *Tartan*, the college's paper. In this evangelical college we find a Dr. Buhler objecting to those who take a strong prolife view on the grounds that they "[don't] seem to have a feel for, or interaction with, complexity. . . . One positive achievement of secular thought in America has been toleration and acceptance of other points of view." Dr. Buhler concluded his remarks by stating that he felt the most sensible stance was to be "antiabortion but prochoice." In the same paper, a Dr. Bishop criticizes a prolife activist on the grounds that he is "unwilling to admit that abortion is a complex issue with room for differences of opinion."

Why this endless nonsense about "complex issues"? Some issues are not complex. Slavery is not a complex issue. Gassing Jews is not a complex issue. Nor is abortion. Maybe a historical analogy will help here. Let's say it's the year 1858 in America, and let's transpose some of these remarks into that context: "I believe that the most sensible stance is to be antislavery but prochoice." This would have been patent nonsense in 1858. If you were antislavery, you believed not only that it was wrong for *you* to own slaves but wrong for *everyone* to own slaves. If you did not believe that it was wrong for everyone to own slaves (that is, if you were "prochoice" on slavery), you were not antislavery. You were proslavery. And it is *exactly* the same in America today. If you are antiabortion, you believe not only that it is wrong to kill your own offspring, but it is wrong to kill any baby, born or unborn. If you do not believe that abortion is wrong for everyone (that is, if you are "prochoice" on abortion), you are not antiabortion. You are proabortion. There is no middle ground. You can't have it both ways—antislavery but "prochoice," or antiabortion but "prochoice." Not in 1858. And not today. There is no such thing as a moderately enslaved black or a half-dead baby. You are either enslaved or free, dead or alive. Let those "evangelicals" who think it is perfectly all right for people to kill human offspring come right out and say so, and let us hear the biblical, medical, and theological basis for their position. But let us hear no more about this "complex issue" nonsense, this "I'm antiabortion but prochoice" foolishness. We are weary of your cant and humbuggery.

When *Christianity Today* magazine in 1983, ten years too late, finally did a cover story on abortion, even then they could not take a forthright approach. Instead they fell into the secularist trap by titling the article, "If Not Abortion, What Then?" and subtitling it, "Why pro-life rhetoric is not enough." They fell into the trap precisely because the secularist abortion argument revolves not around absolutes and the sanctity of life but around *pragmatism;* or in other words, monetary concerns, convenience, poverty-wealth issues, happiness. Anything to avoid the real issue. *Is life precious? Is it sacred?* Abortion has been sold to us as a solution to poverty and to unwanted pregnancies for poor people, or to help the Third World. The reality, however, is that abortion has become a middle-class casual birth control method, as well as a not-so-subtle antiminority genocidal action to reduce in number the "poor" (read blacks). *Christianity Today,* by discussing abortion in terms of its impact on "poor people," once again was up to the same old evangelical trick of trying to appear fashionable while half-heartedly stating the Christian position. Having their cake and eating it too. Fashionable, because poverty is in while abortion is out. Fashionable, because in trying to hector the prolife movement for supposedly too much rhetoric and not enough compassionate action, they became a shill for the secular media version of the prolife movement and its activities. They appeared blind to the *vast strides the prolife movement has made, not only in antiabortion "rhetoric," but also in positive prolife solutions.* For every group around the country that pickets an abortion clinic, other people, and often the picketers themselves, are also involved in crisis pregnancy centers. The same people who have indulged in prolife "rhetoric" are also the ones involved in compassionate alternatives.

By discussing abortion in the way they did, *Christianity Today* was following the secularist ploy for avoiding moral issues. You connect one issue to another until you have erected such a vast set of unmanageable problems that all action is stifled. By framing the discussion of abortion in terms of its impact on the poor in America, one then has to deal with the whole question of poverty as well as abortion. Why not throw in the Third World at the same time, nuclear weapons, and for that matter the possibility of cultivating vegetables on the moon? Tangible actions are put so out of reach of everyday life that ordinary Christians can do nothing more than *discuss* problems while doing nothing to solve them. If one sufficiently complicates the issues, one never has to deal with them.

This is the "what if" ploy. It is easier to discuss endless hypothetical questions of "ethics" rather than deal with real and immediate pressing issues. One way to see this absurdity for what it is, is to apply this ploy to well-known historical moral questions about which there is general agreement. For instance, imagine a series of *Christianity Today* stories like the following:

If Not Slavery, What Then:
Why Abolitionist Rhetoric Is Not Enough.

We have learned of the economic hardship that emancipation will cause plantation owners. Cotton will rot unpicked. . . . Where will the slaves live? Will their quality of life really be improved?

Pro-Jewish Rhetoric Is Not Enough:
If Not Gassing Jews, What Then?

Studies have shown that many Jews feel themselves to be unloved and unwanted . . . Is this full, meaningful humanhood?

Anti-Child Pornography Rhetoric Is Not Enough

If church leaders are going to rail moralistically against child pornography, they must be willing to provide alternative employment for the young citizens of our great land. . . . Without presenting such loving alternatives ourselves, how can we criticize those of other traditions?

There is always a "what if" in a fallen world. There is always a price to be paid for principles. Laws and moral taboos can never be applied completely consistently. For instance, laws against rape notwithstanding, rapes still happen. But because they still occur do we then drop laws against rape? "If we do not decriminalize rape it will continue to take place in dangerous and unsanitary back alleys. Therefore, it should be legalized so those undergoing the procedure will have the opportunity to see that it occurs under the most favorable conditions . . ." Or some such nonsense. There are footnotes to every moral issue. But does that really provide an excuse for having no absolutes we are willing to enforce, no moral framework? I think not. Not everything is to be frittered away by dilettante conversationalists seeking to avoid commitment at all costs. The games jellyfish will play.

Extra Baggage

Sadly, some Roman Catholics, like Cardinal Bernardin of Chicago, have also become fans of linking each question to a larger question which leads to more questions. For instance, Bernardin has linked standing against abortion to pacifism and has claimed that this necessitates being against capital punishment as well. All of which is patent nonsense. Surely we should be able to understand the difference between an innocent unborn baby and a convicted murderer. Or the difference between attempting to prevent war by maintaining a strong national defense and the slaughter of the innocent for reasons of mere convenience. Such linkage causes a sense of being overwhelmed. We are told that if we wish to stand against abortion we must also carry four or five hundred pounds of Cardinal Bernardin's ideological baggage for him. But it is not so. It should be noted here that Cardinal Bernardin has never wavered in his opposition to abortion and is to be applauded for his long-standing faithfulness on this issue. I am merely trying to point out the fallacy of linking the prolife issue to other questions like nuclear disarmament, a linkage which needlessly reduces the number of people who will be committed to stopping abortion.

Eternity and the Christian Legal Society

In *Eternity* magazine (December 1982), in an article entitled "Civil Disobedience" by Lynn R. Buzzard, the president of the Christian Legal Society
(CLS), Mr. Buzzard takes to task those who would urge an activist approach to crucial issues of the day: "Frankly, a little less noise and a little
more spiritual consistency in the religious community would be well advised." This reminds me of the Old Testament passage in Amos, in which
we hear, "Peace, peace, when there is no peace," the message of the false
prophets. In the parable of the Good Samaritan, when the religious leaders
passed by on the other side of the road, ignoring the battered body of the
miserable Jew who had been robbed, lying helpless, no doubt they too were
hurrying to religious functions and espousing "more spiritual consistency in
the religious community." The irony is that if there is any position in society
(other than perhaps Senate Chaplain) where one could expect a little *more*
noise, activism, and visibility, it would be that of Christians involved in the
law, the Christian Legal Society.

"The Law is no more, and the prophets find no vision from the
Lord" (Lamentations 2:9).

Professor of law Bill Stanmeyer (a Roman Catholic and one of the
few activist members of the Christian Legal Society), states in his book,
Clear and Present Danger (Servant Books, pp. 198-200):

> Furthermore, the secular state is no longer "neutral" to Christianity. This
> point is hard to get across to many Christians; like the frog placed in
> lukewarm water that was gradually heated to boiling, we do not see
> how radically our country has changed. The government has now made
> itself, spiritually, our enemy. If anything should be clear to the readers of
> this book, it is that whole segments of our governing apparatus—the
> federal judiciary, the educational administrators, the media elite, and
> much of the governmental bureaucracies in charge of tax-collecting and
> educational regulation—are by and large hostile to Judeo-Christian prin-
> ciples and values. Moreover, many Christians in these and other
> branches of society's leadership elites—such as lawyers who make rules
> and doctors who deal with ultimate ethical questions—have absorbed
> the materialism of their peers to such an extent that they allow the
> world to set the agenda for the church. In short, many Christians think
> that the Christian's calling is to do no more than imitate the faddist
> enthusiasms of their secularized fellow citizens. As someone has
> quipped, too many Christians pride themselves on being "trendier than
> thou"; they are indeed "salt which has lost its savor."
>
> Assuming, as I do, that most of these persons are *privately* "good
> Christians," I can only conclude that they are philosophical schizophren-
> ics. They have two minds: their private and family mind for home and
> Sunday mornings: their public and social mind for work and public
> affairs. . . .

It is also clear that many Christians do not really hold their private principles very deeply.

This nonconfrontational, unprincipled form of appeasement on the part of the CLS was underscored and confirmed in the Fall 1982 issue of *The Barrister,* a national journal for lawyers, in an article on the Christian Legal Society. The CLS, because of its accommodating attitude, received the good boy pat on the head: ". . . The Society [CLS] insists that it does not want to impose its values and principles on others." "It would be improper . . . to impose biblical principles . . . on the secular courts." The statement exhibits what I call being taken in by the myth of neutrality. The CLS position could have been scripted by the ACLU, Planned Parenthood, or the National Organization for Women, and applauded by every abortionist in the country who wants to be left to do his own very lucrative work, unhampered by Christians trying to "impose their morality." The CLS sentiment is a dream come true for the IRS beaureaucrat or state official attempting to regulate citizens or close Christian institutions.

The CLS has in recent months participated in more cases involving religious liberties. Their involvement in prolife cause has been virtually nil, however, and they have chosen to keep an unfortuantely low profile in general. Most distressingly, the organization has not yet come out with an official statement on sanctity of life issues.

Secular Observations

Other observers of the national scene have also been aware of the gradual erosion of traditional orthodox Christianity by the "new evangelical left." Lloyd Billingsley (a well-known California journalist, commentator, and author of the novel *Fear No Evil*) wrote an article in the *National Review* (October 28, 1983) entitled, "First Church of Christ, Socialist," in which he made the following observations:

> Anyone who has regarded the evangelicals as a bastion of conservatism, need only leaf through the two main monthly publications . . . —the *Other Side* and *Sojourners*—to see otherwise.
>
> Based in Philadelphia and co-edited by John Alexander, the *Other Side* bills itself as "a magazine focusing on peace, justice, and economic liberation from a radical Christian perspective." *Sojourners,* formerly the *Post American,* operates out of Washington with a wider circulation and higher profile. . . . *Sojourners* is edited by Jim Wallis, the author of *Agenda for Biblical People* and *The Call to Conversion.*
>
> So much for the differences; the magazines are nearly indistinguishable in content and format. They constitute, for the most part, a recycling of the partisan left, and 60's radicalism. The cover type tends to say a great deal: MAYBE WE SHOULD SAY WE ARE SORRY (after

the Iranians took the hostages): ASSAULT ON THE POOR (after the Reagan budget): and THE U.S. WAR IN CENTRAL AMERICA (ongoing).

Jacques Ellul, a French theologian, often quoted by both magazines, when he agrees with them, points out in his book *Violence* that revolutionary Christians defend only the "interesting" poor, "whose defense really is an attack against Europe, against capitalism, against the U.S. The uninteresting poor represent forces that are considered passé. Their struggle concerns only themselves."

Every issue of *Sojourners* and the *Other Side* exemplifies this double standard: the poor of the U.S., the Philippines, and South Korea, are often mentioned, while the poor of Cuba and the Eastern Bloc are ignored. In 1978, Jim Wallis wrote that the Vietnamese government had been "harsh" with the boat people, but added that some of these people had adopted "Western values" during the war.

The radical journals are often silent or negative regarding the long standing philanthropic efforts of evangelicals—the numerous hospitals, orphanages, skid row missions, and untold millions of dollars in donations. American-based foreign missions are sometimes portrayed as citadels of cultural imperialism.

The pacifism of radical Christians also has two sides. The Sermon on the Mount and other texts apply to anyone who believes he may, as a Christian, serve his country's armed forces, but special exemptions are made for those engaged in class warfare. Witness the interview with a Sandinista apologist in the *Other Side:* Question: "Was the relocation of the Miskito Indians a violation of human rights?" Answer: "One could argue that it was . . . it was a long walk . . . people were upset . . . militarily it was a move that had to be made." Every benefit of the doubt is extended to socialist regimes, even, in certain cases, the USSR— "Most Americans are not aware that we once invaded Russia, but the Soviet people have never forgotten it." (*Sojourners,* Nov. 1982). . . . This is presented as the Christian view with no space allotted to opposing perspectives, . . .

Why are certain evangelicals drawn to discarded radical causes and phantom kingdoms of heaven on earth of the type allegedly under construction in Nicaragua? A new Gibbon may have to explain; meanwhile, others have attempted to. George Orwell believed that the extreme leftist creeds were rationalizations of emotional problems. Jacques Ellul observes that the defense of the poor, although prompted by Christian sentiments, often crowds out the rest of Christianity. . . . Malcolm Muggeridge's judgment is the harshest. He sees the pacifist adulation of the revolutionary as the little brow-beaten boy looking up to the big bully. People believe lies, Muggeridge insists, not because they are plausible, but because they want to believe them.

If Christians want to hear "all sides of the question," why not go right to a nice, fashionable non-Christian source? If you want to know what the left is saying, read *The Village Voice, Mother Jones, Rolling Stone,* or subscribe to the *New Yorker.* Then you will at least know what the true American left is saying, not just their Christian hand-me-down imitators. It would be better to read Marxists, liberation theologians, and forthrightly proabortion literature put out by such groups as The Religious Coalition for Abortion Rights, than something so ineffectual as is represented by so many Christian publications. Those of the true left know why they are publishing *and* what they want. By reading their literature you are educating yourself as to what we are up against.

To the extent that magazines like the *Reformed Journal* and *Christianity Today* have lost their savor and direction, they are neither fish nor fowl. One might as well read the Sears catalog; at least one would then get some interesting photographs and a better understanding of middle America! Like most evangelical institutions today, these publications often seem so busy trying to understand the other person's point of view that they have forgotten what their own is. If a magazine is to be good, it must have a strong premeditated editorial line, enthusiasm for creatively pursuing its agenda, and an understanding that it is in business to make its stand. The secular left understands this but we, ever fearful of being branded "narrow-minded," apparently do not.

Trampled Salt

A pitiful irony is apparent here. Just as magazines such as *Christianity Today* and the *Reformed Journal,* through their "new evangelical" luminaries, are discovering the joys of accommodation with the secular world, diehard secularists themselves, surfeited on the sickening excesses of secularism, are beginning to turn away from secular solutions. While "evangelicals" such as *Sojourners* move left, secular Jewish writers like Ben Stein are increasingly critical of the secular immorality as exhibited, for instance, in television. While institutions such as Wheaton College try to accommodate all points of view (even inviting proabortion John Anderson to speak in chapel, though they will not invite Jerry Falwell), secular and liberal theologians such as Harvey Cox of the Harvard Divinity School (to which Falwell did speak in 1983) worry increasingly about the secularistic and humanistic trends in our society.

Solzhenitsyn has commented that the only people who take Marxism seriously anymore are in the West. In the countries where it has actually been tried, no one will discuss Marxist ideas with anything less than a "sneer on their lips." Marx may look good from Wheaton, but is not so appealing when perceived from Leningrad.

Vladimir Bukovsky, in the book *Who Is for Peace?* (Thomas Nelson, 1983), addresses this point clearly:

The Soviet rulers are a totally cynical lot, much more preoccupied with their own privileges and pleasures than with Marxist ideas. They probably hate Communist dogma more than any Western capitalist. Moreover, the majority of the Soviet people are as cynical as their leaders. There are many more sincere Communists to be found in the West than in the USSR. (p. 76)

Evangelicals for Social Action

Bukovsky's observation is borne out by the ideology of such naive, often good-intentioned groups as Evangelicals for Social Action (ESA). The group was described in the *Evangelical Newsletter* (Vol. IX, No. 19, October 15, 1982, p. 4) as follows:

> . . . ESA has developed a working outline in its "Theology and Strategy" for tackling these problems [poverty, etc.] through the church. This outline forms the foundation of the organization's prophetic stand and social critique. Summarized briefly, this critique claims that the social problems Christians in this nation are most concerned about (i.e. crime, abortion, lack of prayer, secular humanism, etc.) are important, but actually symptoms of much larger problems—unjust social structures in the United States—which underlie these legitimate Christian concerns.
>
> The obvious answer, then, is to attack the causes of the disease so the symptoms will go away. ESA spends much of its educational effort trying to acquaint biblical Christians with crucial areas of basic injustice in society and the need to change these for the better.
>
> What are these basic "unjust structures"? ESA believes most of them (but certainly not all) stem from poverty and the maldistribution of wealth, both on the national and international levels.
>
> . . . Dr. Ron Sider (author of the book *Rich Christians in an Age of Hunger*) is its President. He has personally shaped and guided ESA since its beginning. Since 1973, ESA has become a nationwide movement promoting peace, liberty, and justice. . . .
>
> Ultimately, ESA wants to build into the church and the individual Christian a penetrating social awareness of what causes injustice. . . . Poverty drives persons to despair. *Only when someone relieves that hopelessness, can the poor find Christ* [my emphasis].

These people seem to have revised Christ's statement to perhaps read, "It is harder for a poor man to enter heaven than for a rich man to pass through the eye of a camel."

Let us take a moment to analyze these Christianized socialistic solutions to the world's problems. First we find that apparently society's problems lie not in sin or an understanding of man's fallen nature, but in ESA's newly discovered "unjust structures." (In other words, if GM and IBM can be eliminated, "crime" and "secular humanism," not to mention Beelzebub, will just fade away!) Second, it is assumed that our society is built on "unjust social structures," which also cause "crime, abortion, lack of prayer, secular humanism, etc." Third, we find that poverty drives persons to despair. "Only when someone relieves that hopelessness, can the poor find Christ." So it seems that the first duty of the Christian is no longer to preach the gospel and offer spiritual solutions to sin, which then lead to compassion, but the reverse. We are to alleviate poverty (read "raise taxes") and "unjust structures" (read "eliminate traditional Western freedoms") first.

The interesting thing about Evangelicals for Social Action and friends is not that they are espousing something new. Quite to the contrary, this is essentially the same philosophy the liberation theologians of South America have built upon. To them, the heart of all problems is "maldistribution of wealth." These people are not economists, have not made a study of *why* the West is wealthy and, despite abundant resources, the Third World is poor. But, nevertheless, they wish to "redistribute" wealth and bring "social justice." Nor have these people made a study of the fact that where redistribution has been attempted in the East, freedom has been lost, and economic prosperity stalled rather than improved. Even in the socialistic countries of Scandinavia, freedoms have eroded to a point where many have begun to recognize nations like Sweden as subtly totalitarian. For instance, tax law is so arranged as to force all mothers to work and thus to hand over their children to socialist propaganda via day-care centers. Deliberate tax codes and state policy have combined to virtually secularize the church. U.S. tax codes, too, are increasingly antifamily. But none of this is new, so I will not dwell on it. What *is* new, however, is that leftist groups such as the ESA are now regarded as "evangelical," even "moderate" and mainstream.

The tragedy is that evangelical Protestantism is going down the same divisive and disastrous path that some of our brothers in the Catholic church have taken in embracing "liberation theology." One compromise after another will follow. This kind of Christianity will eventually come to resemble totalitarian Marxism, much more than it will leaven the Marxist lump into something "Christianized." One has only to look at the record of the liberation theologians in Nicaragua and their gradual accommodation with the totalitarian regime which now rules there. There came finally a point of no return. Instead of Marxism having a human "Christian face," the priests involved merely became Marxists themselves and joined the regime. Michael Novak in his brilliant book *The Spirit of Democratic Capitalism* (Simon and Schuster) on page 286 recounts in chilling detail the final steps of some of the Nicaraguan clergy's accommodation with Marxism. Lest evangelicals think there is any convenient point at which they can draw back once they are actually on this slippery slope, let them read the fate of Father D'Escoto described by Novak:

Perhaps clergymen resent being on the "periphery" of economic activism. Perhaps they imagine that socialism will place them more at the "center" of things. Father Miguel D'Escoto of Nicaragua, formerly the editor of the *Maryknoll* magazine, became the foreign minister of Nicaragua. Father D'Escoto dispatched emissaries to the Soviet Union, Eastern Europe, and North Korea to sign pacts of accord and fraternity. His emissaries gave speeches pledging war on the "imperialists" until they are destroyed. His party postponed elections, suppressed dissent, murdered a key opposition leader, took control of all the media and communications, launched a massive indoctrination campaign throughout the countryside, raised the largest standing army (next to Cuba's) in South America, and established a bloc system of domestic political control. Father Ernesto Cardinal, the Minister of Culture, had offices in the palace abandoned by the former dictator, Samosa. Father Cardinal, we might say, moved from the "periphery" into the "center." He did so in the name of "liberation theology" and the gospels.

Learning from the example of orders such as the Maryknolls, who now are virtually an arm of Marxist "liberation" movements across the world, we must ask ourselves this question: Why is it that evangelicals have to get their own fingers burned before they understand that it is, as Orwell put it, dangerous to "play with fire"?

Surely it is not too much to speculate that Matthew 7:15-23 might have something to tell us about the image of machine-gun toting "revolutionary priests" in South America. These verses might instruct us as to the way in which we should judge the "evangelical" leftists who acquiesce to violent revolution.

"Beware of false prophets, who come to you in sheep's clothing, but inwardly they are ravenous wolves. You will know them by their fruits. Do men gather grapes from thornbushes or figs from thistles? Even so, every good tree bears good fruit, but a bad tree bears bad fruit. A good tree cannot bear bad fruit, nor can a bad tree bear good fruit. Every tree that does not bear good fruit is cut down and thrown into the fire. Therefore by their fruits you will know them.

"Not everyone who says to Me, 'Lord, Lord,' will enter the kingdom of heaven, but he who does the will of My Father who is in heaven. Many will say to Me in that day, 'Lord, Lord, have we not prophesied in Your name, cast out demons in Your name, and done many wonderful works in Your name?' And then I will declare to them, 'I never knew you; depart from Me, you who practice lawlessness!' "

In our innermost hearts, as evangelicals, can we really relate the "will of My Father who is in heaven" to the Marxist and socialist agenda? As believing Christians, can we equate the economic failure and poverty brought on worldwide by socialist antieconomics, the loss of freedom, the tyranny of leftist coercion with "good fruit"? In reference to Novak's quote cited above, does it take too much imagination to see that someone who says, "Lord, Lord, did we not prophesy in Your name," and then "dispatched emissaries to the Soviet Union, Eastern Europe, and North Korea to sign pacts of accord and fraternity," will find himself in a rather tenuous position on Judgment Day as he explains these actions of "fraternity" to the Head of the Church which has been so mercilessly persecuted by these communist regimes?

Redistribution

The biggest deficiency in the ideas of "redistribution" and "maldistribution" is simply this. First, as the wrecked economies of every socialist country on earth stand ready to testify, it doesn't work. (One need only study the comparative statistics cited in *The Economy in Mind* by Warren T. Brookes, Universe Books, to see this.) Second, and most importantly, we live in an age in which the power of the government is increasing by leaps and bounds, almost unbridled. The only agency which is going to do any "redistribution" is the state. Man's nature being what it is, one will not see people lining up to voluntarily "redistribute" their hard-earned wages to those the government indicates, on a wholesale communistic level. Under the guise of talk of "Christlike behavior," we see the ESA and similar groups appealing not to real Christian solutions, *but to the power of the state.*

Alexander Solzhenitsyn, in an article entitled "Three Key Moments in Modern Japanese History" (*National Review,* December 9, 1983) had this to say of socialism:

> This is an appropriate place to touch briefly upon a fashionable and widespread myth about socialism. Although this term lacks any precise, unambiguous meaning, it has come to stand, the world over, for some vague dream of a "just society." At the heart of socialism lies the fallacy that all human problems can be solved by social reorganization. But even when socialism promises to take the very mildest of forms, it always attempts to implement by force the contrived and unattainable notion that all people must be equal. One of the most brilliant thinkers in Russia today, physicist Yuri Orlov (now ill and close to death after more than five years' confinement in a Communist labor camp), has demonstrated that *pure* socialism is always and inevitably totalitarian. Orlov shows that it is immaterial how mild and gradual the measures of advancing socialism may be: if they are consistent, then the conveyor-belt-like sequence of socialist reforms will hurl that country (or the entire world) into the abyss of Communist totalitarianism. And totalitarianism is what the physicist calls an "energy well." It is easy to tumble in, but it takes extraordinary effort and exceptional circumstances to effect an escape.

The State as Redistributor

Is the ever-expanding power of the state the "Christian solution" to poverty? Is the coercive Marxist barrel of the gun, or intimidation by the IRS, truly the "Christian" standard that in the end will bring "justice"? If this is not the direction evangelicalism should take, then we must carefully examine what the ESA, Ron Sider, Jim Wallis, and people like them are really saying. If what they say is deliberately unclear, then ponder the logical conclusions of their programs. You will not find them honestly talking about guns and forced redistribution, but their philosophy, taken to its logical conclusion, must always lead in the direction of force. The natural love of freedom in human beings does not comply easily with Marxist utopian idealism. (This explains the need of every Marxist revolution to end in a bloodbath.) There is a great hypocrisy here. Those who speak the most of "love, pacifism, compassion, redistribution" seem to be, more often than not, the very ones who bring about results opposite from those they are advocating. Evangelicals must consider long and hard whether they wish to join the Maryknolls and others in their quest for "a more just society." In the last analysis, it all comes down to the barrel of a gun or, in the United States, a prison term for those who will not comply with the state as it taxes its citizens. An IRS auditor, FBI agent, or some other bureaucrat will in the end be designated to wring "compassion" out of our hard hearts as we attempt to hang on to some of our freedoms and property. The theories are all lovely, but let us ask *how* they would be achieved. Would it not all come down to a call for more *government* action? And even if we willingly gave up our freedoms, would it work?

In Conde Pallen's book *Crucible Island* (New York, 1919), he makes explicit the catechism of statism (as quoted by Herbert Schlossberg in *Idols for Destruction*).

Q. By whom were you begotten?
A. By the sovereign state.

Q. Why were you begotten?
A. That I might know, love and serve the sovereign state always.

Q. What is the sovereign state?
A. The sovereign state is humanity in composite and perfect being.

Q. Why is the state supreme?
A. The state is supreme because it is my creator and conservor, in which I am and move and have my being, and without which I am nothing.

Q. What is the individual?
A. The individual is only a part of the whole, and made for the whole, and finds his complete and perfect expression in the sovereign state.

Individuals are made for cooperation only, like feet, like hands, like eyelids, like the rows of the upper and lower teeth.

Some Christians may call for "redistribution of wealth" and cite "maldistribution" as the source of all problems. They may even go further to say that the poor must be lifted from poverty *before* they can hear Christ. Strange, considering Christ's *own* poverty! Whether or not they themselves know it or admit it (whether they call themselves evangelicals, Anabaptists, Mennonites, or liberation theologians, it does not matter), the road they have chosen leads to state power, state action, state coercion, and finally economic collapse. Their catechism ultimately is Pallen's quoted above. To such "evangelicals" the Lord's Prayer should perhaps be rendered as follows to mirror their new "relevant" Christianity:

> Our parent [no male chauvinism here] in heaven, hallowed be your name, Your social justice come, Our collective will be done, In our ecosystem as it is in heaven. Give us today redistributive justice. Forgive us for not attacking structural injustice and maldistribution, As we have also forgiven corporate polluters and those who deprive consumers of their rights. And lead us not into democratic capitalism but deliver us from traditional American antifeminist freedoms, and help us bring peace and justice on earth forever and ever.   Amen.

Real Economics
Christians who wish to go beyond rhetoric and emotional appeals to "love," who wish to really help the poor and the Third World, must first acquaint themselves with *facts* rather than the worn and failed Marxist dogma now disguised as Christianity. Two books mentioned previously, which ought to be read by every Christian with even the slightest economic concern, are Michael Novak's *The Spirit of Democratic Capitalism* and Warren T. Brookes' *The Economy in Mind*. A third is Herbert Schlossberg's *Idols for Destruction* (Thomas Nelson). Fourth is Julian Simon's book, *The Ultimate Resource* (Princeton University Press). These four books provide a much needed dose of ice water in the form of factual analysis, rather than Bible verses taken out of context to support pseudo-Marxist ideology, which itself has been taken out of the context of its glaring worldwide failures and repackaged now as "Christianity." We should also make a careful study of the books and lifework of John Perkins *(Let Justice Roll Down* and *With Justice for All*, Regal Books). Perkins, a black who has spent a lifetime working with and for the poor, proposes some practical Christian solutions to poverty, *not* the coercive power of the state or "redistribution" and the enslaving welfare state. Rather, he proposes helping poor, blacks, and others build *equity* in their homes, places of work, and communities, so that they can prosper privately without coercive state power intruding.

Evangelicals are now at the point Catholics were twenty or thirty years ago in their attempts to deal with the idea of "social justice." Let us learn from Michael Novak who, as a liberal Roman Catholic, trod this particular path up to the bitter end and was forced, because of his own honesty, to take another look at what he had presumed to be "socialist truth." Let us not, through our own blindness and romanticism when faced with ESA's utopianistic world view, be forced to make the same historical mistakes that some Catholics have made in their "liberation theology."

Before evangelicals swallow the Sider or Wallis vision of the world and "social justice," perhaps they should ponder the remarks of economist and historian Herbert Schlossberg (*Idols for Destruction,* pp. 133, 134). He describes the shortcomings of looking to the ever-expanding state for solutions to human problems, particularly problems of poverty.

> The hatred revealed in such statements [redistribution of wealth] is all that can be expected in a society that has institutionalized envy and uses the term social justice to describe a system of legalized theft. That should alert us to the cant in the old fraud that property rights can somehow be separated from human rights and are inferior to them. There are no societies that are cavalier toward property rights but which safeguard human rights. The state that lays its hand on your purse will lay it on your person. Both are the acts of a government that despises transcendent law.
>
> Those who think they will replace the competition of capitalism with the cooperation of socialism know nothing of either. The novels in C. P. Snow's *Strangers and Brothers* series illustrate that the rapacity, hatred, and back-stabbing that are endemic in academic and bureaucratic settings are fully as destructive as those that take place in commercial life.
>
> Another of Archbishop Temple's colleagues contended forty years ago that when capitalism was replaced by socialism, it would mean the end of the reign of greed and the start of a new order based on cooperation. He looked forward to "comradeship and the zest for efficient public services" that would follow, and cited the Soviet experience as evidence for the soundness of his expectations. He used a good example: Soviet "cooperation" cost by 1959 some 110 million lives. The alternative to free economic activity is not cooperation but coercion. . . .
>
> Those who bought stock in the redistributive state before it began its dizzying rise have done well. Professors of the social sciences, powerful business executives, high government officials, successful politicians, recipients of tax money and implicit grants in an almost infinite variety of forms, heads of research institutes, lecture circuit gurus, international consultants, humanitarian leaders with well-watered reputations for benevolence—they all radiate the aura of wisdom belonging only to those who buy at the bottom and ride their investment up a one-way

escalator. It is only now that the exterior is rotting away that ordinary people can see that the foundations are lacking, and the general shabbiness of the position belies its former glory. It is becoming ever more difficult to cover up the fact that redistribution is a Ponzi game that can pay off old victims only be producing new ones. The moral justifications fade and are replaced by force.

Warren T. Brookes, in his definitive book *The Economy in Mind* (p. 211), gives us what I think is the final word on the subject.

The underlying theme of most of this activity seems to boil down to the demand side premise that income redistribution and the fully socialized welfare state are the highest human expressions of the Judeo-Christian ethic of compassion, that distribution is in some way more Christian than production, that one (distribution) equates with compassion and the other (production) with exploitation. With all due respect to these religious leaders, at best they seem guilty of a shallow interpretation of their own biblical teaching (not to mention economic reality) and, at worst they appear to have a strange kind of death wish, through the sacrifice of the metaphysical initiative for the frustrations of power politics.

It must be transparently clear to any thinking person that the ultimate effect of the creation of the fully socialized welfare state is not merely the destruction of human liberty (and true economy—the unfoldment of ideas) but the shift of human trust from dependence on God to dependence on the state—the exchange of worship of Deity for the idolatry and tyranny of Leviathan.

As theologian Peter Berger admonishes, "Socialism may be an ideal, but its empirical realization removes from the scene yet another limiting factor to the power of the modern state" and this modern state is fundamentally dangerous because it represents "the most massive concentration of power in human history since the demise of Nazi Germany." He notes, "All totalitarian societies have been socialist."

Even so-called democratically socialist countries annihilate what Michael Novak calls the mediating role of the church, as the state and its welfare programs become the repositories of an increasingly secular faith.

Fashion at any Price

The above notwithstanding, the evangelical community scurries around attempting to curry favor from a secular world that couldn't care less. It manifests itself as pitiful rather than broad-minded, treasonous rather than accommodating, and finally as in the case of the now theologically liberal Fuller Theological Seminary, willing to abandon even the basic tenets of the faith, such as the inerrancy of Scripture, rather than appear unfashionable.

Talk about a broken reed to lean on!

Johnny Carson, not usually known as a pillar of the church, told a little story on his talk show, that went something like this:

> A very rich man went up to a beautiful woman he knew, at a party, and asked her if she would sell herself. To which she said, "Of course not." He then asked her if she would sleep with him for a million dollars, just once. At that she said, "Well . . . for a million, I guess so." He then said, "Well, how about for five dollars?" To which she indignantly replied, "What do you think I am!" He answered, "We've already established *what* you are, Madam; now we are only quibbling about the price."
>
> (Johnny Carson, September 21, 1983)

Like the young woman in Johnny Carson's story, many in the evangelical establishment also seem to have a price—acceptance by the liberal secular world and the liberal theological world. And they are just as indignant when their true nature is exposed.

Like peasants shivering in their hovels on the grounds of a magnificent manor house, evangelical leadership often seems to be longing for a place inside the palace—with its bright lights, ballroom, and fashionability—or at least to have their theological views validated by the World Council of Churches, or failing that, to get published in the *Christian Century*. A pathetic servility, an attempt to always see the other point of view while never defending one's own, and incessant compromise embody much of evangelicalism today. What else can explain the extreme lack of vigor of Christian institutions of higher learning? Berkeley, Stanford, Harvard, and other elite secular institutions are the deliberate breeding ground for the secularistic and left-wing thinking that dominates the culture. Where is the dedication and radicalism, the fervor and vision, in the evangelical community to match the dedication of the secular religionists? Where is our fighting spirit?

Herbert Schlossberg has said (in a letter to the author, October 19, 1983):

> In my view the real mission field is the evangelical colleges which have, to a degree, lost any vision for confronting the world. They seem to have a vision, rather, for assimilating what they think is the best of the world into Christian life.

Schlossberg and others have recognized the need to develop clearly an idea of the Christian mind as *distinct* from the world. But if Christianity is Truth, it is the world that must learn from Christianity, not vice versa.

While evangelicals work hard at compromise, Michael Novak, the formerly liberal Roman Catholic theologian, rediscovers in his book *The Spirit of Democratic Capitalism* the great worth of the West as opposed to the economic and human failure of the East, and the bankruptcy of socialism and liberal theology. Notwithstanding, evangelical "thinkers" barely notice that they are crossing Novak's path on the way out toward left field just as he is coming back in toward the center! Just as secular, formerly liberal thinkers, Jewish and Christian, such as Michael Levin, Irving Krystol, Norman Podhoretz, and many others are rediscovering the heritage of Judeo-Christian Western democracy, we find many evangelical historians such as George Marsden and Ronald Wells of Calvin joining the revisionist throng and downplaying America's Judeo-Christian heritage. *Boston Herald-American* columnist Warren Brookes rediscovers conservative economics in his book *The Economy in Mind,* just as *Christianity Today,* twenty-five or so years late, discovers the attraction of liberation theology via friendliness toward the World Council of Churches! Strange, the ships that are passing in the night . . .

All this underlines the fact (to be discussed further later in this book) that orthodox believers from all branches of the church must band together and reject the creeping secularization in evangelical and Catholic circles that is taking place.

If we are anxious to learn from the world, then let us at least learn the world's lessons. Secular modern philosophy, whether dressed as Marxism, humanism, liberalism, or in any other guise, is failing, and failing miserably. Why do we seem bent on imitating the mistakes of the secular world and traveling its own worn and blood-strewn paths of failed movements and intellectual suicide? If we as Christians are interested in what the secular world is thinking, let us begin to read writers such as Irving Krystol, Malcolm Muggeridge, Michael Novak, Yale Burton Pines, or William Kilpatrick, who having trod the liberal secular path and found it wanting are returning to the answers of traditionalism and orthodoxy. Still, many Christians, under the sway of the evangelical establishment, seem bent on trying the secularist state's solution to the world's problems in spite of what the world has learned. Like teenagers who dabble in drugs rather than listening to the experienced warnings of a former drug addict, so the "teenage" evangelicals, many of whom are old enough to know better, insist on experimenting with secular humanist solutions to the problems of sin, greed, and sorrow, solutions which have already proven to be failures. Just as the world is looking toward Christianity for answers, Christians are only now discovering the agenda of the secular left: the Third World, the benefits of taxation to redistribute wealth from the rich to the poor, and liberal theology. How pitiful! As the world realizes its need and calls for salt, Christians busily dilute their salt and refuse to dispense it!

The Secular Quest for Tradition

Other evidence of the world desperately seeking traditional, religious, orthodox alternatives is the number of student newspapers starting up on secular college campuses across the United States which take a traditionalist or even orthodox religious view. Again, there is an irony here. Just as our "evangelical" institutions, ever the tail on the dog, become more open-minded (secularistic) secular people are hungering for religious solutions to the world's problems. As latecomers at Fuller Seminary, Ron Sider, *Sojourners,* and the *Other Side* (to name but a few) discover socialistic solutions to poverty, anti-American collective guilt, and, better late than never, F E M I - N I S M , campus magazines at secular institutions are beginning to look toward traditional Western ideas and values. In the *National Review* magazine (September 1983), an article titled " 'Right On' on the Campus" by Phillip Marcus details this phenomenon.

> Alternative journalism [alternative to secular liberal college papers] is the newest fashion on nearly 40 elite campuses, a change among students not only in dress and style but also in sensibility. Tired of the 60's nihilism, bored with the 70's narcissism, looking for a future with more than designer jeans, students at leading institutions are taking to the printed word in a new display of traditional (what, until recently were called bourgeois) values.
>
> Last spring more than 35 new campus publications sent their editors to New York City (to the Harvard Club, no less) for a National Conference for Young Journalists. . . .
>
> The roll call of alternative papers is an impressive list: *Berkeley Review, California Review* (UC, San Diego), *Claremont Review of Books, Common Sense* (Brown), *Counterpoint* (Chicago), *Dartmouth Review, Florida Sun,* the *Guardian* (Georgetown), *Harvard Journal of Law and Public Policy, Hawkeye Review* (University of Iowa), *Louisville Scholar, Madison Report* (Princeton), *Marquette Free Press, Michigan Review* (Ann Arbor), *Morningside Review* (Columbia), *Northwestern Review,* the *Observer of Boston College,* the *Primary Source* (Tufts), the *Red and Blue* (Penn), the *Salient* (Harvard), the *Sequent* (George Washington), the *Statesman* (Hobart), *Student Magazine* (Colorado), *Texas Review, University Review of New Mexico, Washington Spectator* (Seattle), *Wesleyan Adversary, Williams Republican, Yale Free Press,* and *Yale Political Monthly.*

At the conference the student journalists attended at the Harvard Club, Midge Dector (of the Committee for a Free World) gave a keynote speech entitled, "What Is the New Alternative Journalism?" In her speech she brought up some points which many evangelicals involved in Christian media seem to have forgotten, or at least seem to be eager to forget. She said:

The way to battle against wrong ideas is by a constant, unrelenting, and hopefully cheerful effort to replace these ideas in the minds of reasonable people. . . . As members of a minority, you will be burdened with what you might think of as an unfair responsibility: you will have to do better than the other guys in order to be considered as good. . . The other side is choking on its political and social conventionality. . . . The fresh talent, the new thoughts, the intelligence, the energy are with you. . . . If you remain silent, you grant those who would silence you, a victory.

What a shame that there are vocal students at Harvard, Yale, and Dartmouth who are grasping these ideas and acting on them while the ranks of our own "Christian" student organizations such as Inter-Varsity, especially in their books and magazine, continue to slide toward the ill defined, pacifist-Gandhi-Sojourners-feminist-Ron Sider-collective-guilt-"it's always America's fault" mishmash. An "evangelical" Logos Bookstore in Chicago, for example, has even refused to carry books espousing traditional views by authors such as Cal Thomas, vice-president of the Moral Majority. So much for liberal tolerance. Talk about narrow-minded provincialism! (Meanwhile, the secular bookstore chain B. Dalton has recently increased its line of religious orthodox books and the *New York Times* and *Washington Post* have run op ed pieces by Cal Thomas.)

We might take encouragement from Midge Decter, who concluded her remarks optimistically by noting that there is a bright side to speaking up. She reminded us of "how much fun all this is. I mean fun in the very highest sense: of being energized, entertained, and uplifted by what one is doing. Earlier I used the word cheerful. Nothing is more cheering than to speak one's mind openly and clearly."

We tend to forget that the radical secularist alternative to the Judeo-Christian vision is no longer an "alternative" or even "radical" but has, in fact, become the *establishment*. We tend to forget that we who are Christians, orthodox and traditional in our views, are the *new radicals and the true alternative minority*. How exhilarating to be on the real cutting edge instead of merely repackaging and Christianizing socialistic pablum for a wearied evangelical public that has grown too feeble to resist hand-me-down ideas.

But the drive to be more like the world, both in it *and* of it, continues. As the world discovers the bankruptcy of "values clarification" and "a psychological approach to human problems," Robert Schuller, TV preacher, discovers the modern psychology of self-esteem. A Houston "superchurch" of 8,000 members recently built an eight-lane bowling alley as part of a $32 million "worship complex." Evangelicals are beginning to pooh-pooh uncomfortable Christian absolutes by accepting divorce, and to regard those who call for absolutes as the enemy while embracing Gandhi (and Carl Rogers' psychology or bowling alleys) as the way to God.

Many evangelical Christians now apparently believe that to be fashionable (on the left) or successful at any price (on the right) has superseded repentance, holiness, or a willingness to be the despised, unfashionable, unquoted minority. "God wants you to go first class," says crass materialism; or "God wants you to bring social justice and redistribution," says socialist utopianism. But rarely is heard the distinctly difficult *Christian* alternative.

Meanwhile, as the evangelical establishment sells us down the river, writers such as Walker Percy (*Lost in the Cosmos*), Larry Woiwode (*Poppa John*), Harold Fickett (*The Holy Fool*), and others are showing us, through the art of storytelling, that the same God who was alive to inspire Dante, Milton, Shakespeare, and C. S. Lewis is still at work. However, from the evangelical establishment we increasingly receive only secularist ideas repackaged in Christian garb. It is perhaps to the artistic community within the Christian world that Christians must begin to turn for moral leadership, and away from the evangelical establishment structures. The Christian vision in Percy's *Lost in the Cosmos* is piercing and poignant. Even secular writer Richard Grenier, in his thriller *The Marrakesh One-Two*, or secular screen writer Ben Stein in his book *The View from Hollywood Boulevard*, or Nat Hentoff in some of his articles, seem to understand more of the Christian traditional point of view than is exhibited in a catalog of books printed by a typical "evangelical" publishing company. How can this be?

As *Sojourners* led by Jim Wallis organizes expeditions to Nicaragua to stand between American "aggression" and the Nicaraguan people (read Sandinista communist regime), Jean François Revel, France's most famous leftist philosopher and writer, has recently turned away not only from communism but from socialism as well. As French intellectuals rediscover the importance of freedom, "evangelical" groups have finally caught up to about 1955 and are discovering the left. Oh, wow, man, you mean like redistributive justice and solidarity against the CIA . . .

Ironically, while some evangelicals dismiss the idea that the secular and liberal elite use the media for their own biased ends, secular humorist and commentator Mort Sahl, in his book *Heartland* (Harcourt, Brace, Jovanovich, 1976), had this to say on page 100:

> It is not paranoia to seek to understand how information and entertainment are dispensed to mass audiences in America. A few scores of people do really decide what goes on networks, what goes over wire services, what appears in mass market paperback books, what goes onto radio. . . . Reactionaries [read "orthodox Christians"], in America attack the press because essentially they don't have access to the mass audience. Liberals rarely attack the press in America, because they do have

access and they feel virtuous because they once had a flirtation with good intentions.

Nat Hentoff, writing in the left-wing *Progressive* magazine (February 1983), in an article entitled "When Nice People Burned Books," took the left and liberal elite in the United States to task for their censorship (now imitated by the Chicago Logos Bookstore) of conservative and orthodox ideas. How amazing that Hentoff seems to understand these issues so clearly and that he presents them frankly and without embarrassment when many so-called evangelicals who supposedly have a reason for defending orthodox views will not do so. Hentoff, in his article on liberal censorship, spoke of the way in which secular and liberal institutions, particularly colleges, have been hounding conservative opinion from the scene.

Here is an excerpt:

Take the case of Phyllis Schlafly and Wabash College. The college is a small, well-regarded liberal arts institution in Crawfordsville, Indiana. In the spring of 1981, the college was riven with discord. Some 50 members of the 90-odd faculty and staff wrote a stiff letter to the Wabash lecture series committee, which had displayed the exceedingly poor taste to invite Schlafly to speak on campus the next year.

The faculty protesters complained that having the sweetheart of the right near the Wabash River would be "unfortunate and inappropriate." The dread Schlafly is "an ERA opponent . . . a far right attorney who travels the country, being highly paid to tell women to stay home fulfilling traditional roles while sending their sons off to war."

"Furthermore," the authors wrote, "the point of view she represents is that of an ever-decreasing minority of American women and men, and is based in sexist mythology which promulgates beliefs inconsistent with those held by liberally educated persons, and this does not merit a forum at Wabash College under the sponsorship of our lecture series."

This is an intriguing document by people steeped in the traditions of academic freedom. One of the ways of deciding who gets invited to a campus is the speaker's popularity. If the speaker appeals to only a "decreasing minority of women and men," she is not worth the fee. So much for Dorothy Day, were she still with us.

And heaven forefend that anyone be invited whose beliefs are "inconsistent with those held by liberally educated persons." Mirror, mirror on the wall . . .

But do not get the wrong idea about these protesting faculty members: "We subscribe," they emphasize, "to principles of free speech and free association, of course.

"All the same, it does not enhance our image as an all-male college to endorse a well-known sexist by inviting her to speak on our campus." If Phyllis Schlafly is invited, nonetheless, "we intend not to participate in any of the activities surrounding Ms. Schlafly's visit and will urge others to do the same."

The moral of the story: if you don't like certain ideas, boycott them.

Why is it that we have left-wing writers like Nat Hentoff courageously exposing liberal hypocrisy while the leaders of the evangelical establishment sneer at the "secular humanist bogeyman" and glibly ask, "What's the problem?" Again, it is a case of ships passing in the night.

Escape from Reason

Empirical observation shows that secular, socialist, totalitarian ideologies have failed on a greater and greater scale to solve the problems of societies. We need only consider indigent socialist Africa, beggared socialist France, stifling Sweden, chaotic Greece, declining Mexico, arthritic England, to name but a few. It may be argued that imperialism played a part in the economic and social problems of Third World countries, but France, Sweden, Greece, England? Socialism, given enough time, will turn even thriving Western countries into Third World, underdeveloped nations.

Why, then, this irrational tolerance of liberal, socialist ideas? Because we live in a world populated by people who seem to have abandoned rationality, along with their Judeo-Christian tradition, in favor of utopianisms: leftist political ideology and Eastern religious mysticism. As Novak writes, we are not *really* interested in solving the problems of the Third World; we are more interested in ideologically categorizing them in terms of "liberation," "rich," and "poor."

We are not *really* interested in the issue of abortion either; as Joseph Sobran has said, we would rather mask the issue in a hypothetical discussion of "poverty." We are not *really* interested in ideas of trade, government, the arts; we would rather mask these things in vague essays about "goodness," "virtue," "exploitation." Finally, we are no longer interested in *facts,* empirical observation, nonideological scholarship to uncover the truth. We live in an age of liberal irrationality.

What accounts for Christians and their publications ignoring the words of warning of Solzhenitsyn? When he was a dissident in the USSR (as I have pointed out in my book *A Time for Anger*), the secular media were enamored with Solzhenitsyn and took him seriously. When he moved to the United States, the secular media dropped him like a hot potato because now he was criticizing their own godlessness. Likewise with the Christian media. In *Christianity Today* (September 16, 1983) there is a report that "Evangelicals Praise Nicaragua, Criticize U.S." We find that eleven educators from U.S. "Christian colleges" noted "amazing strides in literacy, education, health and humanitarianism since the Sandinistas came to power four years ago. They found little evidence of the Communist takeover that the Reagan Administration warns about." Later we read, "The eleven educators on the tour were from the following colleges: Bethel College, King's, Gordon, Goshen, Wheaton, and Whitworth, and from Seattle Pacific University."

These impossibly gullible "educators" have embraced the same view adopted by the secularist *New Yorker* or, for that matter, Castro's propaganda radio station beamed from Havana into the United States. They have swallowed the *fashionable* Marxist line.

Ironical, once again, is the juxtaposition of the gullibility of these "evangelicals" compared to the secular world. National Public Radio, a liberal news organization, was highly pro-Sandinista all through the Sandinista revolution and continues to "see their point of view." Nevertheless, even National Public Radio has had an entire series of programs detailing the human rights abuses of the Miskito Indians and others by the Sandinistas. Tim Coulter of the Indian Resource Center was interviewed at length on the National Public Radio program, "All Things Considered" (January 10, 1983). He detailed the irrefutable evidence of the displacement of one hundred thousand Miskito Indians by the Sandinista regime. He also recounted the following facts: more than forty Indian villages had been burned to the ground; there had been widespread torture and rape; Indians had been led on forced marches to Sandinista-regime concentration camps. In addition, he told of the recent unpopularity of the previously fashionable Indian Resource Center with the liberals in the United States because of its exposure of these facts. One wonders if this information was unavailable to the Christian "scholars" who visited Nicaragua. However, we find our evangelicals, like the first ping-pong teams to go to China, returning from Nicaragua all ga-ga and goofy in their eulogies for the Sandinista government. Irrationality is the only explanation.

Truth versus Irrationality

But there is a problem in all this, and that is that the Bible itself is the book of truth. Not only is the Bible concerned with truth, but we as Christians are to be concerned with truth in all areas of life (not just theological truth, but political, economic, and artistic truth as well), whether this leads to convenient fashionability or not. Evangelical Christians who have little regard for the facts concerning the Sandinista government, Gandhi, or the World Council of Churches seem scarcely interested in truth as a subject beyond their own *personal religious experience* or borrowed ideological orientation. And this is the crux of the matter: emphasis has been placed solely on an irrational "personal experience of Christ." Meanwhile, in other areas of life, we go our own merry way thinking and behaving essentially no different from the world, and in some ways more worldly than the worldly. The contemporary pop group Culture Club could well be describing the fawning evangelical establishment in their hit song "Karma Chameleon" when Boy George sings, "I'm a man of no conviction."

It is time that all authentic Christians—Roman Catholics, Protestants, evangelicals, fundamentalists, charismatics, Eastern Orthodox, and any others who hold a world view of biblical truth concerning theology and factual truth about the world, fashionable or unfashionable, band together. We simply can no longer paper over the differences between orthodox Christianity and fashionable, servile liberal Christianity (no matter under what guise it comes—evangelical, Catholic, or mainstream) and pretend all is well. All is *not* well. The Beatitudes, after all, do not read, "Blessed are the servile, the pragmatic, the cringing, and the compromising." We must not confuse genuine humility and love with being faceless nonentities. We find in the Bible a curse for false prophets who cry, "Peace, peace, when there is no peace."

Similarly, we do ourselves a disservice by pretending that everything is fine with magazines like *Christianity Today* that give more favorable coverage to the WCC and NCC than *Time* and *Newsweek* do. We cannot pretend that evangelical colleges which have prochoice professors on their faculties are taking a proper stand on human life issues. We cannot pretend that our seminaries are doing the job they should when, like Fuller, they turn out theologians and pastors who are less sure of their own faith and the Bible's clarity than are their congregations. We have been here before. Do such "evangelicals" seriously wish to repeat what American liberalism did at the turn of the century? Do they really want empty churches, congregations who find it useless to go to church, where they only get more of what they get every day in the world? Do they really wish to blend in with society so well that they become anonymous? Do they wish to lose all their savor? If not, it is time to speak up. It is time to see that proabortion professors teaching at evangelical colleges are called to accountability. Would proslavery faculty have been tolerated in 1858? Jonathan Blanchard, founder of Wheaton College, was an ardent Abolitionist. Board members, trustees, donors, and parents sending children to evangelical colleges all have responsibilities they should shoulder. Donors should stop giving money to colleges and seminaries that no longer subscribe to orthodox Christianity. The prolife issue is paramount. If an institution claims to be evangelical on one hand, what is it doing tolerating proabortion professors on the other hand? Institutions like Wheaton College, that have allowed themselves to be compromised on this issue, should be openly challenged as to why they have done this. And if they refuse to change, support, students, and recognition should be redirected to other more faithful institutions. In short, it is time to clean up our act. We should not accept as inevitable the drift towards liberalism and secularism. Rather, we should assume that this secularist tide can be reversed. And we can begin by salvaging our institutions from the maw of secularist ideology. There are enough worthwhile Christian causes to support without contributing tithe money to help pay the salary of a proabortion professor. The least we can do is to refrain from funding our own demise. One cannot put it more plainly than the words in Joshua: "Choose you this day whom ye will serve," to which we all must answer, "As for me and my house, we will serve the Lord" (Joshua 24:15).

The Biblical Challenge

We evangelicals and other Christians who feel that having a "dialogue" with the world and its spirit is an overriding concern, who have been swallowed by fashion and a greed for men's approval, may be instructed by the timely warning in Matthew 10:32-39:

> "Therefore whoever confesses Me before men, him I will also confess before My Father who is in heaven. But whoever denies Me before men, him I will also deny before My Father who is in heaven. Do not think that I have come to bring peace on earth. I did not come to bring peace but a sword. For I have come to 'set a man against his father, a daughter against her mother, and a daughter-in-law against her mother-in-law.' And, 'a man's foes will be those of his own household.' He who loves father or mother more than Me is not worthy of Me. And he who loves son or daughter more than Me is not worthy of Me. And he who does not take his cross and follow after Me is not worthy of Me. He who finds his life will lose it, and he who loses his life for My sake will find it."

If we are to put following Christ above love for even our father or mother, daughter or son, is it too much to ask that we put our fidelity to Christianity ahead of seeking approval in the staff room at Christian colleges and secular institutions? Can we afford to put our Christian agenda ahead of acceptability by the media? Can we risk our church growth programs and fund-raising drives or subscriptions to magazines on behalf of steadfast principle? Above all, when Christ says, "I did not come to bring peace, but a sword," can we infer from this that principles, truth, integrity, and a biblical faith are more important than "getting along" with other people and being "nice"? Yes, we are to "turn the other cheek," but we are also to obey all Christ's commands in the light of his overriding command to be faithful to him. To be silent about Christian principles that are being destroyed is not to "turn the other cheek," but merely to acquiesce and to deny God. To not be willing to incur the wrath and back-stabbing in the academic community that will follow from a clear statement of Christian belief is not to "love our neighbor," but is instead *to deny the faith,* and to rob its power to save the next generation."

To those of us who are Christians and who truly believe, even with all our frailties and weaknesses, all our biases and giving in to temptation, all our sin and daily struggle, it is well to remember that the verse which reads, "But whoever denies Me before men, him I will also deny before My Father who is in heaven," *means something.* These are not mere words. We must be willing to go a long way and risk a great deal rather than running the risk that the living and risen Christ, the King of creation, will deny us and disown us before his and our Father in heaven. If the eventuality of being turned away by Christ does not fill us with dread, we must ask ourselves, *Do we really believe Christianity is true?* We may be evangelicals, but are we Christians?

It is interesting to note the difference in Peter's attitude toward denying or acclaiming the faith before and after his experience with the Holy Spirit. Before Pentecost, he did deny Christ three times in order to save his own skin, be fashionable, fit in. After he received the Holy Spirit, he reacted quite differently to a challenge, to the command to be quiet and stop teaching. In the Book of Acts we read that when he was filled with the Holy Spirit his resolve was hardened, and that he did not accept peace at any price but instead said, "Whether it is right in the sight of God to listen to you more than to God, you judge. For we cannot but speak the things which we have seen and heard" (Acts 4:19, 20). For giving such an answer he was rewarded with flogging and imprisonment. Stephen was rewarded with stoning. Unlike the evangelical establishment of today, the early church was anything but apathetic. For in Acts we read that Peter would have been killed had it not been that the Sanhedrin feared "the multitude." We read that over five thousand believers had been converted and because the leaders feared public, political reaction—a nonapathetic, nonevangelical reaction—Peter was spared by the Sanhedrin.

It is well to remind ourselves as Christians that we have a higher calling than being "open-minded" or even of being "good Americans" or "pluralistic." *Our calling is to acknowledge Christ before men.* If we think acknowledging Christ before men is without cost, or that injunctions to not deny him refer only to private mental attitudes on the historicity of Genesis or other points, we have fooled ourselves. We are deluded and beyond that we risk falling under Christ's words, "whoever denies Me before men, him I will also deny before My Father who is in heaven." We risk this because we have "spiritualized" a concept that is not spiritual at all, but a matter of fact and common sense. To acknowledge Christ before men obviously will cost us something, or else the warnings against not doing so would make no sense. If this were an easy thing to do, why would Christ have to threaten us, as believers, with denying us before the Father if we did not carry out this command? Obviously, then, to acknowledge Christ must cost us something in our daily lives, right where we are.

It is not theoretical. If a staff member at a secular or Christian college is acknowledging Christ in his discipline, he is *not* going to get on well with either the secular world that has already thrown out all absolutes or the compromising element within the evangelical establishment (today's Sanhedrin). If the Christian surgeon is going to acknowledge Christ in his work, he is not going to get on well with his fellow-surgeons who perform abortions, or hospital administrators who allow them. If a Catholic Christian writer such as Walker Percy is faithful, as he has been, and writes a book such as *Lost in the Cosmos,* there is no reason for him to expect a glowing review from the secularistic anti-Christian *New York Times.* A price must be paid, and the first price we as evangelicals need to pay is a willingness to give up fashion as our false god. Our postfundamentalist, reactionary attitude to all things conservative and traditional must stop. Our adherence must be to the truth of the Bible itself, and not to fashion, *even* if this makes us look unfashionable, "fundamentalist," or narrow-minded. For there are worse things than the wrath of the *Christian Century, Sojourners,* the *Other Side,* the *New York Times, Newsweek,* and NBC. There are things that the believer should tremble in his boots about, but to be thought of as unfashionable by the secularist elite or compromising evangelical establishment is not one of them. However, here is one. "But whoever denies Me before men, him I will deny before My Father who is in heaven."

It is highly disturbing that we must spend time even arguing such points as I have been discussing in these last few pages. Highly disturbing, because while the secularistic world never rests in its attempts to obliterate true faith from the face of the earth, we must waste time pointing out to out fellow-evangelicals how useless appeasement of secularism is. This should be patently obvious. Meanwhile, the secular juggernaut charges forward, grinding up and spewing out millions of unborn babies, not to mention untold Infant Does and Baby Jane Does. How disconcerting to find that it is one's fellow-firemen who are slashing the hoses and vandalizing the pumps, making it impossible to fight the secular conflagration which is raging out of control. It is also tragic that things have gone so far without those leaders responsible within evangelicalism drawing a line. Surely we could all be pulling together in the same direction. We face the threat of secular leftist destruction of the church, but to be destroyed by rot from within has the same consequences as being destroyed by attack from without. Therefore, it is worth taking the trouble to decide in fact *who* is *who.* We must look with discernment at the books coming out of Christian publishing houses. We must look with discernment at the magazines, the colleges and their professors, and what is being taught in our churches. We simply cannot continue to subscribe to and financially support these things uncritically. We are beset and undermined from without, and now we are beset from within as well.

Selling Ourselves Down the River

There are three kinds of "evangelicals" selling us down the river: those who are genuinely misled and who, with a rigorous program of reading, praying, and thinking, can find the way back to true orthodox Christianity; those who are questing after acceptance for personal psychological reasons (for example, because of their uncouth, embarrassing fundamentalist or charismatic mother, they are rejecting the Christianity they were brought up with and have thrown out the baby with the bath water); and those who have truly gone over to the other side but do not like the empty churches of liberal denominations and low subscriptions to their magazines. These *pretend* they are evangelicals to gain the audience built by conservative orthodox views, and yet have the egocentric pleasure of subtly foisting their own new nontraditional views on that audience. They should *not hide in Christian institutions built by orthodox Christian conservatives with blood, sweat, and tears over years of work, using those same institutions to purvey views that would make the founders of such institutions roll over in their graves.* This is patent dishonesty and lack of integrity.

A good example of this phenomenon can be seen in InterVarsity Press. Built in the sixties and seventies on the sales of such well-known orthodox authors as Francis Schaeffer and Jim Packer, InterVarsity, moving into the late seventies and early eighties, has begun to "expand" from this solid orthodox base established by a conservative group of writers. In publishing the writings of those such as Ron Sider and others pushing a socialistic and sometimes feminist world-view, IVP has followed the trend of accommodating itself to the world's passing whims.

For a few years, those who trust the credentials of these evangelical institutions do not seem to notice that a massive ideological shift is taking place. Eventually, however, Christians come to realize the shift and begin to abandon the idea of publishing with such an institution, or counting on its books. The danger is that there is a rather muddy patch during the transition when many people are fooled and still go along without realizing that infiltration has occurred. Thus the warnings in this book.

Of course, recent volunteers for bearing the torch of American liberalism dressed as Christianity are treading a path well-worn by faltering Christian soldiers, opened by such companies as William B. Eerdmans of Grand Rapids, Michigan. Eerdmans, which has quietly specialized in publishing books that subvert traditional orthodox Christianity and conservative points of view, continues to deluge the market with such social and theological commentaries. For instance, in the Eerdmans book *A Documentary History of Religion in America,* edited by Edwin S. Gaustad, the left is highly praised. As a review in *Chronicles of Culture* (Vol. VII, December 1983) noted:

> . . . On feminism and on the no nukes movement, he reveals a decidedly modern liberal bias. The introduction to a pastoral letter from a Catholic bishop, "Withholding 50% of my income tax as a means of protesting our nation's continuing involvement in the race for nuclear arms supremacy" (the last document in the collection) is almost adulatory. Half believers of the sort Eerdmans now seems willing to let edit and write their books may share the fashionable illusion that denying Caesar half his due is a valid act of contemporary worship. True Christians who know that this concedes to Soviet atheists the right to abolish every western congregation will recognize that, like other forms of modernism, it is suicide.

It is interesting to note that the editors of *Chronicles of Culture* seem to have a good understanding of what Eerdmans and others like them represent today, while our evangelical media refuses to draw such distinctions!

Whatever Happened to Evangelicalism?

Earlier I cited an article by Ronald A. Wells that appeared in the *Reformed Journal.* In this article, entitled "Whatever Happened to Francis Schaeffer?" Mr. Wells calls on Dr. Schaeffer and his kind to step aside while he and the other "new evangelicals" take over. He openly states his ambition to assume the teaching, training, and molding of those who have been brought into the evangelical fold by conservative thinking. Once they are in the fold, Mr. Wells wants Francis Schaeffer and others to conveniently disappear, go off into the sunset or whatever, and leave him the privilege of having the large audience produced by *traditional Christianity,* while foisting upon that audience a liberal ideology that *never could have produced the audience in the first place.* Here is what Mr. Wells has to say in his article:

> It is not mere academic patronization to note Francis Schaeffer's own characterization of himself as an evangelist, not a scholar. . . . Francis Schaeffer recognizes the needs of broken people in broken societies out there in the real world. We in the academic world recognize that need too, but our calling is the more subtle and refined task.

Wells then makes an analogy with Francis Schaeffer as an evangelist-"medic" compared to Wells as a scholar-"surgeon."

Evangelism is to the kingdom work what the E Unit is to medicine, while Christian scholarship is to the kingdom what surgery is to medicine. . . . And (before this analogy breaks down) let me say honestly that I hope Francis Schaeffer and his friends in the ambulance corps do not take it personally that we undo some of the stitches they did out on the highways of life. They did good work with the tools available to them: *otherwise we would never have the patients to work on.* I hope that Francis Schaeffer resists the seductions of some whom he has helped and who are close to him that he and they are now ready to found a hospital and school of medicine on their own [emphasis mine].

Traditional orthodox Christianity may be good enough to get them in off "the highways," as it were, but it is not good enough to build "scholarship" on! In other words, we are grateful to traditional orthodox Christians like Francis Schaeffer, C. S. Lewis, Malcolm Muggeridge, Billy Graham, and others, who *because of their orthodoxy* attract millions of otherwise secularized people to Christianity, but once we've got hold of them, "move over and let us have at 'em!"

Unless Christians in the academic community stop casting themselves in the role of liberal debunkers and instead begin to serve the cause of Christ by building up believers, Christian colleges will soon be as secularized as their secular counterparts. Indeed, this seems to be what someone like Mr. Wells desires when he calls for a "definitive repentance from the evangelical ethos."

If Mr. Wells wants to hear from the "mainline" churches, let him ponder this from Roman Catholic historian James Hitchcock (*What Is Secular Humanism?*, Servant Books, pp. 136, 137):

There is no finer irony than this, that the people who have been so sure that they were making Christianity "relevant" to the modern world turn out to be those who are losing followers, while the supposedly outmoded denominations are attracting them. . . . The liberal churches are losing members both because they have driven away many of their more orthodox supporters and because they have "liberated" their parishioners from traditional religion to the extent that these people see no need for religion of any kind. . . . Thus, by a strange irony, the churches themselves are among the principal agencies of secularization in America. . . . Unless they choose carefully, people who join a church may find themselves less religious than before.

I doubt that this is the sort of wisdom that Ronald Wells wishes to hear from your "traditional mainline" churches. From what he has written, I suspect he would be more comfortable with the "mainline" Presbyterians or Episcopalians of America and their views on modern society; they certainly are ambiguous enough!

The bottom line is this. In answer to Wells's rhetorical question, "Whatever happened to Francis Schaeffer?"—nothing happened to him! Schaeffer and other orthodox Christians have not changed; what *has* changed is the evangelical establishment. It has moved leftward and is embarrassed by former allies who are refusing to make this liberal pilgrimage with it. Like some *nouveaux riche* modern couple embarrassed by a quaint old grandmother with all her outmoded ideas, Wells and his fellow-travelers wish to pack conservative Christianity off to a nursing home and be left to wreak havoc unexposed.

In moving toward liberalism, Wells and friends should be honest enough to admit that *they* are the train leaving the station; the platform is where it always has been. To do otherwise is to rely on a sort of intellectual optical illusion.

Os Guinness clearly made this point in an interview in the *Wittenburg Door* (October 1983) in the context of an interview:

> I would like to say that maybe it isn't Schaeffer who is moving, but evangelicalism. Maybe evangelicalism is not so critical and clear about its distinctives as it used to be. For example, look at a sample of [evangelical] reviews of Gandhi, the film. Most of them contain the most amazing, naive, uncritical statements ranging from a mildly uncritical one from Christianity Today, to a review which was grossly uncritical and thoroughly antibiblical like the one in the Sojourners. The evangelical reaction to Gandhi tells you more about where evangelicalism is than it tells you about Gandhi, the man or the film."

(The answer quoted above was to the following question posed by the *Door* interviewer, "To be quite honest, we have been surprised to see Dr. Schaeffer aligning himself with people like Jerry Falwell. Is Schaeffer moving to the right?")

Perhaps the most blatant example of the evangelical sell-out is the case of George M. Marsden, professor of history at Calvin College, who went so far as to testify, *on behalf of the ACLU and against fellow-Christians,* in a court of law in the Arkansas creationist case. With friends like these, who needs enemies?

Fiddling While Rome Burns

There is much argument about terminology such as "secular humanist," "humanist," "America's Christian origins," and so on. Most of the time this discussion, as in the examples in this book, is used only as an excuse for ducking the real issues. A Dutchman was asked in World War II to hide a Jew and, instead of taking immediate action, asked, "What is a Jew?" Then he stood discussing the question until the Gestapo arrived. Like the Dutchman, those who seek to do nothing in the culture and to remain comfortable love to debate endlessly the precise meaning of the words "secular humanism," or "America's Christian origins," or "love" vs. "persuasion," rather than admit that something is drastically wrong with society, no matter *what you call it*. And further, they admit no responsibility to *do something*. Terminology is not the point; reality is. Some evangelical historians quibble about which had more influence on America's founding fathers—the French Enlightenment or European Reformation thinking. Meanwhile, in the *real* nonevangelical world, the *culture goes down the tubes*. The real issues here are not definitions, or to what degree America had or did not have a Christian origin, or how much the founding fathers had adopted Christian or Enlightenment thinking.

The real issue is simple. *What do we do now?* It is a choice, not between competing slogans and word games, right or left, but between godlessness and godliness. Between inhumanity and humanity. Between life and death. Between Joseph Fletcher and Jesus. Between dignity of the individual (whether handicapped, unwanted, born or unborn) and death as a "liberal" solution for social problems such as poverty, race, and medical costs. Between a sanctity of life ethic and the bestial gaggle of ethicists, judges, and doctors who cry for the blood of the innocent, all in the name of economics and "compassion," not to mention convenience. Between freedom and prosperity, or subservience, slavery, and the ever-expanding power of the welfare state.

Those of us who are Christians today must finally choose. We can conveniently play games on the sidelines, even games played in "holy" surroundings, like those of a Midwestern university buried in comfortable obscurity or a Christian magazine with a long tradition. Or we can throw ourselves heartily into the manifold tasks which confront us.

"Christian intellectuals need the courage and confidence to stand fast, if need be, against the near unanimous weight of scholarly fashion," writes Herbert Schlossberg in *Idols for Destruction* (Thomas Nelson, 1983, p. 323).

Psychological Battles

Many evangelicals spend more time "reexamining America's Christian origins," or debunking "secular bogeymen," or "learning from other traditions" such as Gandhi and Hinduism than actually dealing with issues. But in the end it all comes down to embarrassed, embittered, postfundamentalist evangelicals who have thrown out the baby with the bath water. The blind compromise is carried on so comfortably because most of it is done within the Christian ghetto, Christian magazines, superchurches, colleges, and other inbred institutions. It would be harder to continue carrying this grudge against "ignorant fundamentalism," "strict Catholicism," "unenlightened evangelicalism" if one was living in an apartment on Sunset Strip, trying to make it as a screenwriter (as opposed to an editor at some obscure, secure Christian magazine), shouldering past whores, abortionists, homosexual salacious TV producers, shopping bag ladies, and all the rest who now gravitate towards the cultural centers of the twentieth century.

Christians are so eager to *not* be confused with some particular branch of the church, or their grandparents they don't like (i.e., evangelicals carefully stating they are "not fundamentalists"), so eager to be accepted by the academic community (i.e., being careful to distance themselves from Falwell), and torturously trying to look "academically respectable," that they do not see the real battle. (See Appendix 6 by James Hitchock for the equivalent events in the Roman Catholic Church today.)

William Kilpatrick, in *Psychological Seduction,* tells of his own personal move to secularize his faith as he attempted to "fit in" with his academic surroundings. A Harvard psychology student at the time, Kilpatrick's own journey toward secularization was naturally through the ideas of psychology. His story has been repeated *countless times,* however, by Christian students in many other disciplines and is representative of the gradual intellectual emasculation that has overtaken so many Christians. Fortunately for us, Kilpatrick found his way back to orthodox Christianity.

My personal introduction to the world of encounter, and to other expressions of humanistic psychology, was through a minister. Once he invited me to a party given in his honor by students who had taken his workshop in human sexuality. When I arrived, the celebrants had already divided into standing circles of six or seven. Almost as soon as I walked into the house, an arm snaked out from one of these circles and pulled me in.

"What's your name?" someone said.

I told him.

"We love you," he said, and the others murmured, "We love you," as we rocked gently back and forth, arm around shoulder. I felt nothing—some sort of deficiency in my nature, I guessed— but I lowered my head anyway and made a murmuring noise.

Meanwhile, I had developed a mental habit of seeing harmony in all things. I was fond of the phrase "all knowledge is one." I sought synthesis everywhere. Religious, philosophical, psychological, and sociological ideas blended easily and conveniently. Maslow's thoughts merged with those of the Jewish theologian Martin Buber in one tributary of my mind, splashed over whatever sluice gates stood in the way, and joined with numerous other tributaries, swirling together toward oceanic oneness.

Soon I began to blur other lines: those that separated good and evil. It was possible, I found, to transmute good into evil and evil into good by minor adjustments in definition: the loosening of a spring here, the turning of a spindle there. But it was hardly necessary to do so. My consciousness of sin was at a low ebb—the result, no doubt, of a habit of almost total self-acceptance. I had learned to trust my instincts; if I desired something, it must be good. It was hard to see how I could go wrong as long as I was true to my desires and strove for self-fulfillment. . . .

In all this—this "maturation" process—I saw no need for sacrifice or hard choices. I felt no need to renounce cherished beliefs. They simply melted away like March snowmen. More often than not, the melting-away process was aided and abetted by theologians who were eager to remove difficult parts of the faith. Anything that might separate one from the world was considered a fair target. Before long, however, it was the world that had my allegiance. As a child I had been deeply moved and delighted to be a member of the church. But like the child of immigrant parents, ashamed of their accent and anxious to assimilate, I had now arrived at a stage of life where I would have been deeply embarrassed just to be associated with it. It would have been awkward all around. I was now prepared to abandon most of my Christian heritage to the realm of mythology or antiquity, and adopt in its place the new streamlined beliefs that talked very little about anything except love.

Later in Kilpatrick's book we find something more to help us understand the tragedy of the evangelical community's desperate scramble to become secularized and fashionable.

And there is this to consider. People turn to the Christian faith in the first place because they are looking for something more than the secular world has to offer; it is a disservice to give them back more of the same. . . . Finally, it doesn't work. According to every index, these attempts at modernization only serve to weaken the faith of church members. Nor do they attract new members. When you end up telling the world what it already knows, it will have no further interest in listening to you.

The Baby and the Bath Water

A major Christian publishing company recently told me not to bring them "any more issue books." "What do you mean?" I said. "What sort of books are you interested in?" The answer: "Spiritual books—things like Christian cookbooks, personal testimonies, uplifting material. Our biggest business comes from Sunday school curriculum and we sell to many diverse denominations, including those who approve such things as abortion. We cannot risk alienating large sections of our market by printing books on divisive issues. Anyway, a lot of our own staff do not know what their position is on things like abortion."

"But in the time of their trouble, they will say, 'Arise and save us.'

But where *are* your gods that you have made for yourselves? Let them arise, if they can save you in the time of your trouble; . . ." (Jeremiah 2:28).

Solzhenitsyn feels it's too late now. I do not know. But as Solzhenitsyn says, "It is better to fight from one's knees than not at all" (see Appendix 1). He speaks of confronting with courage the totalitarian and monstrous Soviet Union. But the same words would also apply to our own passive, blind evangelical community and its leaders and young people in the face of the march of totalitarian, antireligious, antilife secularism in *our own* country.

John Whitehead notes in his book *The Stealing of America* (Crossway Books, 1983):

> Christians naively believe that they can *retreat* (note that Christian seminars are often called retreats), into a zone of social and political impotence and, therefore, social and political irresponsibility (just as they have done for over a century). . . .
>
> As a whole, modern evangelism, because of its pietistic base, has had little effect on our modern culture. As a consequence, the enemy is at the gates. . . .
>
> Like Joab, contemporary Christians are discovering that the horns of the altar no longer protect them from destruction (1 Kings 2:28, 34). They can no longer be "nice" Christians, the beneficiaries of the endless fruits of a former Christian culture, hiding in their "nice" colleges, "nice" churches, and "nice" ministries. . . .
>
> There are no safety zones in the combat of faith. The only way to be effective is to apply true Christianity consistently to the culture in all its aspects.

High Stakes

This is not to say that all is well with American middle-class conservative evangelicalism/fundamentalism. Far from it. But are we saying the foibles of those who *are* taking a stand on the crucial issues of the day provide us with an excuse to do nothing? Just because some Dutch Calvinist fundamentalist wore funny clothes in 1943, does that mean you would *not* have helped him hide Jews in his attic? Or would you have felt more comfortable working with an enlightened professor of theology from Tübingen University, who wore tweeds, smoked a pipe, loved your favorite authors, and served communion to SS guards at Auschwitz on Christmas Eve?

So you don't dig white shoes, matching belt, and burgundy pants. But if this clown is the only one standing up for life and liberty, are you saying that you'd rather die than work with him?

You may get your wish.

Yeah, I know. The local prolife chairman doesn't know the difference between a Renoir and a Rembrandt. Sure, the Gospelight Trio's Greatest Hits, as replayed by the Stringspiration Orchestra, lacks something as far as artistic merit goes. Not only is polyester gauche, but it makes the hairs on my legs itch.

But there are more important things at stake. All of the above is true and there is more of it. Hey, you could write six books on it (as the *Wittenburg Door* has found, fat preachers make easy targets), but the point remains *that the secularist left is even worse.* As Ellen Wilson writes: "Surely some of the [leftist] theologians . . . have crossed a line that even the crankier traditionalists, for all their faults have not crossed" (*National Review,* October 28, 1983, p. 1348). In other words, folks, make sure you're throwing out just the bath water and not the baby. Sure, have a glass of vino, and your films by Visconte and Fellini, but don't mess around with Marxism just because some fundamentalist preacher doesn't like it and you don't like his leisure suits. Don't abandon evangelism just because some TV evangelist looks like he should be running Crazy Eddie's stereo discount emporium. Don't swallow the garbage mishmash of some "leading" Christian magazine just because its editors can read without moving their lips and quote Gandhi. Don't pooh-pooh the prolife cause just because your mother is all for it and likes Tammy Bakker, too. *Life is too short for such games. The stakes are now too high.*

It *is* possible to be prolife *and* proart. It is possible to be realistic about the Soviets *and* be well read. It is possible to be orthodox in your beliefs *and* recognize a good Bordeaux. It is possible to read the novels of Percy and Fickett *and* be conservative in your theology. Don't be forced by the "new" evangelical compromisers into thinking it's them or Bob Jones. There are *other* possibilities.

In William Shakespeare's play *The Merchant of Venice,* we find that Bassanio must, in attempting to win Portia, choose between the three boxes housed in Portia's estate, Belmont. His decision is similar to that we Christians must make today: to choose the box made of gold with its flattery, self-conceit, and in the end, worthless fashion; to choose the box made of silver with its promise of riches, acceptance, and outward beauty; or to choose the humble box made of lead, "which rather threat'nest than dost promise aught." The lead box, like truth and Christianity itself, threatens more than it promises, asks, it seems at times, more than it gives, and we must risk *all* upon it.

Bassanio, and through him Shakespeare, would, it seems, understand today's compromising, gutless evangelicals. Just before he makes his choice between the boxes, he has this to say.

So may the outward shows be least themselves:
The world is still deceived with ornament.

In Law, what plea so tainted and corrupt
But, being seasoned with a gracious voice,
Obscures the show of evil? In religion,
What damned error but some sober brow will bless it,
And approve it with a text,
Hiding the grossness with fair ornament?
There is no vice so simple but assumes
Some mark of virtue on his outward parts.

(Act III, Scene II)

Part III

GOOD NEWS FOR EVERYONE

6 AN ECUMENICISM OF ORTHODOXY

The ecumenical movement as we have known it up to this day has a deservedly bad reputation among orthodox Christians. Bad, because the "ecumenical movement" has seemingly been based on an ecumenicism of *unbelief.* A liberal Roman Catholic, an apostate Protestant, and an atheistic Unitarian can agree on just about anything related to their "faiths," simply because they have little faith left to quibble about. The ecumenicism of unbelief represents one more secularized movement with religious trappings.

The Challenge

The very word *ecumenical* now understandably scares many worthy people, but in the absence of a new word to do the same job, I must use this word, *ecumenical,* to describe what I feel is the challenge before us. The challenge, simply put, is this: Our backs are against the wall and we are facing an aggressively secularistic society whose powerful elements are deliberately attempting to eradicate what little remains of orthodox religious influence in society. The majority of Christians are either asleep or simply do not care. The minority of activist believers no longer have the luxury of concentrating solely on denominational and church affairs and petty theological differences. *The time has come for those who remain to band together in an ecumenicism of orthodoxy.* Unlike liberal ecumenicism which is bound together by unbelief, this ecumenicism is based upon what we *agree* to be the essence of the Christian faith, including an orthodoxy of belief in social concerns and priorities.

The need for an ecumenicism of orthodoxy is self-evident. Daily we are confronted with court-ordered reversals of religious freedoms, new amoral inroads by groups such as Planned Parenthood in the school systems, the secularization of Christian colleges, feminist "translations" of the

Bible, and other sacrilege. With these and the myriad of other problems which beset us, it is clear that no one group or individual can stem the tide, or even build a fortress in which to ride out the storm.

One compelling reason to embrace an ecumenicism of orthodoxy is that people do not function well alone. Those of like mind must stand together. In Herbert Schlossberg's book *Idols for Destruction* (pp. 321, 322) we read:

> As sociologist Donald Kraybill says, "It is not psychologically healthy to be the only oddball around." Vladimir Bukovsky, whose principled obstreperousness, both in and out of prison, nearly drove the Soviet authorities wild, acknowledged that without a closely knit band of like-minded partisans he could have accomplished nothing. The churches will be able to fashion effective groups of Christians, living in community, only when they acknowledge the bankruptcy of the larger culture, just as the Soviet dissidents have done.

How? What? When?

But let me be specific. What is it that an ecumenicism of orthodoxy can and should be achieving?

First, there is the need for the development of *a body of literature which I shall call the Literature of Christian Resistance.* (In chapter 7 I shall go into this in some detail.) This obviously cannot be drawn from only one branch of the church. Take, for example, the following books: *What Is Secular Humanism?* by James Hitchcock, a Roman Catholic professor of history at St. Louis University; Francis Schaeffer's *A Christian Manifesto,* an orthodox evangelical theologian; *The Stealing of America* by John W. Whitehead, an evangelical attorney; *Psychological Seduction* by William Kilpatrick, a professor of psychology at Boston College and a Roman Catholic; *Lost in the Cosmos* by Walker Percy, a Roman Catholic novelist of international standing; *The Spirit of Democratic Capitalism* by Michael Novak, a Roman Catholic theologian and economist; *Christ in the Media* by Malcolm Muggeridge. All these books have one thing in common—rather than joining the throng of anti-Christian debunkers, they are with one voice, somewhat unorganized as yet, adding strength, vigor, and interpretation to the orthodox traditional Christian view. They are not taking away from what little remains but are building it up.

Western culture, since the Enlightenment, has suffered repeated blows from the cynicism of unbelief and secularism. This cynicism has pervaded every area of life. It has led to abortion as a solution to unwanted pregnancy, lack of confidence in the system of free economics developed in the West, a muddle-headed view of the part psychology should play in our lives, and a general loss of perspective and meaning in every area of life. It has created the "latchkey" child, the day-care center fiasco, the broken home, child pornography, and a loss of decency in many other areas. It is through ideas in action, books, that the balance can be redressed and, in some instances, *is* already being redressed.

Ideas, as Richard Weaver has noted, have power and consequences. Books, our TV media age notwithstanding, are still the best way to present ideas to those who *do* think and therefore can make a difference in our society. Part of the expression of an orthodoxy of ecumenicism, then, will be a continuing cross-fertilization and willingness to work together among orthodox believing authors.

A heartening and recent example of such cooperation can be seen in the book *Who Is for Peace?* Here, Francis Schaeffer, an evangelical, and James Hitchcock, a Roman Catholic, join together with Soviet dissident Vladimir Bukovsky to produce a book which takes a hard, skeptical look at the "peace movement." Coauthored books, shared research, mutual encouragement, and discussion are what is called for. Authors of like mind in various areas must take the trouble to seek out one another. Christian publishers must make the effort to broaden the scope of the kinds of books they are publishing and the branches of the church they represent.

Most important of all, the authors and publishers involved in developing a Literature of Christian Resistance must keep their priorities clearly in mind. There are only so many books a year that a publisher can print, and a high proportion of these books should have some purpose beyond the whimsical standards so often applied in choosing them. The agenda of orthodoxy of belief, evangelization, standing for the dignity of human life, the uplifting of the family, child-rearing by committed parents, clearheadedness in military preparedness, fine fiction and literature, and other crucial issues of the day which fly in the face of liberal secular thinking must be kept high on the list of priorities. The other side of the coin is that Christian publishers should think very hard before promoting secularization, even if it comes in Christian garb. The secular world has plenty of space and opportunity for expressing its antireligious bias. It is a shame when we use the precious few outlets remaining to us to promote secular ideas dressed in a Christian cloak. For example, one expects to see the *New Yorker* promoting Jonathan Schell's views—total pacifism and ultimately a one-world state. But to see these views promoted by leading evangelical publishers in the regurgitated Christianized form of Sider's books is disappointing.

One understands *MS* magazine publishing articles by radical feminist theologians exhorting the ordination of women, abortion rights, "inclusive language" translations of the Bible, and the whole panoply of "women's issues." But one wonders why Zondervan Publishing House of Grand Rapids, Michigan (whose principal income is derived from the sale of Bibles), finds it necessary to jump on the bandwagon by publishing a book called

Women and Church Leadership by Margaret Howe. In this book, Howe discounts church tradition as an argument against the ordination of women, cites a few biblical passages out of context to bolster her own feminist ideology, and then in the end claims that the Bible is "curiously silent" on these issues and shows "no clear pattern." As Michael Anderson, reviewing her book in the *New Oxford Review,* notes:

> What does this really mean? Since she regards tradition as irrelevant, and scripture as inconclusive, human reason is left to decide the issue. What results is a system of church governance in which, apparently, those "creative influences" which happen to be in vogue will win the day.

Real Alternatives

The second large area of endeavor for those who band together under an ecumenicism of orthodoxy must be to *challenge* and *answer* the encroaching secularism of the day and *not* accommodate it. My father, Francis Schaeffer, has written in *A Christian Manifesto,* "Truth equals confrontation." This should be, and can be, the banner under which we develop a response to the world and its antihuman liberal agenda. Those who wish to join in the ecumenicism of orthodoxy cannot be a silent majority. We must be an aggressive, feisty, dig-in-your-heels, kick-and-scream bunch; we must work twice as hard because there are fewer of us. As authors, we must join in the fight by pushing the agenda discussed in this book. As preachers, we must preach on these topics. As laymen, we must study and inform ourselves and then act upon our knowledge in a vocal, political, cultural, and visible way.

For example, Christian academia needs to offer real alternatives in scholarship to those proffered by the anti-Christian world. Education serves as one example, particularly "moral" education, or lack of it, in the public schools.

There has been a great failure in education's modern sociological approach to history and life. We read in the *Washington Post* in an article called "Moral Teaching Urged in Maryland Public Schools" (October 10, 1983):

> Maryland's Governor's Commission has issued a program to promote "value education," without religion but with a strong measure of traditional morality in the public schools. . . . Values that schools should develop were widely praised as a statement of "civil morality" that could offset charges that schools are indifferent to ethical behavior. . . . Its list of desirable values starts with "personal integrity and honesty, rooted in respect for truth." It includes "respect for the rights of all persons, regardless of their race, religion, sex, age, physical condition or mental state: . . . a sense of discipline and pride in one's work: . . . patriotism:

love, respect, and loyalty to the United States of America, and the willingness to correct its imperfections by legal means: . . . respect for legitimate authority . . . and allegiance to the concept of democratic government as opposed to totalitarian rule." . . . It also recommends an effort to put moral values into the curriculum, not through "values clarification" exercises that ask students to solve hypothetical dilemmas, but by strong programs in history and government, literature, and the arts that illustrate important moral points. The Voice of Capital Reason, the group that sponsored yesterday's conference, was formed two years ago to counter attacks on "secularism" in the schools by conservative religious groups such as the Moral Majority led by the Reverend Jerry Falwell. "There are an increasing number of people who are choosing private schools if they can afford it, because they say they do not like the moral atmosphere of the public schools," said the founder of the group, Rabbi Sherwin T. Wein of Farmington Hills, Michigan.

And so we have a bland and belated acknowledgment of the total failure of thirty years of the "values clarification" approach which has fallen on its backside so badly that it must now dust off the ancient moral customs of the past: "personal integrity . . . respect for the truth, respect for rights, patriotism," etc. Like Elijah on Mt. Carmel, one is tempted to laugh at the gods of the secularists and ask them if their gods have been asleep or on a journey while they have destroyed the entire moral fabric of public education in America. Here is an acknowledgment, then, that we need to return to moral values, but in what way—a return to the Judeo-Christian base that can give us real moral answers? *No.* What they are going to teach is "civil morality," as writer Cal Thomas put it, "like a doctor realizing his patient needs to take some pills for his illness but prescribing placebos instead of capsules with real medicine in them." It is a form of godliness, while denying real substance. The frail secular attempts to recreate morality now need some sort of a god, but it is a god with a small *g*.

There are several interesting points to be learned from the *Washington Post* article cited above. First, modern values clarification, or a value-free view of history, has failed so badly in producing the kind of people our society wants that Rabbi Wein and many others are now turning to traditional values while at the same time attempting to deny their ultimate source. They are not about to change educational methods; they are merely going to prescribe a slightly different form of indoctrination for young people, based not on a newly discovered godliness, but rather on mere expedience. The schools will teach people not to steal, not because it is wrong, but simply because we do not want our living room window smashed and our stereo system stolen. But we have seen that without real principles, mere pragmatic expedience fails. To say "be good," but to have no ultimate reason why, is nonsense. So the course of the social sciences will continue to run amok until Christians abandon the psychological and socio-logical approach to history that is now being taught, combat it with their own unique view of morality, and lead the way in Christian schools.

The Social "Sciences" as Religion

One of the tragedies of the late twentieth century, which has unfortunately overtaken the Christian community as well as the secular, is the ascendancy of the social sciences. Psychology, sociology, and now history have been overtaken by relativism, and history, knowledge, and even human beings are being reduced to only amoral statistics. As novelist Harold Fickett once said to me, "The only commandment now in force at universities such as Berke-ley, California, seems to be 'Thou shalt not make value judgments,' " which, of course, is a value judgment of its own. As the humanities in academic circles had given way to the silicon-chip-statistical-study-sociological-inter-pretation-modern-psychological approach, history, morals, and value judg-ments have taken a back seat, if any seat at all. Statistical averages, which are now presented as fact and absolute truth, have replaced moral interpre-tation. Truth is without value judgments and is based merely on available statistics.

Sadly, the Christian academic community has not met this challenge. Far from it. Sociology and psychology classes at many Christian schools are almost totally secular in their content. At the end of a one-hour class, five minutes perhaps may be tacked on to bring certain Christian relics up from the past as a kind of benediction on an otherwise totally secular, antimoral sociology course. So, for instance, divorce might be studied only from the point of view of statistics showing upward mobility, or self-fulfillment might be put ahead of obligations toward the family, without morals, right, wrong, absolutes, or God's sovereignty even being discussed. After teaching such a statistical session at a Christian school, to merely tag on a little Christian trailer at the end, noting that "of course divorce is wrong," is no better than thinking that a weekly church service will somehow redeem your week, even if you are not integrating your Christian principles with your daily work.

What is needed is not only a return to viewing history and man primarily as nondeterminist and moral in character but also an answer and rebuttal developed from the Christian academic community to meet head-on the pretensions of modern twentieth-century sociology and the other social "sciences." One way toward this is to stress the paramount moral importance of teaching the humanities—art, literature, drama, music, etc.—over and above merely statistical studies of society. The blinking and beckoning tube of the computer has, in a sense, hypnotized Christians and non-Christians alike into thinking that all life can be reduced to computer studies and printouts. It cannot. Man's nature is moral first; and most statistics, while perhaps elegant when presented in a scientific vacuum, do not in any way assist or inform unless they are tied to that moral nature. Statistics are a reflection of moral choices, not the cause of them. To argue otherwise is a gross example of putting the cart before the horse.

It is not coincidental that the value-free interpretation of history and the social "sciences" has also led, through psychologists such as Carl Rogers, to what has been known as "values clarification" approaches to personal "moral" teaching in schools. It is also no coincidence that this has led not to more clarification but to confusion, as absolutes and man's moral character have been removed from the scene. High crime rates, high divorce rates, high abortion rates, and all the other woes of the twentieth century cannot be merely analyzed statistically by the "social sciences." They need, above all, to be interpreted as moral acts by moral beings exercising moral choices for which they will answer before a living moral God. For Christians involved in the social sciences—psychology, sociology, and other related fields—not to bow first to God, in more than a token way, and submit their discipline to him, is to put the new gods of the social "sciences" *ahead* of Christianity. Not to come up with an alternative approach to the value-free modern approach is to acquiesce to it. To teach courses without comment and analysis throughout and have Christianity just tacked on in the last five minutes of each lesson relegates the Christian faith to a level of merely a nice superstition that one keeps around. In the same way that there are breaks on television saying, "This program is sponsored by . . ." much sociology taught at Christian colleges is simply modern secularist sociology or psychology with an occasional nod to "This program is sponsored by God."

Open to Ideas
None of this means that we do not wish to acquaint ourselves with ideas foreign to Christian principles or indeed even anti-Christian ideas. Those involved in Christian inquiry, particularly in the Christian academic community, have a responsibility to look at questions honestly. We cannot claim that Christianity is truth unless we are willing to hold it up to questioning from ourselves and others. In this spirit, we are of course open to reading, thinking, watching films, listening to music, and conversing with people who represent anti-Christian ideas.

We do this for several reasons. First, because all men are created in God's image, whether they are espousing a Christian point of view or not, we should be interested in what they have to say because they too are his creatures and their ideas therefore have intrinsic value, even if they are wrong and must be vigorously refuted. We cannot expect to fight wrong-headed ideas unless we understand them. Second, we should be interested in the ideas of non-Christians because sometimes they are correct. Christians often have wrong ideas and non-Christians correct ones simply because all human beings, Christian or not, are fallen. This means that, for instance, one will go to a good doctor, whether he is a Christian or not, rather than a poor doctor who happens to be a Christian. Thus in the area of ideas, interpretations of history, and other scholarly academic and artistic pursuits, we must look for quality and truth in all areas over and above religious ideology. What is dangerous is to dress up anti-Christian secular ideas and *pretend* that they are in fact Christian or compatible with Christianity. I do not fear for someone who reads an openly left-wing magazine such as the *Village Voice* with understanding and discernment. What I do fear is the leftist and feminist ideas of the *Village Voice* being toned down, dressed up, and disguised as Christianity, and re-presented to the gullible, in a mushy pablum form by an evangelical magazine as supposedly a legitimate "Christian viewpoint." To teach modern secular ideas in a Christian school, from the point of view of teaching modern secularism *as* modern secularism, is not dangerous when it is done with understanding, discernment, and a good critique. What *is* dangerous is to teach some subject such as modern sociology and present it as "fact" without discernment and without a Christian interpretation. It is not ideas, art, or literature therefore, that we should be afraid of and shy away from; it is ideas uncritically addressed and swallowed without understanding.

Most unfortunately, the fundamentalist tradition has at times attempted to ban the mere discussion of ideas or the viewing of films or the reading of books as a shortcut for having to work at understanding them. While one can admire the attempt to keep one's thinking pure and unsullied, one can hardly encourage this shortsighted form of censorship which has produced so many naive and bitter Christians who are vulnerable to secular ideas and indeed welcome them because they have been embittered and deprived by their fundamentalist backgrounds. Art, culture, learning and much of the accumulated thought of mankind are ignored at our peril. This will not do. We have to develop *real* alternatives.

Resisting Extinction

What are some of the specific areas where we must especially resist, areas where the last vestiges of Christianity are being hounded out? First, there is academia. For every Christian orthodox lone voice, like William Kilpatrick crying out from his position as a professor of psychology at Boston College, there are a thousand acquiescent believers in the academic community who seem satisfied to drift with the tide and rely on their Christianity only as a "personal faith." This pietism has now become quietism, producing disastrous results. Christians within that community, both in secular and Christian schools, must trade their respectability for outspokenness. The ecumenicism of orthodoxy can help in making this a less lonely endeavor. Orthodox, believing Christians in academia must seek out one another and strengthen one another through writing, journals, conversations, seminars, speaking invitations, visiting lecturers, etc. But above all, the self-effacing silence must end. Christians in academic circles should concentrate less on camouflage and more on resistance. If cars were built in evangelical colleges, I suspect that in recent years they would be equipped with only a reverse gear!

The media is an area that I have spoken about at some length in my two previous books *(Addicted to Mediocrity* and *A Time for Anger).* However, let me reiterate several facts here. Because of the pietistic trends in the church which falsely separate "spiritual things" from "secular things," Christians have often abandoned the media as an area that is not "spiritual" or "Christian." This has left a tremendous vacuum which has been very willingly filled by a secular elite who now are exceedingly grudging when asked to share their opinion-making platform. For instance, when was the last time you saw an overtly Christian book sympathetically reviewed by the *New York Times?* The media must be re-invaded on every level: from the top by those Christians with enough money to buy media outlets and then unabashedly influence them; from the middle by journalists who wish to pursue a dedicated profession in the media, *with an agenda;* and from the bottom, if I may put it that way, by those of us who are inverterate letter writers. I am told by Russ Pulliam, an editor at the *Indianapolis Star,* that if Christians would only write more intelligent letters, they could have a great influence. To write intelligent letters to the editor means we must acquaint ourselves with the issues and not spread ourselves too thin, following our agenda clearly. Before writing a letter on a subject, one must obviously read enough to know something about it. Again, this emphasizes the need for a body of work on Christian resistance in every area.

The law and the courts, as we have seen in the first chapter of this book, have an undue influence over our society. Law should be considered a mission field by Christians. It should be a profession many Christians enter in order to change society. Specifically in this area, I would recommend as an absolute must, reading two books—*The Second American Revolution* and *The Stealing of America* by John W. Whitehead. These books, along with The Rutherford Institute and its newsletter, founded by John Whitehead, give us a base for changing the way law works in this country, vis-a-vis the issues on our agenda. (The address of The Rutherford Institute is P.O. Box 510, Manassas, Virginia 22110.) I would urge every Christian interested in seeing something done through the law to write to The Rutherford Institute, support it, and get on its mailing list. With The Rutherford Institute established, Christian lawyers in this country who wish to do more than have seminars, play golf, and share good feelings now have a point of focus around which they can rally (much as the ACLU is the legal center of gravity for the secularization of society).

The necessity for an ecumenism of orthodoxy in the medical profession is evident. Why didn't the evangelical doctors in the Christian Medical Society leave the AMA en masse when it endorsed abortion? A new Christian medical society, based on an ecumenism of orthodoxy in human life issues as well as theological belief, must be founded to replace the inactive and discredited present one. Evangelical Protestant, fundamentalist, and Catholic doctors must join to form a vocal, undignified, unfashionable, kicking, prodding, and yelling association. The medical profession, along with the legal profession, has a special burden of guilt, an extra spattering of blood on its hands. Christians in these professions *must* fight like cats and dogs to redeem them.

I have a friend, a Christian doctor, who left Great Britain when abortion became legal, simply because under nationalized state medicine he then automaticaly became part of the abortion industry, willing or not. He felt complicity and therefore moved to the United States where he could still practice what he believed was more Christian medicine. He now feels that with the trends evident in this country, the same thing will happen here sooner or later. That Christian doctors of good conscience will find it very hard to be doctors *and* Christians.

Another friend of mine, a hospital administrator, has left that profession and gone into banking. Having changed hospitals six times in ten years as each hospital in turn began to allow abortions, he finally left the field altogether. Do Christian doctors really want to wait so long to speak up that ultimately they have to choose between their profession and their faith? If they do not, they had better band together in an ecumenism of orthodoxy *now*, and begin fighting vigorously for the sanctity of life. With amniocentesis (a search-and-destroy technique for discovering handicapped babies in the womb so that they can be eliminated), "wrongful life" suits, infanticide, and abortion itself, it seems unnecessary to labor long here to establish the reality of the danger signals! If *now* is not the time to act, then I predict that for the deliberately blind the time will *never* come . . . "He died in his sleep."

A friend of mine in Congress once told me that some Christians ask him, "How can you be a Christian and be in politics?" To which he said he replies, "How can you be a Christian and *not* be in politics?" The point is well taken. Where is the ecumenism of orthodoxy banding together those in government who are Christians? There are those in government who call themselves Christians but certainly cannot in any way be seen as part of an ecumenism of *orthodoxy*. Where is the united voice of orthodox Catholics and orthodox Protestants in government? This ecumenism must be based on an orthodoxy and a clear agenda, not merely on the good feelings we have because someone claims he is a "Christian" or attends prayer breakfasts. We must vote on the basis of the clear agenda, the sanctity of human life, religious liberty, and the other points discussed in detail in the final chapter of this book. We must run for office on these issues. We must fight and defeat those who run for office who oppose our views. We must write letters and agitate on behalf of our agenda, put our own candidates forward, and fight tooth and nail for those candidates who do represent an orthodox Christian agenda.

Who Governs Whom?
Since we live in a representative democracy, we can take the Apostle Paul's admonitions to respect government as an admonition for *us* to govern well. After all, the people are supposed to be the government in this democratic nation, and therefore as citizens we have a special responsibility to be good governors.

Under our constitutional system of government, the people are as much the governors as anyone else. Or at least that is how it is supposed to be. We cannot merely duck the issue by taking out of context some of the Apostle Paul's verses on Christians' duty to "rulers" and applying them here. In the United States even today, we are as much the "rulers" as we are the "ruled." William B. Ball, distinguished constitutional attorney (who has won more First Amendment cases in the field of religious education than any other attorney), writes:

> The Preamble to the Constitution of the United States begins with the words, "We, the people, . . ." "We, the people," it says, in essence, create our Constitution and, through it, our government, in order to provide for a number of things which we need in order to live together as a society. You will note that there is a very important double concept of "we" in those words. First, it is "we"—not "they"—who make the government. Government is "us" in the American concept. If some people in government today, particularly in the administrative branches, begin to forget that, it is of course our job to bring them down to reality and let them know that they work for us. (*The Separation of Church and Freedom,* p. 15, published by Calvary Press, 400 South Bennett St., Southern Pines, NC 28387.)

It is clear, then, that American Christians have less excuse for undue subservience than Christians in any other culture in Western history, let alone the totalitarian world.

Because Christians must be dedicated to quality (it is as much a Christian carpenter's religious duty to be a good carpenter as it is to go to church on Sunday) it is our duty to be good citizens. And under our constititional laws, being "good citizens" means being good governors. It is therefore more than appropriate for Christians to involve themselves in matters of state, governments, and moral law. It is our *duty* to take advantage of all the many means available under our Constitution, to bring change for the better in our society.

The arts are another area in which we need to make our presence felt. The arts can no longer be regarded as our poor cousins. To be a painter, dancer, journalist, writer, songwriter, or violinist is every bit as much of a holy profession, so to speak, as being a minister or an evangelist. In the arts, as in other disciplines, we must establish our agenda of priorities. Beyond that, we must endeavor to make clear what the true Christian thinking and ethic is versus the secular ethic, or lack of ethics, in all these fields. We must excel in the artistic professions. God is a creative being, and creativity and art need no further justification than that they are good gifts from a creative Heavenly Father.

Seizing the Initiative

Having formed an ecumenicism of orthodoxy, developed our ideas, re-invaded the various disciplines, rejected leftist ideology, what then? Quite simply, the next challenge is to reverse the role of subservient cowering on the sidelines and move into positions of influence through which the compassionate Christian world view can dominate our culture. To those who, at such a statement, jump up and down and yell, "theocracy!" let me simply state that this is *not* what I am putting forward here.

Christians, *of all people,* do not want a theocracy. The idea of theocracy denotes the lack of checks and balances. Christians believe in sin and therefore, above all, do not want any one group, even Christians, to be absolutely, totally dominant. This is well expressed by Michael Novak in his book, *The Spirit of Democratic Capitalism* (page 353):

> The perception of each of us is regularly more self-centered than our ideal selves can plausibly commend. We are often as objective as we would like to be. That is why the separation of systems is appropriate to our weakness. At the heart of Judaism and Christianity is the recognition of sin.

Earlier in the book (page 68) we read:

> In the world as it is, humans as they are, are often and unavoidably enmeshed in lies, betrayals, injustices, and sinful energies of every sort. Prematurely, before the end time, to attempt to treat any society of this world as "a Christian society" is to confound precious hope with sad reality. Human beings, even the most devout and serious Christians, cannot be expected to act always and in all ways as Christians ought to

act, under the sway and impulse of God's grace. A political system based upon such expectations must necessarily end in disaster.

Therefore, what we must call for is an involvement by Christians *as citizens,* who act on what they believe like everyone else, not religious crusaders, in this society—no more, no less. Unfortunately, we have abdicated the stage. It is not a call to theocracy or a naive "Christian society," but instead a call to active participation in our society and an attempt to mold its views toward compassion and fundamental morality. In a pluralistic democratic society, Christians have only ·themselves to thank if they are conspicuous by their absence. Supposedly democracies and pluralistic societies operate on the basis that all persons are free to speak and to attempt to impose their view of society on others. This is of course what elections are all about; one group votes for their candidate over and above another group's candidate. The party that wins gets to drink the champagne and is then in a position to try to impose its views on the rest of society. To pretend that the only people who are trying to do any imposing are Christians is ridiculous. To say that only secular people and interests can speak up and change things is outright bigotry and discrimination. To not have school prayer, for instance, is just as much an imposition by secularism as *to* have school prayer is a recognition of the religious nature of all life, not to mention free speech! To allow permissive abortion is as much of an imposition of the secular "ethic" on the aborted fetus as to ban abortion is an imposition of a Christian view of the sanctity of life. If this is really "an open society," then for better or worse Christians too must have a voice. Orthodox Christians too have a right to make their views known and struggle to have them implemented.

In this light, we would do well to be instructed by Charles Colson's remarks made in his book *Loving God* (Zondervan, 1983). In Chapter 17, pages 165 through 172, we find the following thoughts challenging Christians to take direct action to change their culture around them:

Believers today have many ancestral radicals in their family tree. In fact, the kingdom of God is full of them. John Wesley passionately argued that there could be "no holiness but social holiness. . . and to turn Christianity into a solitary religion is to destroy it." Wesley was branded a radical for his St. Mary's speech, an angry, but accurate denunciation of his fellow Oxford faculty members for their weak-kneed faith (he was never invited to speak there again). Later he captured the essence of radical holiness when he wrote: "Making an open stand against all the ungodliness and unrighteousness, which overspreads our land as a flood, is one of the noblest ways of confessing Christ in the face of his enemies." . . .

Government, then, is biblically ordained for the purpose of preserving order, but, as Francis Schaeffer writes, "God has ordained the state as a *delegated* authority: it is not autonomous." So when government violates what God clearly commands, it exceeds its authority. At that point, the Christian is no longer bound to be in submission, but can be compelled to open and active disobedience. Dr. Carl Henry sums up the Christian duty: "If a government puts itself above the norms of civilized society, it can be disobeyed and challenged in view of the revealed will of God: if it otherwise requires what conscience disallows, one should inform government and be ready to take the consequences." . . .

Furthermore, the Bible provides clear precedents for civil disobedience. Moses' parents are cited approvingly for their decision to hide their child from Egyptian officials, as are Daniel and his friends for their refusal to bow before the statue of Nebuchadnezzar. In the days following Pentecost, Peter and John defied the orders of the Sandedrin, the Jewish governing body, who ordered the disciples to stop speaking of Jesus.

. . . [As to] whether men and women who seek to be faithful to Christ can serve in public office . . . My answer is yes. For if Christ is not only truth, but *the* truth of life and all creation, then Christians belong in the political arena, just as they belong in all legitimate fields and activities, that "the blessings of God might show forth in every area of life," to quote the great Puritan pastor Cotton Mather. Indeed, it is the Christian's duty to see that God's standards of righteousness are upheld in the governing process. This may be accomplished from within the structures themselves or from the outside by organizing public pressure to influence the system.

Molding Events

What then are some of the areas in which we could do with a little less servility and "trying to see the other side's point of view" and more of an attempt to *mold events?* First, as we have seen, the area of *ideas* is paramount. Second, *education,* which includes self-education—reading, thinking, subscribing to fine journals, discussing and analyzing, *and* educating our children through our homes and the Christian school movement. Third, the *electoral process*—participating in becoming powerful through selected candidates, voting, protesting, and taking action. Fourth, helping to shape *the national agenda.* By this I mean constantly identifying the heart of the changing battle and promoting an awareness of it and a call to do something about issues as they emerge. Fifth, *protest.* This includes everything from letter writing to picketing abortion clinics (which is the only way to shut them down), even extending to the spirit of Elijah against the prophets of Baal—a mockery of today's false gods, the inflated claims of secularism and its enormous failures on every front. Sixth, *the media,* which can be approached in two ways—from within (the profession of journalism), or from without. Seventh, exposing the wolves in sheep's clothing in our own midst. We simply cannot tolerate any longer liberal Christianity or Christians who claim it is all too "complicated" and who take no activist stand on issues such as abortion. What are Christian colleges doing with proabortion professors? Where are their alumni, their boards, their presidents? Are we to assume that a century ago they would have welcomed slave-holding teachers? Or that during World War II they would have tolerated anti-Semitic professors in a spirit of "Christian love" and "diversity of viewpoints"? The new orthodoxy of ecumenicism cannot include people who waffle on the issues or have been so overwhelmed by the spirit of the age that they no longer know where to stand.

Finally, we must *strengthen the family.* The family is the basic building-block of society, but it is also (and this is a little recognized point) the basic bulwark against totalitarianism. For totalitarianism has much difficulty in piercing the four walls of a Christian family that has a loving mother, a father, and children. A family in which the mother and father are dedicated *first* to their children and second to their jobs. A Christian family in which the loving mother *is* the mother *who stays at home when her children are preschool,* who raises them, and does not commit them to the day-care latchkey fiasco. We must fight against antifamily tax structures and the feminist agenda, which have the effect of forcing mothers into working outside the home even when they wish to remain at home to faithfully discharge their duty—as well as experience the joy—of raising their children. Such a bulwark is a bulwark in which free ideas can be expressed and nurtured aside from state intrusion. In protecting our families, we must also protect our children's education against state manipulation. This means, always providing an antidote to state teaching through home education after school, and where possible, by sending children to Christian schools or a home school. It also means steadfastly resisting state intrusion into and control over Christian schools. The family is paramount.

Secular commentator Rita Kramer in her brilliant book *In Defense of the Family* (Basic Books), writes on pages 14 and 15:

> While mothers turn to factory jobs or clerical work, who will mind the children? As Nathan Glaser points out, we no longer have the large families' older siblings, the live-in grandparents, or the dedicated religious orders and "simple village girls" who used to care for other people's children. The irony is that the same feminist logic that sends mothers of young children out of the home to fulfill themselves in the labor pool makes it unlikely that anyone but those at the very bottom of the heap would be willing to take their place in the home. It also makes it unlikely that most working women—excepting, of course, the well-

educated and well-connected class from which most published feminist writers come—can earn much more than they would need to pay for adequate substitute mother care.

Is publicly-funded, publicly-provided child care the answer? The authors of the MIT-Harvard Report on The State of the American Family tell us that the "traditional suburban nuclear family lifestyle" (families with children, male workers and female homemakers) is rapidly becoming obsolete. What they expect to take its place is "a new combination of work and family life that uses nursery schools, day care centers and paid child care help more extensively." They add, "it seems likely that the families in 1990 will be looking to non-family sources for help with the care of children," by which they mean that some child care services *may become the responsibility of government."*

Is this the direction family life in America will take in the near future? If so, it seems ironic in view of how it all began [emphasis mine].

To me, the MIT-Harvard Report quoted by Rita Kramer underlines the basic imperative that the family become a *bulwark* against the ever-expanding state. Once the home is broken by feminist ideology which removes a mother from the care of her children, the last resort in the care of the young is an appeal to the state to "do more for working mothers." The state becomes the final baby-sitter in the absence of the family.

Judging by the state's results in secular education, Christians should be the last to allow the breakup of their homes by putting jobs and career ahead of raising their children. To hand preschool children over to state or private care outside of the family is disastrous on two counts: (1) the child is deprived of the love and joy of a true family (not to mention what the parents are missing!), and (2) the child is handed over at an extremely early and vulnerable age to the care, ideology, and eventual control of others. As Christians who have tried to oppose the state public school system have found, *to wrest control back from governing agencies is much harder than to give it to them.* Christians who do not put their families first, and the care of their children above jobs and careers, are signing a death warrant for future generations.

The Open Field
Before concluding this chapter, it should be noted that to call Christians to an ecumenicism of orthodoxy is not to call them to agree, or even pretend agreement, on every point of doctrine. This is an ecumenicism of orthodoxy in friendship forged as alliances are forged in war. It is an orthodoxy with a purpose: to win the war of ideas, culture, politics, and the life of the nation. This is not to say that theological differences do not matter; they do. But there is a time and place for everything, and the ecumenicism of orthodoxy of which I speak is one forged of desperation, not one made in

the spirit of synthesis and the pretense that there are no differences between orthodox Catholicism and Protestantism. With this realistic and hardheaded approach, letting theological differences stand for the moment until we have, like Nehemiah, rebuilt our wall, we can truly accomplish great things. The great divide is between liberal Christianity, including "evangelical" liberals, and orthodox true belief and faith, which includes Catholics and Protestants alike.

If we cannot manage to unite on the issues of the day, if we cannot manage to throw off the yoke of liberal and left-wing thinking, if we cannot manage an orthodoxy on the basic doctrines of Christianity, and if we cannot join with others who hold the same views, we will not achieve the ecumenicism of orthodoxy. Nor will we have a Literature of Christian Resistance. Nor will we have a community of believers who are a light in a dark world. The result will be the advance of darkness, the unbroken night of the new dark age—endless secularism, the inky pit of Marxism, a world which from sea to shining sea is submerged in totalitarianism. We will be asked to make a choice between chaos or totalitarianism. I would prefer to have a third, nonsecularist alternative, that of following the Judeo-Christian world view. But this will not happen by itself. Wishful thinking and even prayer is not enough. God needs willing hands. What will you do? Truth, orthodox Christianity, and the life of faith are as varied as there are people and talents. But we can each do something.

Homemaker. Confrontation. Activism. Evangelism. Protest. Civil disobedience. Uprising. Work. Dedication. Quality. Arts. Family. Media. Children. Love. Care. Compassion. Writing. Painting. Music. Jazz. Symphony. Ballet. Dance. Law. Medicine. Politics. Business. Wealth. Sharing. Civil rights. The right to life. Justice. Mercy. Spirituality. Entrepreneur. Obedience. Poetry. Prose. Bach. Handel. Rembrandt. Shakespeare. Milton. C. S. Lewis. Walker Percy. Vivaldi. Lasagnia al Fourno. The Apostle Paul. St. Francis. The Eucharistic tradition. The Book of Common Prayer. Lent. Christmas. Easter. J. R. R. Tolkien. Solzhenitsyn. Francis Schaeffer. William Kilpatrick. Harold Fickett. Michael Novak. Joe Sobran. Old Testament. New Testament. The Milky Way. Save the whales. Supernova. Great blue heron. Whooping crane. Eagle. Hawk. Prolife. Prochild. Prohandicapped. Prolove. Chemical engineering. Steel. Labor. Management. Italy. Ireland. USA. *Commentary* magazine. *Debate* magazine. The *Human Life Review.* Priest. Pastor. Nun. Midwife. Plumber. H. R. Rookmaaker. Peter Brueghel. Lucca Della Robbia. Andrea del Sarto. Massaccio. Dante. Van Eyck. The Uffizi. The Academia. Ponta del Vecchio. Medici Chapel. Vasari. Brunnelleschi. King Oliver's Jazz Band. Actor. Agent. Banker. *Fight! Unite!*

7 THE LITERATURE OF CHRISTIAN RESISTANCE

As Christians abandoned their culture throughout this century in favor of a quietistic pietism, perhaps the most serious loss, which has caused the most suffering and borne the bitterest fruit, has been the abandonment of the Christian mind. An inability and a lack of desire to think through the issues, or in fact to think at all, is our legacy.

If we are to produce an ecumenicism of orthodoxy, a spirit of resistance to the secularism of our age, we are going to have to start by developing a truly Christian world view. It must not cover only theology and spirituality but, in these fast moving times, the issues of the day as well. This development of the Christian mind is so important that I feel justified in dedicating this entire chapter to a short guide to the more recent contributions by current authors to the Literature of Christian Resistance.

This guide is by no means complete. However, I offer it here in the hope that it will provide a good starting place for many people, both for self-education and for texts to be used in schools.

As Christians we must realize that we have a great heritage of Literature of Christian Resistance, going all the way back to the Book of Genesis. More recently we have writers such as Malcolm Muggeridge, C. S. Lewis, Francis Schaeffer, and G. K. Chesterton, to name but a few faithful stalwarts in our own century. These writers, and others, have laid a foundation on which the new emerging writers are building the present Literature of Christian Resistance. The list presented here is drawn especially from current writers who challenge the present secular onslaught in detail and specifically. Unashamed conviction combined with a precise knowledge of the subject matter is the common thread running through all of these books. None of these authors are willing to accept the status quo, to give up, to learn to lose gracefully, and none of them are willing to take our present situation lying down. Each of the works listed below seeks to give new life to our nation.

Books

Human Life

1. *Whatever Happened to the Human Race?* by Dr. C. Everett Koop and Francis A. Schaeffer (Crossway Books; Westchester, Ill.)

   This book is one of the most complete and accurate works available on the issues of abortion, infanticide, and euthanasia. Updated and fully revised to be current, the book also includes a Plan for Action chapter at the end. Written by Dr. C. Everett Koop, currently Surgeon General of the United States, and Francis A. Schaeffer, leading evangelical theologian and philosopher, the book carries the argument of the sanctity of life so completely and thoroughly that it remains *the standard evangelical work* on the subject.

2. *Abortion, the Silent Holocaust* by John Powell (Argus Communications; Allen, Tex.)

   In this powerfully written, highly recommended book, one finds a combination of profound analysis of the implications of abortion and a discussion of historical facts and figures such as the 1973 Supreme Court decision "constitutionalizing" abortion. Most helpful is a "key question" section with questions and answers.

3. *The Zero People,* edited by Jeff Hensley (Servant Books; Ann Arbor, Mich.)

   A collection of essays on different aspects of the abortion issue, this book is easily read because each essay stands alone, and many can be read in a matter of minutes. The book is comprehensive and because of the scope of its authorship, particularly thought-provoking.

4. *Single Issues* by Joseph Sobran (available by *mail order only* from The Human Life Foundation, 150 E. 35th Street, New York, NY 10016. Send $12.95 to cover the cost of the book and shipping.)

   Joseph Sobran is probably the finest writer in America to have consistently taken up the cause of the prolife movement. His essays in *Single Issues* are the most readable, beautifully written, and expressive on the subject. Sobran's style is reminiscent of the very best of G. K. Chesterton and C. S. Lewis, and his writing combines high literary value with tremendous moral perception. This is the best book of its kind and should be read by everyone who espouses the prolife cause and enjoys truly great writing.

5. *A Private Choice* by John T. Noonan, Jr. (The Free Press, Macmillan; New York)

John Noonan, professor of law at the University of California, Berkeley, and considered the foremost legal expert on abortion, puts forward the most careful argument against *Roe v. Wade* and subsequent proabortion decisions over the years. *A Private Choice* is generally accepted as the most important book yet written on the Supreme Court's 1973 abortion case and following rulings. In John Noonan the Supreme Court has found a formidable opponent to its prodeath decisions.

6. *Rachel Weeping* by James Tunstead Burtchaell (Andrews and McMeel; Fairway, Kan. Soon to be published in paperback by Harper & Row.)

The definitive antiabortion statement, this book is a storehouse of invaluable information—biological, medical, ethical, sociological—establishing beyond a doubt the fact that human life begins at conception and documenting the havoc resulting from *Roe v. Wade*. Absolutely irrefutable in its objective and dispassionate presentation of the prolife position, it makes a unique and lasting contribution to antiabortion literature by clearly and exhaustively detailing the parallels between the language, attitudes, and mentality of slavery and the Nazi holocaust, and those of the proabortion forces in America.

The Law, the Deterioration of the American Court System, and the Loss of Religious Liberty

1. *The Second American Revolution* by John W. Whitehead (David C. Cook; Elgin, Ill.)

The Second American Revolution is the definitive statement now in print on what has recently happened to the American judicial system. If you want to know how we have come to the place where the Supreme Court of the United States endorses abortion-on-demand as a "constitutional right," if you want to know how we have reached the place in which the Supreme Court of Indiana allowed the starving to death of Infant Doe, if you are perplexed by the federal bench and its attacks on religious freedom throughout this country, if you want to know why and what people like the ACLU are doing, then read *The Second American Revolution*.

2. *The Stealing of America* by John W. Whitehead (Crossway Books; Westchester, Ill.)

A sequel to *The Second American Revolution*, this book summarizes the great American legal tragedy as it has unfolded. America has become a nation in which acts once thought morally impossible are now performed on a daily basis. How has this happened? What can we do about it? The answers are contained in this book.

3. *A Christian Manifesto* by Francis A. Schaeffer (Crossway Books; Westchester, Ill.)

This best-seller has become a landmark in the battle for religious freedoms and traditional Judeo-Christian ethics. This is indeed a call to *action*. What is the base for Christian civil disobedience? Has the time arrived when Christians should "take to the streets"? This is the most provocative book to date on the subject of resistance to the secularistic trends in our society.

4. *Clear and Present Danger: Church and State in Post-Christian America* by William A. Stanmeyer (Servant Publications; Ann Arbor, Mich.)

Here is a book that clearly describes why we are confused by attempts to muzzle the Christian voice through talk of "separation of church and state" and "the establishment of religion." Is the First Amendment meant to protect the freedom *of* religion or freedom *from* religion? Here is a basic book that explains this and other problems. Any Christian wanting to be effective in this day and age must read this book.

5. *The Freedom of Religious Expression in the Public High Schools* by John W. Whitehead (Crossway Books; Westchester, Ill.)

The title is self-explanatory. Christians involved in work with students in both high schools and colleges *must* read this book and have it at hand as a most necessary handbook. Christians who wish to be effective in this area must understand what rights they still *do have* and be willing to *fight to keep them!*

6. *Home Education and Constitutional Liberties* by John Whitehead and Wendell R. Bird (Crossway Books; Westchester, Ill.)

The best book available concerning parents' rights to educate their children free from state interference both in Christian schools and at home. Every Christian involved in education and every Christian parent must read this book before it's too late. Positive and practical discussion on questions of the law, this book also is one of the best explanations of what Christian education really is, can, and should be.

Living as a Consistent Christian Minority in a Secular Culture

1. *How Should We Then Live?* by Francis A. Schaeffer (Crossway Books; Westchester, Ill.)

This book remains *the* overall comprehensive view of the decline of Western thought and culture, the abandonment of Judeo-Christian ideals, and the replacement of those ideals with secularism and, above all, *statism.* Christians must understand what has taken place in order to respond *effectively* in this day and age. This book is a foundational building-block and should be a priority on any reading list.

2. *Idols for Destruction* by Herbert Schlossberg (Thomas Nelson; Nashville, Tenn.)

Here is the most complete analysis of the difference between a Christian world view and a secularistic, anti-Christian world view that has been written pertaining to economics, wealth, poverty, political systems, academics, government, and a range of other issues. Well-researched, highly readable, fully footnoted, this book is sure to be a popular item and mainstay of Christian students in America for many years. It is a building-block and, in a way, a sequel to Schaeffer's *How Should We Then Live?* Should be a *standard textbook* in *all* Christian colleges and high schools. *Idols For Destruction* should also be mandatory for anyone interested in a Christian view of economics.

3. *Psychological Seduction, the Failure of Modern Psychology* by William Kirk Kilpatrick (Thomas Nelson; Nashville, Tenn.)

This is, without any doubt, the best book available detailing the difference between a modern humanistic, psychological world view and mindset and *a truly Christian one.* Problems of well-being, identity, and all the other modern "psychological problems" are discussed in this book. Kilpatrick, professor of psychology at Boston College, writes from rich personal experience. His style of writing is extremely clear and easy to read. To all Christians involved in counseling, pastoral work, or those who have personal problems of identity, in fact all Christians everywhere, this book is a must.

4. *Book Burning* by Cal Thomas (Crossway Books; Westchester, Ill.)

Book Burning is the ultimate answer to the "liberal" charge that "Christians are bigots and censors." Detailing such unheralded but true *censorship* as the feminist censorship of textbooks, the omission by secular libraries of Christian books, the omission of Christian books from bestseller lists and other areas, this book exposes that the true censorship of the age comes from a liberal secularistic elite, not from the so-called "right-wing bigots." This book is an absolute must. It provides a *positive* case for a Christian view of free speech.

5. *A Time for Anger* by Franky Schaeffer (Crossway Books; Westchester, Ill.)

Showing that we live in an age of "the myth of neutrality," the book details the manner in which the secular media and other news-making and opinion-making elites in this country have denigrated and sought to belittle Christianity. This book hits back hard and informatively, providing Christians with some real ammunition as they attempt to negotiate the booby traps of a secularistic, anti-Christian society and media.

6. *Common Sense Christian Living* by Edith Schaeffer (Thomas Nelson; Nashville, Tenn.)

The title of this book is self-explanatory. Christians are deluged by everything from cults to total unbelief. Christians have been infiltrated by the spirit of the age. Christianity is under attack. Never before have we more needed *Common Sense Christian Living*. This book will be of interest to many, many people. Positive and practical.

The "Peace" Movement
1. *Who Is for Peace?* by Francis Schaeffer, Vladimir Bukovsky, and James Hitchcock (Thomas Nelson; Nashville, Tenn.)

Finally, a book that sorts out what the whole "peace" movement is all about and gives Christians a perspective on questions of arms, war, and the peace movement. That Schaeffer (well-known Protestant theologian-philosopher), Hitchcock (noted Catholic scholar and historian), and Bukovsky (world-renowned Soviet dissident) would combine to write such a book points up the seriousness with which they take the issue. A "must read" for everyone.

2. *Moral Clarity in the Nuclear Age* by Michael Novak (Thomas Nelson; Nashville, Tenn.)

This book is an analysis of the arguments for and against nuclear armaments by noted scholar, writer, and Catholic layman Michael Novak. In this landmark essay, he assesses the bishops' pastoral letter and discusses the effects of pacifist thinking on the geopolitical stage. No one concerned about issues of peace and war can consider themselves informed until they have read Novak's book. The best of its kind.

3. *Who Are the Peacemakers?* by Jerram Barrs (Crossway Books; Westchester, Ill.)

A short, easy-to-read biblical exposition that answers the arguments of Christian pacifism. Barrs, a L'Abri worker and associate of Francis Schaeffer, is an Englishman. The book, therefore, has transatlantic perspective. This book deals in particular detail with the misuse made of biblical passages by pacifist Christians, and ends up presenting the authentic biblical position in relation to issues of war, peace, and justice.

Economics: Toward a Christian View of Money and Wealth

1. *The Economy in Mind* by Warren T. Brookes (Universe Books; New York)

The Economy in Mind is an incredibly informative book. Written by the economics correspondent for the *Boston-Herald American,* this book presents, at last, a balanced view of a Christian economic frame of mind. Based not on Bible verses taken out of context to support either left-wing or right-wing ideology, this book instead deals with economics as economics rather than economics as theology! What a relief to read a book whose arguments are built on facts and empirical evidence rather than on utopian idealism. An *absolute must* for anyone who purports to be concerned about the poor, our culture, economics, or any other related subject.

2. *The Spirit of Democratic Capitalism* by Michael Novak (Simon & Schuster; New York)

The Spirit of Democratic Capitalism is a moving book. Here is a book that explains why we cannot allow left-wing "liberation" theology and other idealistic propaganda to answer all our problems. It is a breath of fresh air to read a book written as well as this one defending the good and just heritage that does form part of our Western tradition. It has become fashionable to see no good in our own nation or Western man and to seek all of our answers elsewhere, seeing what we can "learn from other countries and dialogue." But there are plenty of things in our tradition that are worth defending, and Michael Novak has become their able defender. A book that will leave no one who reads it unmoved or unchanged.

3. *With Justice for All* by John Perkins (Regal Books; Ventura, Calif.)

John Perkins writes from his wide experience and practical involvement in dealing with questions of race and poverty. Perkins, a Christian and a black American who has worked with the poor and disadvantaged, writes not only out of true personal compassion but also from a sensible perspective. Perkins, unlike many who pretend to be "helping the poor," actually has taken the time to analyze what is best suited to help the poor. He is not preaching a massive "redistribution" of wealth or looking for solutions to poverty by readjusting societal structures. Instead, he sensibly realizes that the poor in America must build up an equity of their own and a stake in the economic future of the country. Perkins is the best writer in this particular field. He has also practiced what he has preached by setting up active and working communities in Mississippi to implement his ideas.

(Also see *Idols for Destruction* by Herbert Schlossberg in previous listing.)

Teenagers' and Children's Books
1. *How to Be Your Own Selfish Pig* by Susan Schaeffer Macaulay (David C. Cook; Elgin, Ill.)

Susan Macaulay has written an astounding and highly entertaining book. She explains to teenagers the basic philosophy of Christianity in terms of the issues that confront us in today's world. A Campus Life Book of the Year and Gold Medallion winner. This highly acclaimed best-seller is truly a unique book.

2. *Something Beautiful from God* by Susan Schaeffer Macaulay (Crossway Books; Westchester, Ill.)

If children do not grow up knowing why human life is valuable, how will they stand against the antilife onslaught coming at us from all directions? If you don't like what people like Planned Parenthood are doing to indoctrinate your children, why don't you give them the positive Christian view of human life first? This book is of tremendous value in presenting the development of human life as something positive and beautiful. Indeed, the book itself, with photographs and illustrations, is beautiful, and provides *real answers* to *real questions*. A tasteful and lovely book in every sense of the word.

Fiction/Essays
1. *Lost in the Cosmos* by Walker Percy (Farrar, Straus & Giroux; New York)

Percy is one of America's greatest living writers. Percy has combined his Christian philosophy and his talented writing in an imaginative and incredible way to speak more clearly to twentieth-century unbelief in this book than any other statement I know. Highly entertaining, and very funny in places, this is the ultimate book to give a totally secularized person to help him understand the beginnings of why Christians are, in fact, Christian.

2. *The Holy Fool* by Harold Fickett (Crossway Books; Westchester, Ill.)

Harold Fickett is a brilliant writer. *The Holy Fool* is the best novel to come out of a Christian publishing house. Here this new, young writer has presented us with a book that is funny and entertaining and also has a point to make. That is, there is a way back for the disaffected, lonely, and cynical Christian who has seen too much of "professional Christianity" and not enough of the living gospel. In following the story of such a person, in fact a pastor, Fickett gives us a most entertaining, amusing reading experience and makes a memorable and edifying point. A wonderful book. *The Holy Fool* proves again that Christian writing can be entertaining and of exceedingly high quality.

The Soviet Union

1. *Stalin's Secret War* by Nikolai Tolstoy (published by Holt, Reinhart & Winston; New York)

Though truly shocking in the real sense of the word, it is a book that everyone must read. If you don't understand the Soviet Union today, you do not understand your world.

2. *Confiscated Power: How the Soviet Union Really Works* by Helene d'Encausee (Harper & Row; New York)

The title is self-explanatory. To those who wish to be knowledgeable on current events, a working knowledge of *how* the Soviet Union works in its daily life, government, politics is must knowledge.

3. *KGB Today, The Hidden Hand* by John Barron (Reader's Digest Press; New York)

This is an excellent book for understanding not only the KGB but the gullibility of the West. The fact that the KGB has infiltrated Western institutions, nations, diplomatic missions, and media to the extent they have, unopposed, is amazing. Particularly revealing are the KGB's efforts against religious freedom and conscience as exposed by this book, the tyranny against Christians, and the KGB infiltration of the "peace" movement.

4. *The Gulag Archipelago* by Alexander Solzhenitsyn (Harper and Row; New York)

Solzhenitsyn, prophet and writer, is a lonely voice crying in the wilderness, crying of Soviet oppression on the one hand and Western apathy on the other. Arguably the greatest writer of the twentieth-century. Arch-foe of evil, defender of freedom, a one-man government in exile. The book is a classic, the greatest exposé of Soviet tyranny ever penned. It is also an incredible witness to the indomitability of the human spirit and the unyielding tenacity of authentic faith—a tenacity which is a stinging rebuke to the complacency of American evangelicalism.

Exploding Secular Myths, Doing Battle with New Secular Elites
1. *The Homosexual Network: Private Lives and Public Policy* by Enrique T. Rueda (Devon Adair; Old Greenwich, Conn.)

The organized homosexual movement in its quest for "gay rights" has become one of the most destructive forces in American life today. Perhaps no other organized group is so greatly at variance with traditional orthodox Christian values. The much heralded "attack on the family" has been almost exclusively put forward by this aggressive minority. To not understand the homosexual and lesbian movement is to not understand twentieth-century America. Rueda, in his nonpolemical, highly factual book, has written the be-all and end-all statement on where the homosexual movement came from, what its present aims are, and where it is going. This is a vital book to be read and *understood* by Christians.

2. *What Is Secular Humanism?* by James Hitchcock (Servant Books; Ann Arbor, Mich.)

A simple, well-written exposé of "secular humanism," this book gives an understandable overview of the cultural shift from traditional, Judeo-Christian values toward a secularistic and humanistic point of view. This is the best short, overall summary of the subject.

3. *The Gandhi Nobody Knows* by Richard Grenier (Thomas Nelson, Nashville)

It is no accident that the Gandhi film, so completely and so historically inaccurate, gave such a rosy, one-sided picture of Gandhi. It is also no accident that Hindu Gandhi has, with the advent and rise of pacifism, become such a figurehead for the pacifist movement. What is strange, however, is that so many Christians have been taken in by all this. Here at last is a book that sets the record straight in an amusing and satirical manner. The best book on the subject by one of America's finest authors and movie critics, this book will both entertain and inform.

4. *Addicted to Mediocrity* by Franky Schaeffer (Crossway Books; Westchester, Ill.)

This book is an exposé of Christian attitudes that have been antiart, anticultural, and antilearning. Christians' own attitudes in these areas have contributed heavily to the decline of Christian influence in our society. If we are going to do anything about the secular culture we live in, we must also *get our own house in order!*

5. *In Defense of the Family* by Rita Kramer (Basic Books; New York)

As a writer who has been widely published in secular newspapers—the *New York Times* and many others—Rita Kramer understands the feminist movement and its antifamily propaganda from the inside out. This is the ultimate argument for the profamily, prowoman point of view that allows and promotes the idea of women and families putting their children and home as a No. 1 priority ahead of career and money and superficial prestige. *This is the definitive statement in the field.* A "must read." The best book of its kind.

6. *The Ultimate Resource* by Julian L. Simon (Princeton University Press; Princeton, N.J.)

Here is a book that explodes one of the greatest myths of our time: the "we're running out of resources, let's abort everybody and enforce contraception on a worldwide level because there's no more zinc, oil, copper, or anything else" myth! As the shrinking resources propaganda of the sixties made enormous claims that "everything's running out, the world's coming to an end," the media, always looking for a secularistic and sensationalist approach to problems, pumped and hyped this point of view until it became something accepted unquestioningly by the general public, Christian public included. But have all these predictions come true? No! Says Simon in this well-researched, highly documented, and informative book. Far from running out of resources, the earth still provides abundant resources, many as yet untapped. This book, on a scale of 1 to 10, is a 10. This book stands in the way of a deluge of "limited resource" propaganda which has contributed heavily to the prodeath, Planned Parenthood mentality of population control. Every person who has been affected by the "limited resource" concept should read this book. A must. This book should be *the* basic textbook in all Christian colleges and high schools on the subject. Talk about investigative reporting—*The Ultimate Resource* will make everyone rethink their position on this vital issue.

7. *Panic Among the Philistines* by Brian S. Griffin (Regnery/Gateway; Chicago)

Brian Griffin has written a hilarious and irreverent expose of the "artistic-media community" and its shabby, amoral values. The book paints a refreshingly unorthodox picture of the popular writers, critics, and journalists who celebrate the mediocre and even the depraved "in an age where everything was Great precisely because nothing was very good." The book pops the media elite bubble and exposes the emperor in all his nakedness as never before. He ends this book with a rousing call for renewed dedication to the ancient artistic ideals of "moral, esthetic, spiritual, and intellectual splendor." His book outraged the doyens of the literary and cultural world. Anything the *Washington Post* calls "arrogant . . . singularly irritating" must have something going for it.

Magazines
The following magazine-journals are currently the very best subscription reading—secular or Christian—available in the United States today for keeping up with current issues, national issues, and foreign affairs.

Human Life Issues

> *The Human Life Review.* For a year's subscription, send $15.00 to The Human Life Foundation, 150 East 35th Street, New York, NY 10016. *The Human Life Review* is the single best presentation on a regular basis of human life issues. Abortion, infanticide, enthanasia, and directions in our country that the courts and medical profession are taking are routinely reviewed here. The best writers on the subject write regularly for *The Human Life Review.* This is must reading.

Economics and Foreign Policy

> *Commentary* magazine. For a year's subscription send $30.00 to Commentary, 165 East 56th Street, New York, NY 10022. Foreign affairs, national policy, movie reviews and books as well as other subjects are treated here on a level of good writing and analysis not achieved in any other magazine today. Here is a magazine that truly seeks to understand the world in the light of traditional orthodox, Judaic views. Read by the

most influential leaders in society, this magazine is imperative reading for all those who would understand the culture in which they live.

News and Current Events

National Review. For a year's subscription send $26 to 150 E. 35th Street, New York, NY 10016. This publication is a real alternative to the all-pervasive liberal bias of the new print media. The easy-to-read *National Review* gives comprehension and excellent coverage to news and events, as well as the arts. A fine magazine written by fine writers. Edited by people who know what they think.

Taken together, these three magazine-journals provide regular stimulation and information on a whole range of subjects that will leave their readers informed and competent to deal with the world around them.

Free Newsletter

Schaeffer V Productions, Inc. sends out a free newsletter, the *Christian Activist,* to inform and update Christians on current issues. This newsletter is read widely and provides such things as regular mention of new and worthwhile books, publications, and films, as well as an analysis of current trends. To get on the mailing list, simply write to Schaeffer V Productions, P.O. Box 909, Los Gatos, CA 95031.

Movies and Documentary Series (For Rent, Sale, and Study)

1. *How Should We Then Live?* with Francis Schaeffer. (Ten 35-minute episodes; 16mm or video, color)

   The rise and decline of Western thought and culture, from the first to the twentieth century, and Christian alternatives to a secular view of history.

2. *Whatever Happened to the Human Race?* with Dr. C. Everett Koop and Francis Schaeffer. (Five 50-minute episodes; 16mm or video, color)

   Infanticide, abortion, euthanasia, the sanctity of life, and Christian alternatives.

3. *The Second American Revolution.* (Forty-five minutes; 35mm, 16mm, or video, color)

   A detailed analysis, in the form of a provocative play, of what has happened to our court system.

4. *Common Sense Christian Living* with Edith Schaeffer. (Five 40-minute episodes; 16mm or video, color)

A teaching series on the Christian life. Family, children, sanctity of life, and prayer are some of the issues discussed.

5. *Reclaiming the World.* (Ten 30-minute episodes; 16mm, color)

A teaching series with Francis Schaeffer on the most asked questions about how to live as a Christian in a pagan and secular society.

6. *The Great Evangelical Disaster.* (Thirty minutes; 16mm or video, color)

A *very* funny movie about contemporary values, or lack of them, and the less than adequate evangelical response. A long-overdue satire.

To find out how all these films are available on film, videotape, for TV use, for rent or sale, write to:

Franky Schaeffer V Productions, Inc.
P.O. Box 909
Los Gatos, CA 95031
Or call (408) 395-1785

Legal Action and Defense of Religious Liberty
Christians must be involved in society around them. There are several groups and associations who are truly involved and actually *do something* rather than just talk about it. In the area of law, standing up to the courts and groups such as the ACLU, and defending religious liberty and the prolife movement, two groups stand alone:

The Rutherford Institute
P.O. Box 510
Manassas, VA 22110

This group, founded by attorney and author John W. Whitehead, is the best Christian legal association in America today. This group actually fights cases and actively promotes Christian freedom in the area of education, the prolife movement, and other fields. Every Christian should receive its free newsletter, and every Christian lawyer should be associated with it. Write to them.

The Catholic League for Religious and Civil Rights
1100 West Wells Street
Milwaukee, WI 53233

The Catholic League also has an excellent newsletter and has done good work in actively defending religious and civil liberties.

In the books, films, newsletters, and magazines listed above, a clear agenda is emerging. An agenda, in many specific areas, for Christians who wish to do more than sit on their hands or attend "fellowship seminars" and for those who are prepared to think as well as to act. Ideas do indeed have consequences, and to define one's thoughts about any issue or event is half the battle. We must inform ourselves and act. But action without information is devoid of value. On the other hand, simple knowledge without the willingness to act on it is not a morally defensible position for the Christian. The above list is a happy combination of print media, books, films, and organizations that both inform and give direction to our actions.

8 THE FUTURE AND THE CHRISTIAN RESPONSE

"For I have heard a voice as of a woman in labour, the anguish as of her who brings forth her first child, the voice of the daughter of Zion bewailing herself, who spreads her hands, saying 'Woe is me now, for my soul is weary because of murderers!' " (Jeremiah 4:31).

In J. R. R. Tolkien's wonderful *Lord of the Rings* trilogy, we read of a time when the dark shadows of Mordor have fallen over Middle Earth, a time so forlorn that there is a place that is known as "the last homely house." We have come to such a time ourselves. The minority of Christians living consistently in this world of ours now stand forth as those who occupy "the last homely houses." The undivorced family, the mother who puts the care of her children above career, the father who puts a Christian way of life above selfish materialism, the teenager or adult who is interested in God's Word, art, beauty, life, music, and drama—these are the few who are living the full, beautiful, Christian moral life. They are a minority standing like a beacon on a hill: the last homely house.

Christians who have not been completely co-opted by the world, who have not been hopelessly infiltrated, who are not compromising, and at the same time who are exhibiting beauty, love, and life, have become so rare that indeed they now represent an oasis of sanity in the midst of an insane world. What does the future hold for this dwindling band of consistent orthodox Christians in the United States? Two possibilities can be envisioned.

The First Scenario

In the first scenario Christians will continue to be silent, fashion-conscious pietistic, and apathetic. The world will continue its slide towards antihuman, total secularism, becoming ever more hostile to Christians. Because of its folly, the world will generate more and more excesses, and in the end license and chaos will reign, followed by increased statism and imposed governmental power. Freedom of religion will be gone. AIDS, latchkey children, abortions overtaking live births, and many other evils and sorrows of the day are only the first indicators, the first bitter taste, of where all this will finally end. If humanistic secularism has chosen the death of the human spirit, so be it. It will get its wish.

"All your enemies have opened their mouth against you; they hiss and gnash their teeth, they say, 'We have swallowed her up!' " (Lamentations 2:16).

If this scenario plays itself out to its logical conclusion, the vacuum created by the criminal Christian abandonment of society will be filled by a statist regime bent more and more on curbing all religious dissent. Christian schools will be shut down for opposing "public policy," and those who are religious will be considered the last "deviants" in a society that has accepted all actual devious behavior as "normal." Daniel Maguire, an "ethicist" who teaches at Marquette University, in his book *The New Subversives* refers to orthodox ("fundamentalist") Christians as "subversives." Groups such as the National Organization for Women have stated that they advocate sexual equality in seminaries, denial of tax exemption to churches that do not ordain women, and federal intervention to stop churches from "discriminating." In the view of radical feminists, one of the *advantages* of the Equal Rights Amendment, for which they have been pushing for some time, would be that it would put them in a position to use the courts, always ready to expand the power of the state, to eliminate tax-deductible status for churches that "discriminate" against women by not ordaining them. It would also enable them to strike down the Hyde Amendment in Congress, which now prohibits federal funding for abortions. Thus, Christians would find themselves in churches that faced extinction or antibiblical compromise, would find themselves forced to fund abortion and a host of other evils. The anti-Christian aspects of the ERA, and proposals associated with it, is only one of the many items that could be cited in showing the secularistic direction of our society. Indeed, the antichurch, antifamily, and antiorthodox mood prevails in the courts and para-court organizations such as the National Organization for Women, the American Civil Liberties Union, Planned Parenthood, and the National Education Association, to name but a few. And this is only the beginning of the gloves-off approach that started with the 1973 *Roe* v. *Wade* abortion ruling.

The dedicated secular religionist will not rest until all rival religious persons have been driven from the field, especially those orthodox people who pose a threat because they have a belief system which places God and his Law over the actions of secular man. In this first scenario, then, the church will face greater and greater persecution in this nation until it is either totally destroyed or it fatally compromises its ability to survive.

The Second Scenario

In the second scenario, *which I pray fervently to God will be the one we will see,* a slumbering and decaying church will rouse itself to do battle with the leviathan of secularism, statism, and the deliberate immorality as state policy which threatens to consume us. The church will heed the prophetic writings of George Orwell's *1984* and *Animal Farm,* and Aldous Huxley's *Brave New World.* It will heed the Christian prophetic voices of writers such as C. S. Lewis in *That Hideous Strength,* Herbert Schlossberg in *Idols for Destruction,* Francis Schaeffer in *The Great Evangelical Disaster* and *A Christian Manifesto,* and John Whitehead in *The Stealing of America.*

Christian colleges will become "think tanks" of resistance. Instead of Christian professors and the academic community of Christendom being eager to assimilate the "best" of the world into Christian curriculum, they will instead look for ways in which to be more distinctive and less acquiescent. What will emerge will be a Christian vision that is distinctly Christian in contrast to the secular vision, a vision that is prepared to confront the world and do battle with it in the areas of ideas, politics, morals, social "sciences," law, the arts, the humanities, medicine, and science. The church, Christian educators, and the Christian legal profession will combine to fight for the rights of Christian education that remain to us, and fight to expand those rights to guarantee the ability to teach a new generation of Christians from a Christian perspective. The organized orthodox Christian church, both Catholic and evangelical-fundamentalist Protestant, will be strengthening that which remains by presenting a united front to secularism. By insisting that their parishioners become acquainted with the issues and raise their children in truly Christian families, the church will be strengthened and prepared.

The prolife movement will have its ranks swelled by millions of orthodox Christians who will join in a vocal and outraged body, pouring into the streets to protest the slaughter of the innocent. Never again will an Infant Doe be starved while the church looks on in silence. The one million six hundred thousand abortions a year will be protested, mourned, and rightly denounced. And above all, direct action will be taken to reduce these terrible numbers of killings. The abortion industry will literally be brought to a standstill and closed down clinic by clinic as the sidewalks outside every abortion mill are clogged with righteously angry Christians demanding that the image of God in man be protected from further murder. We can no longer hope only for legislative change. It is time to take to the streets and stop the carnage directly. You may not be able to change all the laws at once, *but you can close your local abortion mill!* Picket! One does not wait for the legal abolition of slavery before starting the Underground Railroad.

Meanwhile, the Christian media, magazines, TV shows, and radio will abandon their long, sad history of pietism and noninvolvement and acquiescence to secularism and throw themselves into the breach. They will inform the Christian public and then call them to specific action. Christians with access to television will begin to use the medium as cleverly as secular humanistic talk show host Phil Donahue has used it. He has relentlessly pounded away at the moral fabric of this country, introducing secularistic and amoral ideas to middle America through the vehicle of a "talk show." ("We have two lesbians who have been artificially inseminated here with us today to talk about their reproductive rights . . ." ad nauseum.) It is time we use our own media as effectively. Linked to the protesting and vocal church and to the now thinking, resisting, and awakened Christian colleges, high schools, and primary schools, the Christian media and arts could be the organizational basis from which the movement moves forward and makes its stand.

If this all takes place, we will not yet have started a reformation in the culture in general, but merely assured, to the best of our ability, the continuity of the faith. However, the foundation for a reformation would then be laid. The future of Christian education will be assured by political involvement to stop the march of groups who seek to eradicate the Christian school movement. The prolife movement will have made it impossible for the abortion industry to expand, and the number of abortions performed will actually diminish as clinics are shut down by daily, round-the-clock sidewalk picketing, godly harassment (consider Christ and the money changers), and counseling action. Christians long overwhelmed by a secular media will now be developing a Christian world view through Christian colleges, newspapers, seminaries, magazines, television, etc., to counteract the omnipresent and overwhelming secular force. The church, no longer preaching a pietistic gospel unconnected to life, will be preaching an applied gospel connected to every area of life, including the life of the mind, the arts, political and social action, and the law. There will be an opportunity to be a true witness, to change the culture, and to bring a reformation, if God so chooses to bless the church's faithfulness.

A New Reformation

Why would this reformation come about? Simply because the secular world has played itself out to the end of a hangman's rope. AIDS is the result of sexual abandonment in the homosexual movement. The latchkey child, the abandonment of the home, the divorce rate at a record level, abortion, and the total unfulfillment of a whole generation of "working" women are the stepchildren of the radical feminist movement. A million six hundred thousand abortions a year, infanticide, and a growing movement toward active euthanasia are the legacy of a medical profession that has been cut off from moral standards and Christian ethics. A legal system pitted against its own people, unable to curb crime and yet anxious to stop religious freedom, is the heritage of those who have separated law from morality and justice from God. Disillusionment is rampant. From the failed Keynesian economics of the liberals down to the last patient who died from AIDS, the whole secularistic world view has proven itself completely bankrupt.

In the first scenario, Christians will merely continue to compound this ongoing tragedy by conceding to secularism, trying to "dialogue," or "be reconciled," refusing to draw the line, and as in the sadly muddled words of Ronald Wells, seeking to hide behind "ambiguity" rather than taking a stand. But in the second scenario the picture is much different. Embittered, lost, directionless, and disillusioned, a secular culture confronted by a church as dedicated as that portrayed in my second scenario could and would change.

How Reformation?

We have arrived at a generation of people so cut off from the gospel that it will be as fresh to them when preached as it has been in the past to completely pagan cultures who have never heard the good news to begin with. When I say a gospel "preached," I do not mean only verbally, though verbal evangelism is *paramount*. Here is what I do mean. One family living consistently as a Christian family in a neighborhood, with a father and mother who are not divorced and would never contemplate being divorced, a mother who stays at home caring for her children, especially preschool children, rather than abandoning them to seek the "fulfillment" of a career, a father who puts his children and family first in a loving relationship which literally glows—this is Tolkien's "last homely house." This is the beacon of love and sanity set on a hill above the decaying mass of secularized, immoral, adulterous Western culture. This is *true* radicalism for truth.

In the New Testament we hear of the conversion of two tax-collectors, Zaccheus and Matthew. Matthew went into "full-time Christian service," but Christ did not commend him to any greater extent than Zaccheus, who redeemed the area of life in which he worked, namely tax collection, by paying back what he had stolen and being honest forthwith. If current evangelicals had written the New Testament, Matthew would be commended on a higher level than Zaccheus, who would have been "merely a tax-collector" (or merely a homemaker or artist or lawyer), rather than a minister or "full-time" Christian servant. But this is not how Christian truth is portrayed in the New Testament.

Instead of being a pietistic belief, Christianity applies to all of life, real life, and applies to every profession and human situation. The mother raising and enjoying her children and producing sweet, loving, compassionate human beings who will stand on principle in the face of any adversity, is contributing more heartily to the Christian agenda than many full-time evangelists and preachers. The doctor who refuses to perform abortions and leaves a practice at a hospital that allows abortions and makes a stand is putting forth a more vigorous defense of both Christian liberty of conscience and of human life than a score of evangelical "leaders" who refuse to take a stand for life. His action will be more likely to bring the much sought after "Well done, thou good and faithful servant," than the work of many a trendy youth minister engaged in spreading the gospel of "redistribution." The Christian teacher, refusing to bow to the pressures of such groups as the ACLU and courageously speaking of the things of God to her students in the public school classroom, has much more in common with Sts. Stephen, Paul, Peter, and John than has many a president of many a Christian college.

Why Reformation?

A revitalized, aggressively Christlike church tuned to the needs of the society and ready to take dramatic action can see a field which is indeed full of wheat ready for harvest. The disillusioned, directionless, and piteously sad teenager today is ready to hear the gospel. The girl about to have an abortion, who has been told that her unborn baby is merely a blob of tissue, is ready for the love and the living alternative that can be given by a dedicated Christian crisis pregnancy center. The thrice divorced mother with two children in day-care centers and a live-in lover who has just left her is ready to hear the gospel from a friend who has put her children first, has a loving husband, and who can outline to this sad person not only the gospel, but a practical way back to "the last homely house."

Our crying, dying, and bleeding country, torn by the ravages of secularism and the social sciences, claiming to give more freedom, has actually enslaved this nation. We are slaves to our hedonism, the child of divorced parents is a slave to the broken home, the AIDS victim is a slave to license and sexual immorality, the person victimized by crime—the murdered, the raped, the pillaged, the robbed—are slaves to a justice system which believes that there is no such thing as sin and instead has given a psychological or sociological interpretation to law. The sexually abused child is a slave to the absurd liberal idea that sex is only good fun and there are no longer any taboos. We have not become freer. Instead we have often legalized those things which should be illegal and made illegal those things which men should be free to do. Child pornography is not aggressively prosecuted, but woe betide the teacher who prays in a public school classroom! James Watt, Secretary of the Interior, was hounded from office for calling a handicapped person "a cripple." But the justices of the Indiana Supreme Court, who *actually starved* a "cripple" (that is, a handicapped person) to death, are still holding their esteemed positions and *being praised by the secularist media for acting so "courageously."* Indeed, the opening lines of Shakespeare's *Macbeth* apply here: "Fair is foul, and foul is fair."

The secular world is untouched by a pietistic and retreating church, a church always trying to "see the other point of view," a church never willing to make a stand, a church which regards all social questions as "too complicated" to warrant involvement, a church enamored with the social "sciences," psychology, liberalism, and every other "ism" but not authentic Christianity. The secular world will pay no attention, and *is* paying no attention, to such a bankrupt church. But a world confronted by a clear, consistent, unfashionable gospel message applied to every area of life, a message on which orthodox Christians are willing to stand and fight, is a world that can be converted. The world is spiritually hungry and distraught and looking for answers, and we as Christians have those answers. There is no need for us to hide, cower, and pretend that we are "broad-minded and pluralistic" in a shabby attempt to camouflage ourselves and avoid drawing embarrassing criticism. Instead, we can stride forth robustly and claim the high ground in the name of our God from whom all truth comes. Freedom, justice, compassion, beauty, life, art, love, and family are ours if we wish to claim them.

The Alternative

The alternatives are stark. The fire has gone out of much evangelical and Catholic Christianity in this country. One has to look no further for proof of this failure of will than the culture around us. Any Christian reading the ridiculous polls, which purport to show that there are forty to fifty million "evangelicals," and drawing comfort from such reports, is truly misled. Why, if there are so many believing Christians, is the culture moving so radically in the opposite direction of the Christian faith? Why, if all these Christian colleges, Christian high schools, and primary schools are doing a good job, do they continually graduate students who are so ill prepared to meet the challenges of the world, unaware of the distinction between the Christian mind and the humanistic and secularistic mind? If our ideas of Christian education are correct, why are the most subservient and namby-pamby Christians often faculty members at Christian colleges, Catholic or evangelical Protestant? Why are graduates from these pale, listless institutions so passive? The answer is simple. Pietism and nonapplied, nonconfrontational, liberal, fashion-conscious, compromising Christianity has overtaken evangelicalism and much of American Catholicism to such a degree that it is doubtful that we are going to be able to make a real stand. But if we can, if we only can, rouse those troops, if we only can have even a small, faithful minority within a faithless majority in the church, ready to stand, what could not be done! We do not fight the good fight for results alone—only

God can give those—but we fight because we believe in doing things *because* they are right in themselves. This is what having absolutes means.

A Practical Agenda

1. *Every church should be involved in the prolife movement.* Abortion clinics *must be picketed* nonstop. Doctors who wish to murder the innocent must be harassed and driven from our communities. To stand silent and allow them to do business as usual, to trade in human flesh, is to acquiesce to their deeds. Picket! Every church must be involved with the positive alternatives to abortion. It must be involved with crisis pregnancy centers, care for the pregnant woman, and an open-home policy for people who need a place to stay while they bring their pregnancy to term. This is a mission field. The church must nurture life. For those who wish practical help and information on how to picket abortion clinics and offer positive alternatives to abortion, two organizations among others that have wide experience in an activist approach to the prolife battle should be contacted. They are:

OMEGA—DEBATE
P.O. Box 11796
Ft. Lauderdale, FL 33339

The Pro-life Action League
6369 North LeMai Avenue
Chicago, IL 60646

There are a number of other excellent prolife organizations that take a more educational and legislative approach toward changing proabortion policies. Among them are the following:

The Christian Action Council
422 C Street NE
Washington, D.C. 20002

The National Right to Life Committee
419 Seventh Street NW, Suite 402
Washington, D.C. 20004

Americans United for Life
230 N. Michigan Ave #915
Chicago, IL 60601

Those concerned with stopping abortion should be in touch with and on the mailing lists of all the above organizations.

2. *Every Christian college and high school should teach a course perhaps called "Living Consistently as a Christian Minority in a Secular World."* This course can be built around a number of books and films outlined in Chapter 7 of this work. To not send Christians, as graduated students, into the world prepared to understand the issues of the day from a distinctly Christian perspective is to send them out to be slaughtered, unarmed. Discussions, lectures, and practical involvement can assist. Every Christian college campus ought to have a branch of a prolife organization that students are encouraged to join. Schools should give encouragment and support to students involved in picketing abortion clinics and hospitals that perform abortions. Working with the elderly in old folks' homes (in opposition to calls for euthanasia) and helping the handicapped (our answer to infanticide) ought to be practical work for which *credit would be given*. There are other areas, but these would be a start. If current evangelical institutions are not prepared to exercise their mandate to equip their students for warfare against secularism, then we must replace these institutions quickly, for the day is late, with new ones. The message must be clear: mend your ways, or we will withdraw support, students, and approval. Declare yourselves openly. Where do you stand? In wartime, only the dead, dying, and vultures occupy the no-man's land between the trenches. Nowhere in Scripture is waffling equated with godliness.

3. *The gospel can no longer be preached in a vacuum.* For an evangelist to say, "I'm just preaching the gospel; I can't get involved in the fight for human life," is for him to join the ranks of the religious leaders in the parable of the Good Samaritan, who passed by on the other side of the road and did nothing for the bleeding man lying there. There is no such thing as "just the simple gospel." The gospel is *not* the gospel unless it is applied to life. The strength of the Whitefield and Wesleyan revivals was that they *did* apply the teachings of Scripture to life in the generation in which they lived. It is no coincidence that Whitefield started orphanages. It is no coincidence that it was those such as Lord Shaftesbury and Wilberforce who, as *Christians* in England, abolished slavery and child labor in their day. Where is this robust vision of the gospel as affecting every area of life today?

The true gospel includes the cross. It is very clear from the New Testament (for instance, in Matthew and Hebrews) that a true gospel speaks not only to every area of life but particularly to the areas in which we are to keep Christ's commands. If one is saved, he will try, however imperfectly, to keep Christ's commands and the teaching of Scripture in every area of life. A nice "salvation or conversion experience" is not enough. This is not to judge any individual's salvation or lack of it; it is merely to state a principle: *a gospel preached without the duties of the gospel being taught along with salvation is not the true gospel.*

Jesus is not our "buddy"; he is our Lord and Master before whom every knee shall bow. And if we do not preach this gospel, this gospel of repentance from sin, bowing before God, and willingly separating ourselves from the world ideologically and morally, seeking to bring life to the dying, then we have not preached the real gospel. To preach "just the simple gospel" is not to preach the gospel.

4. *The arts and media must be vigorously re-invaded by Christians if they wish to make an impact on this society, let alone enjoy this life.* If we look at Paul and the other apostles, and indeed Christ himself, when they wished to teach they went to the places where the people were, in their day typically the market or the Temple. In our day, the marketplace of ideas is in the arts and media.

It is not a coincidence that most of Christ's teaching was done in the form of parables. Storytelling, the short story, the screenplay, the novel—in other words, the parable—are a means of communication which our Lord and Master himself used. The whole of creation is an artistic expression of his character. If we who claim to be created in the image of God do not understand God's creative nature, and do not mirror it in the way we communicate, are not interested in the arts and beauty, and consistency and integrity in communication, then who will be? For Christians to not be joyfully and aggressively involved in the media, the arts, writing, music, composition, painting, photography, and all the other areas of communication and aesthetic pleasure, is for Christians to state in effect that they do not care about communicating with the world, do not care about enjoying God and his creation, and do not care whether or not anyone hears the Christian point of view. It is also a statement that to us, beauty is not important.

5. *The home is of paramount importance.* Christians should put more emphasis on their marriage relationships (simple fidelity for a start!), the raising of their children, and home life than on any other area of their day-to-day existence. The home is the basic building-block of society and by degrees is being destroyed and eroded. One of the greatest tragedies of this century is that Christians have not taken as strong a stand in this area as they could have taken. One looks at a "religious leader," who is a "best-selling Christian author," and at his divorce and remarriage. One wonders why he continues to write "Christian best-sellers" and why anyone has so separated the idea of the purity of the Christian life from reality that they would continue to buy, publish, or sell those books. How can we make a stand against the erosion of the family if our so-called "Christian leaders" do not have the rudimentary decency to carry out Christian principles in areas so fundamental as divorce and remarriage?

A Christian marriage places sacrifice and sharing above career, ambition, or fulfillment. There is no use in pretending that the ideas of modern feminism and Christianity can be merged. They cannot. The naive Christian who thinks that he can merge these ideas will find himself or herself more feminist and less Christian at the end of the process. Such mergings tend to become one-way streets. The idea of Christian sacrifice in all of life is completely incompatible with the generation of me-ism, self-satisfaction, and fulfillment.

Nor is there anyplace in the Christian mind, home, or life for the manipulative, "woman as only an object" philosophy of those such as Hugh Hefner and Playboy Enterprises. Just as on the other side there is no room in the Christian mind for compromise with the attitude put forward by people such as Gloria Steinem and *MS* magazine. *Both* are anathema to the biblical viewpoint and should be utterly scorned and rejected as counterfeit, selfish pseudo-religions trying to fill the vacuum created by the absence of real truth, real love, real compassion, real sacrifice. And this includes obeying the biblical injunctions on order in the home. (If we must look for role models of "working women," let us select Mother Teresa rather than Bella Abzug!)

It is not a question of the man dominating the home in a totalitarian and brutal fashion; it is rather that the man and woman both sacrifice their own egos and "fulfillment" to the other partner *because* of the love they have in Christ for each other. The same is true in child-rearing. We love our children, sometimes at cost to ourselves, and have a willingness for self-sacrifice *because* God loved us first. Paul says that the man who does not care for his own family is "worse than an unbeliever." If we do not rally our forces on this most basic of all points, there is no hope for the future. If Christians cannot present a clear understanding of what the family is, of putting children first, above career, and of putting warm, home-centered activities ahead of things such as television watching and other copouts from active thinking, family life, then we will not be able to build a new Christian agenda. If Christians have lost their understanding of the sacredness of the family, the mother/child relationship, the husband/wife relationship, and the parent/child relationship, then the future is bleak indeed. Where shall this shepherdless generation turn for alternatives if not to Christian homes and Christian families? And what remains between the rapacious state and the total possession of all of its citizens if it is not Christian parents standing between the state and their children, and the Christian home (as a fortress) standing between the state and parents? (And I pray that there are no Christian married couples who have been so infiltrated by the sterility of the twentieth century that they think being deliberately childless is an "authentic Christian option." How sad, how barren, how tragic, how lonely! The greatest warmth, pleasure, and love exchanged for a used Mazda or the time to complete one's doctorate.) And so, indeed, Christian home life, with a mother taking care of her children and a father nurturing the family, must be put first. The greatest act of positive Christian revolution today is the faithful husband and wife raising an informed and Christian family. The woman putting her children ahead of "career" is today's last radical and real revolutionary for truth.

6. *We must make a continued effort to analyze and critique the world around us, particularly the media.* It is no secret that the media is biased against Christian truth—in fact all orthodox religion that challenges its own liberal secular assumptions. But it is also no secret that Christians watch almost as much television rubbish as other people, allow their children to be bombarded by secular ideas without comment, read very little, and subscribe, if at all, mainly to compromised Christian magazines that, as we have seen, often have less to tell them even than good secular ones. With the deluge of liberal and anti-Christian ideas coming from a secular and bigoted media on one side, and a vacuum created by the lack of firm principle in Christian teaching on the other side, ideologically Christians are like sheep being herded to the slaughter. The Christian academic community must bear a great deal of the blame here. Where is the clear Christian agenda developed by Christian colleges now that we need it? Where are the alternatives to the social "sciences"? Where are the seminaries preparing preachers to stride forth as leaders of their society rather than skulking behind the bushes and fringes of today's world, playing word games about redaction theology? Where are Christian magazines with names like *Leadership* actually leading? A great deal of prayer, reading, thought, and study is needed in these areas. We must develop a mental resistance as a vaccine, if you will, to inoculate us against the onslaught. This inoculation and vaccine comes only in the form of information and thinking. We should be a praying, reading, and studying people if we do not wish to be swept away by the persuasive powers of a brilliant and perverse secular media elite.

7. *We must show solidarity with our fellow orthodox Christians.* A Christian nurse who refuses to perform an abortion is fired. A Christian minister or priest is arrested or fined for refusing to allow his church or church school to be state-regulated. A Christian teacher is fired for speaking of the things of God in her classroom. An elder in a church is fired for picketing an abortion clinic and "embarrassing" his pastor. These are examples of instances in which we, as fellow-Christians, should show solidarity. This is *our* business. We read in the Book of Acts that Peter would have been put to death had it not been that the leaders of the day feared the five thousand Christian converts. We should make our authorities and Christian leaders acutely aware of the presence of many thousands of orthodox Christians who are ready to march, picket, protest, vote, write letters, agitate, impeach officials, preach, donate their time and money, pray, and take strong and decisive action on behalf of all those whose rights of religious liberty, assembly, speaking, conscience, and practice are threatened.

Local, state, and federal agencies should be picketed when they unduly interfere with Christians. State and federal officials should be removed at the next election if they have been on the side of those who would curb religious freedom and expression in this nation. Hospitals that do not make provisions for the consciences of their doctors and nurses concerning abortion, infanticide, and euthanasia should be ostracized by the whole community, and picketed and criticized for their intolerant anti-life, prodeath views. Women should *never* have their babies in hospitals that also perform abortions and *never* use the homicidal gynecologists that do perform abortions. (Would you let Charles Manson deliver *your* baby?) The best way to find out if a doctor performs abortions is to call and ask to see him about having one. If he says he won't perform an abortion, you know the doctor is prolife. This tactic is better than just calling up to ask a doctor if he does abortions because if you ask him straight out, he may answer no even if he does do them. Many of these homocidal gynecologists will do almost anything to remain respectable and enjoy "the best of both worlds." The safest course is always to go to orthodox, conservative Roman Catholic hospitals and doctors. The church, as a ministry, needs to collect funds to provide legal assistance for individuals persecuted by the state or other agencies. The vicious, antireligious, and antimoral nature of such groups as the ACLU and Planned Parenthood and the National Organization for Women needs to be constantly exposed and criticized. Our elected officials should understand that they cannot have it both ways. Either they must stand with the orthodox Christians in the United States against the para-legal organizations and their friends in the courts, or we will find new officials to represent us. If your pastor will not support you in your efforts to take a stand, find one who will!

Jails or prisons in which Christians, like the Nebraska seven, are held for the sake of their belief should be surrounded by other believers holding vigils, prayer meetings, and other demonstrations of solidarity. If church school administrators, nurses, doctors, and others are brought to trial by antireligious zealots, they should be surrounded by Christians showing solidarity. Christian communities must provide legal assistance, as I have said, but beyond that, long-term, consistent moral support. We must not be embarrassed by the heat put on our fellow-Christians who *do* take a stand. We should be anxious to *share* in their travail.

If we are not our brother's keeper when someone else faces destruction by the secularist elite or the appeasing evangelical establishment, to whom will we turn when our turn comes? Public policy has dictated that homosexuals are now a "minority," as are radical feminists. One does not need to labor long to see the extensions of this type of policy and how it will be used in the hands of the crusading antireligious zealots and antireligious organizations such as the ACLU. When your Christian institution's number is up, on whom will you call if you have not built up a network of solidarity with other believers who have been under the gun? Christian organizations, schools, colleges, and individuals must find new ways to link up with other orthodox believers. Here is another reason why we need an ecumenicism of orthodoxy. An ecumenicism of militant solidarity will not allow its members to be picked off piecemeal. Our message, like that of the five thousand believers of Acts, is, "If you want to take one of us down, you have to be willing to reckon with all of us!" *We stand or fall together.*

Christian magazines and other Christian media must alert orthodox believers to violations of religious people's rights and call for action on their behalf. From the earliest grades Christian schools should teach their students to resist and to support one another as the world attacks them. Pastors should preach resistance from the pulpit, and it should not be uncommon for whole churches, led by their pastors, to picket local courthouses or IRS offices when Christians are being persecuted. If we do not all pull together, who is going to pull for us? Are we so foolish as to not understand that if we are not willing to support our fellow-believers, when it is our turn God may not support us? Just as God through Christ intervened in history on our behalf, if we love one another, we will intervene for each other here and now.

8. *We have to take the religion out of Christianity and put the truth back in.* We must reassert the idea that Christianity is not a religion but is indeed truth. This means that we must deprivatize our religion; it is not a personal salvation experience we look to, but rather a living faith with *service* to the living God who speaks to *all* areas of life. Of prime importance is the area of Bible reading itself. Bible reading must cease to be merely "devotional-inspirational" on the one hand, or cold theology on the other. The Bible must instead be read afresh, not as a book of religion, but as a book of history, a book of law, a book of God's revealed truth to man in an absolute sense, a book of mini-stories that make a point as only stories and biography can. Somehow we must recapture the freshness of the biblical message, which has been so polluted by professional Christianity, seminaries, and by our Christian academic and media-publishing community. We must, especially in these synthetic times, reread the verses of warning against compromise and abandonment of principle. Consider the Letter to the Hebrews, chapter 10, verses 26-39. Such passages must leap from the Scriptures and convict us in our day and age:

> For if we sin willfully after we have received the knowledge of the truth, there no longer remains a sacrifice for sins, but a certain fearful expectation of judgment, and fiery indignation which will devour the adversaries. He who despised Moses' law died without mercy on the testimony of two or three witnesses. Of how much worse punishment, do you suppose, will he be thought worthy who has trampled the Son of God

underfoot, counted the blood of the covenant by which he was sanctified a common thing, and insulted the Spirit of grace? For we know Him who has said, "Vengeance is Mine; I will repay, says the Lord." And again, "The Lord will judge His people." It is a fearful thing to fall into the hands of the living God!

. . . Therefore do not cast away your confidence, which has a great reward. For you have need of endurance, so that after you have done the will of God, you may receive the promise:
"For yet a little while,
And He who is coming will come and will not tarry.
Now the just shall live by faith;
But if he draws back,
My soul has no pleasure in him."
But we are not of those who draw back to perdition, but of those who believe to the saving of the soul.

How can we read a passage like that and not feel its full force? An inability to feel the strength of such a passage is to "theologize it" or make it "religious" rather than regarding it as a *true* statement and a straightforward *warning*. The Spirit says to those who feel they do not have to put their Christian lives on the line with the *moral* teachings of Scripture: "For if we sin willfully after we have received the knowledge of the truth, there no longer remains a sacrifice for sins." What does this mean if not to warn us against the very compromises we make in accepting divorce, abortion, abandonment of preschool children to day-care abnormality, and all the other selfish evils of the age? Do we not tremble to know that if we turn away from the truth we will come to a point where "there no longer remains a sacrifice for sins"? Have we become such blind and professionally religious Christians as to not be struck trembling by statements like "a certain fearful expectation of judgment, and fiery indignation . . . will devour the adversaries"? Do we not realize that even if we call ourselves "evangelical," we can ourselves become the adversaries of God? If we do not make a stand, *we are the very ones* in our overly religious Christianity to whom this verse applies: "Of how much worse punishment, do you suppose, will he be thought worthy who has trampled the Son of God underfoot, counted the blood of the covenant by which he was sanctified a common thing, and insulted the Spirit of grace?" Surely, it is the compromising evangelical, and oftimes liberal Catholic, establishment which has trampled the Son of God underfoot and has insulted the Spirit of grace. Instead of holding up Christ as an absolute standard to whom every knee must bow, the evangelical establishment and Christian academic community and media have sought ways to "accommodate" Christ to the world. "How shall I pardon you for this? Your children have forsaken Me and sworn by those that are not gods" (Jeremiah 5:7).

Standing Up

Instead of listening to the Spirit and our consciences, which have pricked us again and again to stand up and be counted, we have insulted the Spirit by not standing, by hiding, by being fashionable. Have we forgotten what it means to stand our ground? If we have, we should listen again to these words: "Therefore do not cast away your confidence, which has great reward. For you have need of endurance, so that after you have done the will of God, you may receive the promise." If doing the "will of God" is merely a religious concept, then our privatized, mumbling, quiet, hand-wringing, apologetic religion is good enough. But if instead it is a command founded in truth itself, to which we will be answerable in person on Judgment Day, then more care must be taken in interpreting these verses. Do we no longer wish to receive what he has promised? Can we not reaffirm in a nonreligious, historical way the words, "But we are not of those who draw back to perdition, but of those who believe to the saving of the soul"? Does not the whole Scripture command, cajole, beg, and plead with us *not to shrink back but instead to make our stand*? It may be young King David against the Philistines, Christ not turning back from that bitter cup, or Peter and John being flogged and imprisoned again and again for breaking the law and continuing to preach. Does not all this shout at us, MAKE YOUR STAND?

Surely one has to admit that the overrepetition of Scripture, the religiousizing of it, the theologizing of it, and the deadening effect of our sadly compromised Christian insitutions are responsible for the lack of freshness with which we approach the Bible. Without all these deadening and decaying, trite, Sunday-schoolish interpretations of Scripture around us, would not the biting clear freshness of Christ's teaching in Matthew 13:18-23 leap from the page?

> "Therefore hear the parable of the sower: When anyone hears the word of the kingdom, and does not understand it, then the wicked one comes and snatches away what was sown in his heart. This is he who received seed by the wayside. But he who received the seed on stony places, this is he who hears the word and immediately receives it with joy; yet he has no root in himself but endures only for a while. For when tribulation or persecution arises because of the word, immediately he stumbles. Now he who received seed among the thorns is he who hears the word, and the cares of this world and the deceitfulness of riches choke the word, and he becomes unfruitful. But he who received seed on the good ground is he who hears the word and understands it, who indeed bears fruit and produces: some a hundredfold, some sixty, some thirty."

Can we no longer see how this applies to *us?* Do we not see that when he speaks about "anyone [who] hears the word of the kingdom, and does not understand it, then the wicked one comes and snatches away what was sown in his heart," he is speaking of the fact that a Christianity preached without application and without depth cannot be sustained? Is it beyond our imagination to take warning from "But he who received the seed on stony places, this is he who hears the word and immediately receives it with joy; yet he has no root in himself but endures only for a while"? Is this not an accurate description of modern evangelicalism that has many "joyful" activities—church growth, fund drives, building programs, emotional religious experiences, and the like—but has such shallow roots that the icy blasts of secularism are sweeping this rootless church from our society? And what of this passage: "He who received seed among the thorns is he who hears the word, and the cares of this world and the deceitfulness of riches choke the word, and he becomes unfruitful"? Does this not speak to our hearts if we have abandoned our children in favor of material wealth or career? Does not the deceitfulness of self-fulfillment and materialism, self-gratification, feminism, and all the other forms of me-ism that we seek today choke the Spirit of God? And what of the last verse: "But he who received seed on the good ground is he who hears the word and understands it, who indeed bears fruit and produces: some a hundred-fold, some sixty, some thirty." Notice what must happen. First the ground must be cleared of rubble and prepared. The seed must be sown and then the Word must be understood. Finally it must be applied in faithfulness to produce a crop. In other words, to *believe* is not enough. *The results tell all.* Where are our fruits?

Conclusion

We have, then, as I said at the beginning of this chapter, two scenarios before us, and we can adopt one of two attitudes. The first, a capitulating, quiet acquiescence to the perversity of this world and a gentle drift toward total secularism that in the end will obliterate Christianity in this nation. The second, a robust and viligant faith ever ready to do battle for the cause of Christ and a stand that does not bend before the winds of fashion. Which will it be? Unfortunately for all of us, these are not theoretical questions, for the very hinge of fate and the destiny of not only ourselves but also our children depends upon which course we choose. To *not* think about these issues and to not take a stand is also an activist approach. It is actively passive, giving over the field to the devil and his emissaries: Christians in the act of surrender, running from the scene of battle, coats flapping, foolish smiles on our faces, attempting to save our own hides at any cost. How much better to take our stand in this generation with the saints who have stood before and to affirm the following statement:

Therefore, seeing we also are surrounded by so great a cloud of witnesses, let us lay aside every weight, and the sin which so easily ensnares us, and let us run with endurance the race that is set before us, looking to Jesus, the author and finisher of our faith, who for the joy that was set before Him endured the cross, despising the shame, and has sat down at the right hand of the throne of God. For consider Him who endured such hostility from sinners against Himself, lest you become weary and discouraged in your minds. (Hebrews 12:1-3)

AFTERWORD

Dear reader: As you have read my book, you perhaps will have noticed that I have attempted to be as straightforward as possible. I have not minced words or pulled punches. Instead, I have dealt with ideas and institutions directly and openly. I prefer honesty to back-stabbing.

Having taken this very frank approach, I feel I owe you an explanation of what this book is and what I hope it accomplishes. But first, let me say what my book is not. It is not a work of scholarship. I am not a scholar. Nor is it a work of theology. I am not a theologian. Nor is it a great work of literature. I am not a writer of high art. It is not even a "nice" book—though I believe it is a true book.

What is this book then? It is a blunt instrument—not pretty but, I hope, effective. It stands in the honorable tradition of the outspoken pamphleteering practiced by the American Revolutionaries, the abolitionists, the civil rights activists, the environmentalists, and all others who have sought to redress evil through activist means. It seeks to alert, radicalize, and activate—and above all, to let the cat out of the bag in a way that it cannot be put back in or ignored. Why? Because in my heart, mind, and soul, I believe in the issues for which I am openly agitating. And I believe that open agitation and reform are necessary, indeed paramount.

The heart of the book is that the sanctity-of-life ethic is being destroyed. I am distraught over this, as well as distressed and, yes, *angry*—angry at those who are doing nothing about stemming this tide of inhumanity. Those who are evangelical, and therefore should know better, have been particularly derelict.

Finally, then, as you make up your mind about my book, think of it as a descendant of the old broadsheets, pamphlets, and streetcorner polemics of yesterday. This is a tradition long forgotten in evangelical circles but one I am not ashamed to revive—if the issues warrant it, as I believe they

143

most certainly do. Long live agitation, polemics, and anger directed at real and gross evil! For me to do less would be a dereliction of duty. I hope and pray that what I am saying here will enable more skillful hands to further this good cause. But every now and then someone has to organize a Boston Tea Party to stir things up, to get things started. As Brian Griffin so eloquently states in his book *Panic Among the Philistines* (p. 259), "Let us therefore have some thunder in our anger, and let us finally clear the sullen advocates of the night from our path so that we may yet live again as men and women were meant to live."

As you consider what I have written, your question should not be, "Do I like Franky Schaeffer and how he states his case," but, "Is what he says true, and what am I going to do about it?"

You may have felt the tone of this book was sometimes harsh, but remember this—we are not talking about mere intellectual problems. In the time it has taken you to read this book, thousands of abortions have been performed, no doubt a number of infants have deliverately had care removed and been left to starve, and the zealous secular juggernaut rolls onward unopposed. Cool, collected, and detached tones of "neutral scholarship" at times are morally wrong and callous. If you are in a burning hotel and discover a fire at night, you do not debate the science of combustion, add footnotes, or call a quiet, friendly symposium. You shout, *Fire!!* for all you're worth.

Franky Schaeffer V

Appendix 1
THE LONELY VOICE
OF ALEXANDER
SOLZHENITSYN

(*The Wall Street Journal,* June 23, 1983)
by John Train

When Alexander Solzhenitsyn came to America nine years ago, the then incumbent of the White House declined to see him. Such a gesture might annoy the Soviets, it was thought.

I recently accompanied Mr. Solzhenitsyn and his wife to England. What a difference! He was welcomed by the royal family, addressed over a thousand notables in London's Guildhall to acknowledge the Templeton Prize, spent an evening with the archbishop of Canterbury, was pictured on the front pages conferring with Prime Minister Thatcher and brought a roar of approval from the boys of Eton after addressing them in chapel. Television coverage was extensive. The *Times of London* printed his Guildhall address in full and carried a long editorial on it. Day after day the *Times* ran a stream of letters; its eminent editorialist Bernard Levin wrote a column, and later consecrated an entire page to an interview.

The American press, although present, virtually ignored these events. Indeed, says Mr. Solzhenitsyn, the *Washington Post* through selective editing misrepresented his message. What does he in fact have to say? And why are his words so differently received in the two countries?

The families of the Russian dissidents are exceedingly close to Mr. Solzhenitsyn's heart, and in his London talks he often turned, anguished, to their plight. In the Soviet Union a husband and wife can still barely support a family even if both work. When a dissident, exercising his rights under the Helsinki agreement (which Mr. Solzhenitsyn had always warned the Soviets would ignore), is sent to prison, his wife alone may no longer be able to earn enough to feed the children and herself. Ordinarily, the wives are also deprived of work, and heavy official disfavor falls on any who help such families. So their situation is desperate.

Reasons of Conscience
While still in Zurich in 1974, after leaving Russia but before coming to America, Mr. Solzhenitsyn created the Russian Social Fund to help the families of Russian dissidents imprisoned, contrary to the Soviet Constitution, for reasons of conscience. To this fund of which his wife is president, Mr. Solzhenitsyn assigned all the proceeds of *The Gulag Archipelago,* his most valuable asset.

The fund has assisted many hundreds of families, including more than a thousand children. Its directors inside Russia, who look after the distribution of what is brought in (perforce unofficially), are heroes and martyrs, like a doctor who works on during a plague knowing that sooner or later he must fall victim himself. Such is the hatred of freedom in the Soviet Union that helping the families of prisoners of conscience to stay alive has been declared an act of treason. In 1981 Valery Repin, who ran the fund in Leningrad, was seized and flung into solitary confinement for over a year of the KGB's inimitable treatment, after which, broken, he was exhibited on television to "confess" that the fund was engaged in a witches' brew of anti-state machinations. It was all a fake, since the fund, a Swiss—i.e., neutral—foundation, is purely philanthropic. Mr. Repin has been tried and convicted. The fund's chief Soviet Union representative, Sergei Khodorovich, has just been arrested also. If he, too, can be broken, he may be subjected to a show trial. If, as seems more likely since he is a man of spiritual strength, he stands fast, then, condemned in secret, he will disappear. His only hope is Western public opinion. If we manifest enough concern in the media and in Washington, he may be saved.

A successor, Andrei Kistyakovsky, has stepped into Mr. Khodorovich's place, an act of extraordinary courage. Mr. Kistyakovsky's time of travail has yet to come.

"Do you believe," I asked Mr. Solzhenitsyn, "that the Soviet government is indeed a 'focus of evil,' to use President Reagan's words?"

"Of course. But nobody has a monopoly on evil or good. There is also evil in the West. Still, the Soviet government is the home of communism, and communism is the most dreadful engine of oppression on our planet. Besides bringing about the annihilation of tens of millions, and the physical and spiritual crushing of countless more, it has destroyed the Soviet economy. And no conqueror in history has taken over so much territory."

Does Andropov represent a change?

"Not in the least. I am constantly struck by the ignorance of so-called experts on Soviet matters, who seem to think that the change of one face, or many faces, in the Kremlin can possibly affect how Soviet communism will act. This is a naive view of communism, not based on observation. The only thing that would change the behavior of the Soviet Union would be the accession to power of a noncommunist leader. He would reverse Soviet policy, both domestically and internationally."

What have been the West's chief mistakes?

"Since 1918, the West has made only mistakes, one after another, in dealing with the Soviet Union. Since the discovery of the atomic bomb it had just one good idea—the Baruch Plan, to put the atom under international control—which Stalin brushed aside.

"Sixty-five years ago Lenin pronounced a sentence of death on the Western world. Sixty years ago nobody seriously supported the Russian forces fighting communism. There was a torrent of fugitives, including some of the finest persons in the country, who testified that what was happening was unprecedented, horrible. Rather than listen to them, the West listened to Bernard Shaw. Forty years ago, after the war, there was a second wave of emigrants, bearing witness to Stalin's mass murders. Again, the West was indifferent. Thirty years ago, Kravchenko defected, revealing to the West the terrible things that were going on; people preferred to listen to Bertrand Russell. Eight or nine years ago I described what was really happening—and again, except for a few, the West paid no attention. At that time, I proposed specific political remedies for the desperate problems we face. Nothing was done. Now it is probably too late.

"The single worst mistake of the post-war era was relying on the 'nuclear umbrella.' False confidence in this 'umbrella' relaxed the West, sapping its strength, its moral qualities, its courage. Freedom does not depend on any 'umbrella,' it depends on stout hearts and steadfast men. Today the 'umbrella,' neutralized, no longer protects, but the habit of weakness, of lack of courage, persists. As a result, the West lies gravely weakened before the expansionist aims of the Soviet Union."

What next?

"It is far better to fight on your feet than on your knees, but you can still fight on your knees. The Russian people are still resisting after 65 years. One man in the Soviet Union wrote me to urge Western scientists to invent a do-it-yourself copying machine. In a dictatorship, that would be a lot more valuable than an arms cache."

What hope is there, then, for the West?

"The time when the West could save itself by its own exertions may already have passed. To save itself would require a complete change in its attitudes, when in fact these attitudes are still going the wrong way. Instead of girding itself for struggle, the West is still hoping for outside forces to save it, through some kind of miracle . . . perhaps a miracle in the Kremlin. Solidarity was hailed as such a miracle. But the only miracle that the people of the West can pray for is a profound change in their own hearts."

And what about Afghanistan?

"In the three years of Soviet aggression against that country, the West has in essence done nothing. Had it dared, it could by now have supported several regiments of ex-Soviet soldiers—defectors—who would be ready to fight against this aggression. Then things would look very different."

Could Western broadcasting to the Soviet Union be more effective?

"Yes. In fact, that is a matter of the greatest importance. Today, all broadcasts into the Soviet Union are shackled by the naive and idealistic concept that we need above all to have good relations with the Soviet government: not to vex the Kremlin. As long as this delusion is considered a prime policy objective, the Western governments will be responsible for undermining their own world. Such broadcasting is currently bound by a narrow limitation: It should say nothing against Lenin, it should never insult the Soviet government. This policy is insane. Almost every man, woman and child in Russia is sick of Leninism. The West, standing on the brink of catastrophe, has immensely strong allies of which it makes no use: the people of the Soviet Union, and, indeed, of the other subject nations. It must stretch out its hands to those oppressed people."

'A Need for Selflessness'
Is the Soviet Union serious about arms control?

"There are two Soviet Unions. The people—millions of them—dream of an end to wars, to armaments. The government, on the contrary, does not contemplate that idea even for a minute. It does, of course, want the *West* to disarm. But not one item of Soviet military equipment will ever be given up."

What about our younger people and their concern for disarmament?

"It is normal to be afraid of nuclear weapons. I would condemn no one for that. But the generation now coming out of Western schools is unable to distinguish good from bad. Even those words are unacceptable. This results in impaired thinking ability. Isaac Newton, for example, would never have been taken in by communism! These young people will soon look back on photographs of their own demonstrations and cry. But it will be too late. I say to them: You are protesting nuclear arms. But are you prepared to try to defend your homeland with nonnuclear arms? No: These young people are unprepared for *any* kind of struggle."

Do we have a single main underlying moral ill that one can identify?

"Besides cowardice, selfishness. We hear a constant clamor for rights, rights, always rights, but so very little about responsibility. And we have forgotten God. The need now is for selflessness, for a spirit of sacrifice, for a willingness to put aside personal gains for the salvation of the whole Western world."

Such, then, is Mr. Solzhenitsyn's message. It was received in England as an inspiring evocation of ancient values.

In America, Mr. Solzhenitsyn is often taken as a repetitious Cassandra, whose concerns need not be faced, because even if true, they're not new. As the hostile tide rises around us, we would rather, as he says, hope to be saved by some miracle.

Appendix 2
YELLOW RAIN: THE CONSPIRACY OF CLOSED MOUTHS

(*Commentary,* October 1983)
by *Lucio Lami*

When one investigates the use of Soviet chemical weapons in Laos and Cambodia (and, for that matter, in Afghanistan as well), the difficulty lies not in gathering evidence, which by now is within the grasp of anyone who searches for it, but rather in understanding by what sophisticated mechanisms this evidence has been obscured, discredited, and minimized by the very persons who should bring it forward. And since the great falsifiers are all Westerners, one encounters a second difficulty: how to explain to the victims the absurd game of political complicity by which the "chorus of closed mouths" has come to be organized.

A few months ago, during my most recent visit along the Cambodian and Laotian borders where the guerrillas operate, I gathered so many and such detailed accounts of chemical warfare that anyone in my position would have had enough evidence for a grave and definitive verdict. At Ban Sangae I heard the testimony of Prith Song, the survivor of a gas attack on January 6 in the area of Non Chan, and the testimony of Chun Sarom, survivor of the attack of January 14. These two young men still had symptoms of poisoning, about which I heard the testimony of Miss Garcia, the attending doctor. The nature of the symptoms was confirmed by Dr. Jibbhong Jayarasu, a specialist in these things, who in recent days had treated twenty-eight gassed persons.

Along the Laotian border I heard the detailed testimony of Khommi Vang, the village chief of Ban Nam Jao, who, on December 22, 1982, between 8 and 9 in the morning, witnessed a "yellow-rain" attack launched from a Vietnamese airplane. Eyewitnesses described the effects of the attack, which wounded ten persons in the village, and roughly eight in the surrounding area.

The same description of "yellow rain," launched at the beginning of February on Nam Ngao and on Pa Mon, were heard from the refugees fleeing those villages. From the inhabitants of Ban Hue Sai, a Laotian village under Soviet and Vietnamese control, I heard of deposits of chemical weapons in the former religious house of the Oblates, a building visible from the Mekong.

In the region of Non Chan, in the first days of my arrival, a Vietnamese from the chemical units was killed, and his gas mask was taken by the Khmer Blancs. They insisted that I photograph and examine the mask before it was given to the West German embassy in Bangkok, which had secretly asked for it. The mask was of a new variety and confirmed that Vietnam was obtaining gas masks from various sources.

It is obvious that all countries, through their embassies in Thailand, have been collecting evidence. They have, by now, obtained a bit of everything: samples of infected soil and vegetation, blood samples from victims, samples of yellow powder, "top-secret" autopsy results, photographs of scarred and burned victims of chemical attacks (the photographs remind one of Hiroshima).

The documentation is immense (indeed, the Thai government has a special section of its intelligence service to deal with this material), and for some time the embassies collecting it have considered the evidence irrefutable. But the West is silent. Arrogantly challenging the obvious, the American national press continues to raise subtle questions, as if instead of a tragic reality one were talking about the Loch Ness monster; the press continues to say, "If it is true that 1,500 Hmong tribesmen have been killed by nerve gas," when it is sufficient to go there to discover that the number of dead is closer to 15,000, if not more. The *Washington Post* wrote last February that the "credibility of the charge" (of the use of gas) has been placed in further doubt by the fact that the gathering of evidence has been entrusted to the American secret services. Such evidence—said the *Post*—is used by Reagan to convince Congress to finance American chemical-weapons programs.

Europe is no better. A few months ago a noted French newspaper spoke about Vietnamese gas attacks in these terms: "No definitive proof, but strong suspicions," and thus the dead come to be the objects of black humor like the character in the famous joke. (Alas! If he weren't dead, he would still be alive.)

In the United States, in the meantime, at regular intervals one reads reports from skeptical professors who, with great echoes in the press, deny the evidence of the sampling carried out at the request of the State Department. These statements are not presented for what they are (technical disputations of marginal questions: Was the sample contaminated? Did it contain traces of one or another substance?), but as a general challenge to a reality that they do not wish to accept. Instead of the thousands of deaths (many of them among the Hmong tribesmen, precisely those who remained loyal to the last to the Americans), one hears about learned scientific analyses.

Meanwhile, Western journalists, respecting the Thai veto that obliges them to stay far away from the zones where the gas is used, live their pleasant days in Bangkok. Of the hundreds of "information kamikazes"—the great investigative reporters who crisscrossed Vietnam during the "patriotic war" against the United States—there is not a trace. A mysterious syndrome of disinterest in the phenomenon seems to have spread like an epidemic across four continents.

This silence permits the most shameful and the most aberrant complicities between the Vietnamese and the West. An impressive example: the doctors of the International Red Cross—in violation of all medical standards—refuse to help victims of gas attacks, "because to accept them in the hospitals would create a political problem." Protests are lively, but useless. The International Red Cross in Thailand is under United Nations control, and UN organizations favor with their silence the slaughter of Laotian and Cambodian anti-Communists, guilty of having refused to accept their "liberation" by the Vietnamese.

Amos Townsend of the International Rescue Committee appealed to the UN Border Relief Organization which supervises the International Red Cross in Thailand. At a meeting on November 4, 1982, Townsend officially asked why the Red Cross denied assistance to gassed victims. He was given no answer and—even worse—his question was removed from the transcript of the meeting. The same treatment was given to his second question: "Why were the results of the autopsy of a twenty-two-year-old Cambodian woman, killed by Vietnamese gas and carried to the hospital of Kao I Dang, suppressed, even though the autopsy was performed by Red Cross doctors?" No reply. Question deleted from the transcript.

The assistance agencies that work alongside the UN carry out their own campaign of obfuscation, while the newspapers say that "evidence is insufficient."

Almost all the medical agencies, even the private ones, are under UN control, and they have adapted to these methods and deny help to gas victims. On December 2, 1982, the question was raised by a scientist, Dr. Jibbhong of the Catholic Office for Emergency Relief to Refugees (COER), who pleaded that the doctors "respect professional ethics and put their personal or political interests aside." The appeal was not in the transcript.

All the UN humanitarian agencies make efforts to prevent the truth from appearing in the press: there is no worse enemy of the journalist who tries to work in the area than the United Nations.

Indeed, we owe some of the most brilliant operations of suppressing the truth to UN officials. The most tragic, perhaps, took place some time ago. Two years back rumors were heard in Bangkok to the effect that the Vietnamese were producing new gas mixtures that were capable of deceiving investigators as to their toxic content and their origin. These new substances—it was said—were the result of experiments in a laboratory conducted by a "new Doctor Mengele" who operated on human subjects. No one accepted these rumors, which were so clearly "defamatory" to Vietnam. But in April 1982, Adelia Bernard, of COER, was secretly taken to Phnom Penh where, thanks to a person who worked at the Hôpital Sovietique, she was informed of the incredible truth. The experiments were taking place, in that very same hospital as well as elsewhere, and were being conducted on healthy children ranging from two to ten years of age. The children were kept in special homes and during the experiments were placed in transparent plastic spheres equipped with two valves, one for oxygen, the other for the gas that was being tested. There were approximately one hundred child guinea pigs in the area of the hospital alone, while many others lived in laboratory camps built on the tiny islands of the Mekong. The latter were injected with toxic substances.

Incredulous, Mrs. Bernard asked for proof, and after negotiating the payment of $300, her interlocutor entered the hospital and returned with a plastic sphere, with valves and tubes, inside of which lay the dead body of a three-year-old baby. Adelia Bernard put the sphere in a sack and carried it back to Bangkok, where she deposited it on the desk of Mark Brown, a representative of the UN High Commission for Refugees. Brown did nothing, and no "case" was opened.

Brown has gone, perhaps prudently transferred or removed. But not a word is to be heard of that terrible episode, which takes us back to the days of Treblinka, and which makes us all guilty of a shameful silence.

Appendix 3
SANCTITY OF LIFE OR QUALITY OF LIFE?

(*Pediatrics,* July 1983)
by Peter Singer

The ethical outlook that holds human life to be sacrosanct—I shall call it the "sanctity-of-life view"—is under attack. The first major blow to the sanctity-of-life view was the spreading acceptance of abortion throughout the Western world. Supporters of the sanctity-of-life view have pointed out that some premature babies are less developed than some of the fetuses that are killed in late abortions. They add, very plausibly, that the location of the fetus/infant—inside or outside the womb—cannot make a crucial difference to its moral status. Allowing abortions, especially these late abortions, therefore does seem to breach our defense of the allegedly universal sanctity of innocent human life.

A second blow to the sanctity-of-life view has been the revelation that it is standard practice in many major public hospitals to refrain from providing necessary life-saving treatment to certain patients. Although this practice applies to geriatric patients and those suffering from terminal illness, the most publicized and also the potentially most significant cases have been severely defective newborns. In Britain, Dr. John Lorber[1] has quite candidly described his method of selecting which babies suffering from spina bifida should be given active treatment, and he has indicated, with equal candor, that in his view the best possible outcome for those not selected is an early death.

The decision not to treat an infant with Down's syndrome has also been publicized. In April 1982, in Bloomington, Indiana, the parents of an infant with Down's syndrome and in need of corrective surgery refused permission for the surgery to be performed. Few details are available because the court ordered the records sealed, but the court refused to intervene or to take the child out of his parents' custody.[2]

Although many doctors would sharply distinguish the active termination of life from a decision not to treat a patient for whom the foreseen outcome of this decision is the death of the patient, the distinction is a tenuous one, and the claim that it carries moral weight has been rejected by several academic philosophers. Hence, the acceptance of nontreatment in these situations is rightly perceived as a further threat to the sanctity-of-life view.

Some respond to this situation with a sense of alarm at the erosion of our traditional ethical standards. We already have, these people tell us, one foot on the slippery slope that will lead to active euthanasia, then to the elimination of the mentally feeble and of the socially undesirable, and finally to all the atrocities of the Nazi era. To pull back from this abyss, we must renew our commitment to the most scrupulous respect for all human life, irrespective of its quality.

It is in keeping with this response that shortly after the verdict was handed down in the Bloomington case, the Reagan administration issued, through the Department of Health and Human Services, a "Notice to Health Care Providers" stating that it is unlawful for a recipient of federal financial assistance to withold from a handicapped infant any medical treatment required to correct a life-threatening condition, when the treatment is not medically contraindicated and would be given to an infant who was not handicapped.

Seen from a distance, this notice appears to put doctors in the absurd situation of having to keep alive the most grossly defective infants, for whom life is either quite valueless—because the infant is forever incapable of any conscious experience whatsoever—or else a positive burden, because it is a life of pain and discomfort without the redeeming value of a rational awareness of self or others. Even Lord Justice Templeman, who in a recent English case concerning an infant with Down's syndrome ordered that surgery be performed, did not wish to go so far. He allowed that in a case in which the life of the infant would be "demonstrably awful" there would have been grounds for allowing a child to die. The Reagan administration, it would seem, wishes infants to be kept alive even when their life will be "demonstrably awful."[3]

Is the erosion of the sanctity-of-life view really so alarming? Change is often, in itself, alarming, especially change in something that for centuries has been spoken of in such hushed tones that to question it is automatically to commit sacrilege. There is little evidence, however, to support the application of the slippery slope argument in this context. Cultures that have practiced forms of infanticide or euthanasia—Ancient Greece, the Eskimos—have been able to hold the line around those categories of beings that could be killed, so that the lives of other members of these societies were at least as well protected as the lives of citizens of the United States, where the culture officially accepts no limits to the sanctity of human life.

Whatever the future holds, it is likely to prove impossible to restore in full the sanctity-of-life view. The philosophical foundations of this view have been knocked asunder. We can no longer base our ethics on the idea that human beings are a special form of creation, made in the image of God, singled out from all other animals, and alone possessing an immortal soul. Our better understanding of our own nature has bridged the gulf that was once thought to lie between ourselves and other species, so why should we believe that the mere fact that a being is a member of the species *Homo sapiens* endows its life with some unique, almost infinite, value?

Once the religious mumbo-jumbo surrounding the term "human" has been stripped away, we may continue to see normal members of our species as possessing greater capacities of rationality, self-consciousness, communication, and so on, than members of any other species; but we will not regard as sacrosanct the life of each and every member of our species, no matter how limited its capacity for intelligent or even conscious life may be. If we compare a severely defective human infant with a nonhuman animal, a dog or a pig, for example, we will often find the nonhuman to have superior capacities, both actual and potential, for rationality, self-consciousness, communication, and anything else that can plausibly be considered morally significant. Only the fact that the defective infant is a member of the species *Homo sapiens* leads it to be treated differently from the dog or pig. Species membership alone, however, is not morally relevant. Humans who bestow superior value on the lives of all human beings, solely because they are members of our own species, are judging along lines strikingly similar to those used by white racists who bestow superior value on the lives of other whites, merely because they are members of their own race.

Ironically, the sanctity with which we endow all human life often works to the detriment of those unfortunate humans whose lives hold no prospect except suffering. A dog or a pig, dying slowly and painfully, will be mercifully released from its misery. A human being with inferior mental capacities in similarly painful circumstances will have to endure its hopeless condition until the end—and may even have that end postponed by the latest advances in medicine.

One difference between humans and other animals that is relevant irrespective of any defect is that humans have families who can intelligently take part in decisions about their offspring. This does not affect the intrinsic value of human life, but it often should affect our treatment of humans who are incapable of expressing their own wishes about their future. Any such effect will not, however, always be in the direction of prolonging life—as the wishes of the parents in the Bloomington case, and in several other recent court cases, illustrate.

If we can put aside the obsolete and erroneous notion of the sanctity of all human life, we may start to look at human life as it really is: at the quality of life that each human being has or can achieve. Then it will be possible to approach these difficult questions of life and death with the ethical sensitivity that each case demands, rather than with the blindness to individual differences that is embodied in the Department of Health and Human Services' rigid instruction to disregard all handicaps when deciding whether to keep a child alive.

References

1. Lorber J: Ethical problems in the management of myelomeningocele and hydrocephalus. *J. R. Coll Physicians Lond* 1975:10:1
2. *Deciding About Foregoing Life-Sustaining Therapy,* discussion paper prepared by staff of President's Commission for the Study of Ethical Problems in Medicine and Biomedical and Behavioral Research. Washington, DC, August 1982, chap. 7
3. See Re B, (a Minor). *Times Law Report,* Aug. 8, 1981, p. 15

Appendix 4
Norman Lear vs.
the Moral Majority
THE WAR TO CLEAN UP TV

(*Saturday Review*, February 1981)
by Ben Stein

A battle is raging for control of network television. Storming the citadel of imperial TV power is the new Christian right, allied with the new political right, and its spearhead political-action commando group, the Moral Majority. They have vowed to clean up the moral swamp of contemporary television programming. Says Tim LaHaye, top adviser of the Moral Majority, "A medium that once featured family-oriented programming now makes jokes about homosexuality, incest, wife-swapping, and depravity." It's not only immoral, he argues, "but anti-Christian."

Standing at the battlements is a phalanx of traditional religious leaders, the television establishment of networks, producers, and station owners; and at its head the towering paradigm of American media, television and movie tycoon and emerging political leader, Norman Lear. Lear, who launched two dozen sit-coms and changed the face of television comedy, is serious about the Moral Majority. He says he resents the new Christian right's implication that its positions constitute the "revealed word of God." "I'll fight that way of thinking. I don't want a narrow band of people controlling American politics or what's on television."

This narrow band numbers an estimated 30 million militant Christians. Their movement is headed by the likes of Pat Robertson, James Robison (on the Christian side), Paul Weyrich, Richard Viguerie (on the political side), and most prominent of all, leader of the Moral Majority, prayer-warrior on 400 stations with 15 million viewers every Sunday, the Reverend Jerry Falwell. He and his followers have been mobilized in anger toward abortion, divorce, child abuse, drugs, deficit spending, low defense budgets, weakness toward communism, the Department of Education, and a host of issues that represent to them a lax and Godless America.

Lear and his allies are upset because they know this isn't just empty preaching. They've seen how influential this new Christian militia can be. A few years ago, before the Christian Roundtable, the Christian Voice, the *Old Time Gospel Hour,* the Moral Majority with its computers, and the amalgamation of political and church reactionary radicalism, names like Birch Bayh, George McGovern, John Culver, and Frank Church seemed like permanent fixtures on the American political scene. Then the Moral Majority targeted them for defeat, drawing on its tremendous financial and polemical resources for a media blitz endorsing their conservative opponents and identifying them as "ungodly." No doubt these senators were victims of the general conservative swing last November. Still, George Cunningham, McGovern's administrative assistant, weighs the Moral Majority's contribution as considerable. "They're frighteningly effective," he says. "They can do anything unless someone stops them."

Now the Moral Majority is planning boycotts of sponsors of offensive shows, and its leaders are talking quietly among themselves about making a bid for a controlling interest in one of the three big networks. What they want to do is to scourge from television everything that they consider an abomination in the eyes of God. The Evangelicals are disgusted by seeing homosexuals treated as acceptable jokes *(Too Close for Comfort),* abortions and incest treated as acceptable *(Maude* and *Soap* respectively), extramarital sex presented as cute *(All's Fair, Mary Hartman, Soap, Three's Company, Family, Secrets of Midland Heights, Dallas,* and a hundred others), soap operas awash in sex (again, too numerous to mention), divorce as inconsequential (ditto), and narcotic drugs pushed as socially desirable *(Saturday Night Live, Fridays).* Jerry Falwell, D.D., pastor of the Thomas Road Baptist Church, Lynchburg, Virginia, and his allies, flushed with victory in the November elections, are determined to put some Christian rigor into television.

Television today is a far cry from the days of *F Troop* or *Your Show of Shows.* Since the early Seventies, when Norman Lear and CBS first aired *All in the Family,* television has been casting off the restraints that once characterized the business. Where Robert Young once wisely counseled his daughter about kindness to new girls in school, Ted Knight now screams at his daughter about working semi-nude in a bar—and the mother says it's fine. Where any mention of race was once verboten, Carroll O'Connor routinely calls people spics and hebes. Teenage girls who were at home helping Mom with the ironing on *The Partridge Family* are now out hooking on Eighth Avenue, their veins filled with heroin.

Many television producers feel that liberalization improved television. Certainly, some of the episodes of *Mary Hartman, All in the Family*, or *The Mary Tyler Moore Show*, which reached the highest levels of TV art, would have been impossible in 1959. But equally certainly, once Fred Silverman got onto the formula of teenage prostitutes, veritable striptease on TV, and endless bump, grind, and jiggle, television concentrated on the maximum amount of titillation the censors would allow, rarely bothering with "redeeming social values." It was inevitable that a great many people would get angry and that they would find a vehicle to express their anger. The Moral Majority is that vehicle.

Norman Lear is deeply concerned and committed to fending off this onslaught. For many years a middling successful movie producer—*Cold Turkey, Divorce American Style*—he became one of the major tycoons in media history with *All in the Family*. Lear is retired from the nearly 2,000 half-hour shows produced under his active supervision, but his company owns eight prime-time shows, many cable systems, a great deal of stock in movie companies, including Twentieth-Century Fox, Columbia Pictures, Filmways, and other good things.

Lear now concentrates on motion pictures (he has two in development), collecting modern art, and putting his energies to work on his social concerns. He is a one-man center for support of liberal causes. The president campaign of John Anderson would have been hard-pressed without Lear's support. Lear is one of the largest living donors to the American Civil Liberties Union and an important supporter of Ralph Nader's activities and those of the Constitutional Rights Foundation.

Long before Falwell turned his guns on TV, Lear had become deeply concerned about the burgeoning power of the combined new Christian right and new political right. Last fall, he and a group of citizens, including Theodore Hesburgh, president of Notre Dame, Charles Bergstrom of the Lutheran Church, and Iowa's former Senator Harold Hughes, now an Evangelical minister himself, founded People for the American Way. Their aim was to combat the work of the politically committed Evangelicals that they saw as endangering the separation of church from other areas of American life. PAW aired three anti-Moral Majority commercials. In one, an actor complains, "There's got to be something wrong when anyone, even a preacher, suggests you are a good Christian or a bad Christian depending on your political point of view. That's not the American way."

But Lear and his group have not addressed the question of whether television is undermining the moral foundations of our society. TV, Falwell points out, is crammed with "sexual permissiveness, situational ethics, and outright obscenity."

"America has turned toward humanism," says Falwell, "the wisdom of man, as opposed to Godliness, the wisdom of God, as revealed in the

Bible." Humanists cluster in universities, the governments, foundations (the Asper Institute is the archest of enemies), and in the media. Within the media, the most powerful organ of the humanists—who favor abortion, disarmament, drugs, busing, and moral decay according to Falwell—is commercial television. It was only natural, then, that on December 3, 1980, Falwell and his closest associates met in Lynchburg and drafted a statement of Falwell's next project after his success with Congress: cleaning up TV.

In his statement, Falwell said that his Moral Majority was beginning to form a large national coalition to reverse the trend on television. The new group will not attack specific shows until it has taken a national poll to determine which shows are "most obnoxious" to viewers. After that step, Falwell's new group will contact producers, networks, and sponsors to ask for changes to pro-family, pro-life (anti-abortion), pro-Godly shows. Falwell says that he hopes a boycott will not be necessary, but that if it is, he will reluctantly call for national boycotts of products advertised by sponsors of humanist shows.

Would advertisers ever knuckle under to a boycott, withdraw their sponsorship, insist on programmatic changes, on a more Christian form of programming? While an official of BBD&O, one of America's largest advertising agencies, insists that advertisers will *now* insist that they cannot be boycotted into subservience, they deeply fear such a consumer action. "Remember," the advertiser said, "it only takes a percentage point or two of shift in the retail sales of washing machines or K-cars to make a tremendous difference in profits. If push came to shove, the advertisers would lean on the producers to make sure that the boycott ended fast."

An executive of ABC offered the same message. "We will always deny that we can be boycotted successfully," she said. "If word gets around that we can be boycotted, everyone in town will start boycotting us for every cause under the sun. But if a boycott by a few million people were very successful, it would shake up the programmers a lot. They'd be putting dresses on the girls in bikinis in a hurry." And the smaller affiliates are much more vulnerable to special-interest groups. Even if the big boys could withstand the pressure, with the local stations caving in one by one, they might soon find themselves with no outlets on which to air their shows.

But boycotts are only the beginning of Falwell's plans for television. According to a top California official of the Moral Majority, Falwell's ultimate goal is to actually buy a controlling interest in a network. "It's an ambitious goal," the aide says cheerfully, "but we've never believed in thinking small." Falwell wants a network, as opposed to simply changing program content, "because we have to change the kind of coverage that the network news gives to issues. We're sick of the humanistic bias on the news. There's too much in favor of abortion, too much about evolution and nothing about Creation. We want a nightly network news show which will let people know that they should place their reliance in God, and not in man as an animal."

According to the same aide, Falwell would get the hundreds of millions necessary for such a purchase from "the many very wealthy people who support our way of thinking." Oil billionaires Nelson and Bunker Hunt and T. Cullen Davis were specifically named as people who would make funds available for the take-over bid.

But could wealthy oilmen like the Hunts or Davis actually buy control of a network? "It's a longshot," says Steve van Brunt, an executive of Merrill Lynch's Beverly Hills office. "But it could happen. They could buy effective control of ABC for $150 million if the institutional holders went along—which they might if there was a lot of national heat for them not to fight the Evangelicals. And remember that it wouldn't be a loss for the Hunts or Davis. They'd own a valuable asset that would pay them dividends. It's a long, long shot, but there have been stranger corporate take-overs," van Brunt said.

Marilyn Gross, a financial consultant in Los Angeles, adds that if the Hunts or T. Cullen Davis even *began* to buy blocks of network stock, they would send shivers down the spine of the top management. "People don't like to lose their jobs," she said. "They'd start tacking into the wind, cleaning up the shows to preempt the takeover."

The Christian Broadcasting System? It may sound unlikely to you, but ask ex-Senator McGovern how unlikely it sounds to him.

It does not sound unlikely at all to Normal Lear or to the mainstream church leaders on the board of PAW. They were already deeply troubled by the sight of TV preachers telling viewers that they would be un-Christian and ungodly if they didn't hew to the ministers' positions about a number of key political and social issues. They were further alarmed at the prospect of TV coming under the aegis of the new Christian right. Now, the Hollywood production community is worried, too. Lee Rich, head of Lorimar, the producer of *The Waltons, Secrets of Midland Heights,* and *Dallas* (the highest rated show in TV history), says that "for any group to tell viewers what to watch is a violation of the Bill of Rights. Where does it stop? Will they tell us what neighborhoods we can live in? They're threatening to take away the livelihood of everyone who works on a show they don't like." Even Garry Marshall, one of the most relaxed of producers *(Mork and Mindy, Happy Days, Laverne and Shirley)* is concerned. "I'm so sick of pressure groups," he says. "I wish they'd just stop bothering me."

But, as might be expected, the most serious opposition to the new Christian right's forthcoming assault on TV comes from Lear. Lear agrees that television, along with other American big business, has a poor sense of morality. He talks about the major chemical companies dumping toxic wastes all over the landscape. "TV is dumping its toxic wastes, too. We sell jeans with tush and crotch shots in commercials. And we even use 15-year-olds to do it." But Lear says that he cannot definitively comment on much of the entertainment side "because I simply do not watch enough TV to say," which is perhaps the most devastating indirect comment he could make. When the busman uses trains, he may be telling us how safe buses are.

In addition, Lear says he does not want "a narrow band" of Falwellians controlling American politics or American television; but the major flaw in this argument is that a "narrow band" of network executives and TV producers control American TV *right now*. Their parochialism is one of whispered TV traditions and Nielsen ratings, but is hardly less narrow than the Bible.

A writer once sold to a TV producer a concept about a generous owner of a small manufacturing company. It came back completely revised, the hero now villain. He was advised that in TV, businessmen can never be heroes. Another of his story proposals, about a heroic college professor, was turned down by a couple of Hollywood eminences as a complete impossibility. Everyone knew, they said, that professors are either crazy or fags.

So there we are, in the midst of two warring parochialisms, Lear arguing with Falwell as Falwell beckons to the American people to radically change TV. Who is right? Should either side stop arguing? It seems obvious that in a free society, people should have the right to tell others what is a sin or un-Christian. To deny that right would be an outrage against the Constitution. Just as clearly Lear and the PAW have the right to tell Americans that they should not be bullied by a group of latter-day Cotton Mathers. In a democracy, people often disagree. There will always be tension between and among competing groups in a free society.

But that leaves a nagging question. If, after all the arguing, Falwell and his allies assemble the power to change television, should they succeed? Is TV in need of a Falwellian housecleaning? Is it killing the American soul?

The clear answer to that is that currrent television seems to contribute little that is useful except to the pocketbooks of those involved. It has been shown to lower scholastic achievement, encourage violence, generate lassitude, and paint a wildly untrue and distorted picture of American life. That much is certain. But whether it harms the human soul is an extremely difficult proposition to prove or disprove.

Since it is unclear who on this earth understands the human soul, it is dangerous to delegate to anyone the control of TV because he or she claims such knowledge. Authority derived by reference to such abstractions, unknown and unknowable, leads to Christian republics and American Khomeinis. *Three's Company* is bad, but an Ayatollah for television would be far worse.

164 •   Bad News for Modern Man

To many people, however, *the* problem with TV is that it is so unwatchably, unbearably uncreative, simpleminded, boring, and insulting to the good sense of the viewer. Seemingly, television gets more repetitious, imitative, and inane every year. The few *All in the Families, Mary Hart-mans, Rockfords,* and *Mary Tyler Moores* vanish, and nothing comparable takes their place.

Where is the leader who will rise up from the anguish of Americans and put some dramatic decency into commercial television before it becomes cartoons with groans and oinks? It won't be Falwell. His *Old-Time Gospel Hour* offers only low-key, homogenized religious Muzak, without even the flair of Billy Graham or Oral Roberts.

Lear apparently *realizes* what has to be done to change television. "We have to do what we think is wonderful," he says, "not what we think will get good ratings. We have to go with our own viscera, rather than guessing what the American people will want." But his efforts to put his ideas to work are limited. He is producing a cable show called *Sharing,* about women's problems, "without psychological balderdash," and a children's show called *No Adults Allowed* featuring children acting out real-life stories. While these may turn out to be fine shows, they hardly represent the drastic efforts necessary to turn television around. So Lear may not be the leader either, which leaves us with TV as a creative sludge pit.

Meanwhile, the struggle between Falwell's crusaders and Lear's Hollywood infidels goes on. Stay tuned.

Appendix 5
COVENANT AND CREATION
Theological Reflections on Contraception and Abortion

Adopted by the 195th General Assembly (1983), Presbyterian Church (U.S.A.)

Policy Statement

Biblical faith depicts persons as stewards of life, heirs who are responsible for the care of God's world. This responsibility leads persons of faith not only to an exploration of all creation but also to efforts which maintain order, secure justice, and improve the quality of human life. Because human life, in the Biblical sense, is much more than the perpetuation of physical existence, people of faith should commit themselves to improving its quality spiritually, educationally, and culturally as well as medically. This commitment will often necessitate difficult moral choice in the midst of conflicting values.

The church itself should pattern for society a way of life wherein sexuality, conception, birth and raising children are issues of profound responsibilty, fidelity and care. The way of life inevitably stands in judgment on our present cultural ethos which extols casual and promiscuous sexuality.

Some of the most difficult moral choices persons face in their care of creation are related to contraception, pregnancy and abortion. Christians will make these decisions knowing that the value and dignity of human life are bestowed by God the Creator who calls us into a covenant relationship with our God and with each other. Faith in God surely leads to profound respect for human life.

For the most part, Protestants have affirmed the role of contraception as a responsible exercise of stewardship with regard to procreation. Limiting the size of a particular family or limiting population growth in a whole society is generally understood to be a kind of caring for one's family and for the next generation. Contraception is clearly the most morally appropriate way to control fertility and to plan families.

Current contraception technology is far from reliable. The church is called to exercise social responsibility by advocating more effective contraceptives for males as well as females, and to educate our own membership that family planning must be the concern and responsibility of both sexual partners. A greater emphasis in church and society on contraception would significantly reduce the possibility of unintended pregnancies.

When, however, an unintended pregnancy occurs or a genetic problem with the fetus is diagnosed the question of abortion often arises even though it is not the only solution. An understanding of various kinds of circumstances surrounding unintended pregnancies is especially important.

Tragically, many women become pregnant as a result of rape or incest. All too frequently contraceptives fail, even though conscientious efforts to prevent pregnancy have been taken. In addition, the increasing numbers of teenage pregnancies each year is sobering and presents especially agonizing situations.

There is no point in the course of pregnancy when the moral issue of abortion is insignificant. This serious moral decision is to be made on the basis of the covenantal character of parental responsibility. Bearing children is a process of covenant-initiation which calls for courage, love, patience and strength. In addition to these gifts of the Spirit, parent-child covenants also require the economic as well as spiritual resources appropriate to the nurture of a human life. The magnitude of the commitment to be a human parent cannot be overestimated, and should not be understated.

The decision to terminate a pregnancy may be an affirmation of one's covenant responsibility to accept the limits of human resources. Because we understand the morality of abortion to be a question of stewardship of life, the responsible decision to choose abortion may arise from analysis of the projected resources for caregiving in a specific situation.

Abortion can therefore be considered a responsible choice within a Christian ethical framework when serious genetic problems arise or when the resources are not adequate to care for a child appropriately. Elective abortion, when responsibly used, is intervention in the process of pregnancy precisely because of the seriousness with which one regards the convenantal responsibility of parenting.

Biblical faith emphasizes the need for personal moral choice and holds that persons stand ultimately accountable to God for their moral choices. The freedom to do what one judges most appropriate in an abortion decision is qualified by the fact that the purpose of such decision is the responsible exercise of stewardship. Even in the face of the most difficult decisions, of which abortion is surely one, the gospel assures us that we can trust in God's Spirit to guide us in our decision. Furthermore, given the fact that such hard choices involve some unpleasant consequences whatever the decision, the gospel reminds us again and again of God's grace, which is sufficient for us in spite of our limitations, and assures us that even if we err in misusing our freedom, God's forgiveness restores us in Covenant love. Only in the knowledge of such grace and guidance could we dare to claim the responsibility and freedom to use modern medical skill to intervene in the process of human procreation.

The Calvinist affirmation of conscience as one of the primary junctures at which the power of the Holy Spirit breaks through into human experience is grounded in both a) the Old Testament call to human responsiblity, as set forth in the biblical witness to God's covenant with us; and b) the New Testament assurance of the work of the Holy Spirit as our enabler and guide in the exercise of human freedom before God. When faced with significant moral choices, women and men who prayerfully consider the options set before them can be assured that they are empowered by the gracious work of God's Spirit to make an appropriate moral choice.

Any decision for an abortion should be made as early as possible, generally within the first trimester of pregnancy, for reasons of the woman's health and safety. Abortions later in pregnancy are an option, particularly in the case of women of menopausal age who do not discover they are pregnant until the second trimester, or women who discover through fetal diagnosis that they are carrying a fetus with a grave genetic disorder, or women who did not seek or have access to medical care during the first trimester. At the point of fetal viability, the responsibilities set before us in regard to the fetus begin to shift. Prior to viability, human responsibility is stewardship of life-in-development under the guidance of the Holy Spirit. Once the fetus is viable, its potential for physically autonomous human life means that the principle of inviolability can be applied.

The church is called to model the just and compassionate community in its ministries to members and its witness to society. The church has responsibility to help make acceptable alternatives available to persons struggling with an unwanted pregnancy if they are to exercise their freedom responsibly. Moreover, the church must seek to support persons as they exercise their moral freedom, which it can fulfill through such means as proclaiming the Biblical faith, clarifying alternatives and their probable consequences, and offering support in love to persons struggling with difficult choices. Christians should make their personal decisions in the context of the community of faith.

It is a tragic sign of the church's sinfulness that our propensity to judge rather than stand with persons making such decisions too often means that persons in need must bear the additional burden of isolation. It would be far better if the person concerned could experience the strength that comes from shared sensitivity and caring. The church is called to be the loving and supportive community within whose life persons can best make decisions in conformity with God's purposes revealed in Jesus Christ.

The church should energetically support efforts of family planning, education in contraception and human sexuality, adoption of unwanted children, care for unwed mothers and, in general, advocate wholesome and responsible stewardship of the human body and its procreative process. As the church is able to give expression to these values and commitments, the need for abortion will be reduced. Whatever a woman's decision may be, the caring support of the church should always be hers.

In the area of public policy the church should call upon policy makers in government and industry to form a rational policy for all members of our society in the area of contraception. This would need to include research and development in contraception knowledge and technique, and the provision for unhampered access to contraceptive information and services for all males and females of child bearing age.

The church's position on public policy concerning abortion should reflect respect for other religious traditions and advocacy for full exercise of religious liberty. The Presbyterian Church exists within a very pluralistic environment. Its own members hold a variety of views. It is exactly this plurality of beliefs which leads us to the conviction that the decision regarding abortion must remain with the individual, to be made on the basis of conscience and personal religious principles, and free from governmental interference.

Consequently, we have a responsibility to work to maintain a public policy of elective abortion, regulated by the health code, not the criminal code. The legal right to have an abortion is a necessary prerequisite to the exercise of conscience in abortion decisions. Legally speaking, abortion should be a woman's right because, theologically speaking, making a decision about abortion is, above all, her responsibility.

As Presbyterians and U.S. citizens we have a responsibility to guarantee every woman the freedom of reproductive choice. We affirm the intent of existing law in the United States regarding abortion: protecting the pregnant woman. Medical intervention should be made available to all who desire and qualify for it, not just to those who can afford preferential treatment.

In the United States today, the right to choose abortion is a constitutional right, clarified by the United States Supreme Court *Roe* v. *Wade* decision (1973). We firmly oppose efforts to amend the constitution in order to prohibit abortion. Under terms of the 1973 decision, elective abortions are confined generally to the first two trimesters of pregnancy. This conforms to the moral principle we affirm that elective abortion should be available before fetal viability but only in the rarest instances after that point, for instance, in rare cases involving medical judgment and late diagnosis of grievous genetic disorders.

The Presbyterian Church believes that society must offer good health care, both pre- and post-natal; day care facilities and homemaker services where needed; maternity and paternity leaves and family service centers; and expert counseling services. In addition, we must work toward a society in which life-long respect and dignity for all people is manifest in the opportunities to obtain adequate resources for maintenance of life and health. In these ways the church seeks to strengthen the various alternatives available to women in making decisions about pregnancies.

Obviously the most desirable moral situation is that every pregnancy be intended and trouble free, but our life experience is very different from this ideal. Abortion is not the only solution for unintended or problematic pregnancies, although it may be at times the most responsible decision.

Recommendations

Thus the 195th General Assembly (1983):

1. Urges Presbyterian congregations and their individual members to:
   A. Provide a supportive community in which such decisions can be made in a setting of care and concern;
   B. Respect the difficulty of making such decisions;
   C. Affirm women's ability to make responsible decisions, whether the choice be to abort or to carry the pregnancy to term;
   D. Protect the privacy of individuals involved in contraception and abortion decisions;
2. Affirms the church's commitment to minimize the incidence of abortion and encourages the sexuality education and the use of contraception to avoid unintentional pregnancies while recognizing that contraceptives are not absolutely effective, and;
   A. Commits this denomination and urges its members to encourage research and development of contraceptive knowledge and technique to make this awareness and facility easily available to all and to support legislation and public funding activities which strengthen family life;
   B. Urges Presbyterians to support sexuality education programs in families, churches, schools and private and public agencies;
   C. Encourages mutual responsibility by men and women for contraception;
   D. Affirms the need for research in and development of a range of contraceptives which can be used by men;
   E. Encourages couples to use more than one method of contraception in order to minimize the possibility of unintended pregnancy;

F. Affirms the use of voluntary sterilization by couples who have completed their families.

3. Recognizes that negative social attitudes toward women cast doubt on women's ability to make moral decisions and urges ministers and congregations to work to counter these underlying social attitudes and affirm the dignity of women;

4. Recognizes that children may be born who are either unwanted or seriously handicapped and affirms the church's ongoing responsibility to provide supportive services to families in these situations and to help find appropriate institutional care and adoptive services where needed;

5. Affirms the 1973 *Roe* v. *Wade* decision of the Supreme Court which decriminalized abortion during the first two trimesters of pregnancy;

6. Celebrates the courage of clergy and others who were willing to risk participation in the Clergy Consultation Service prior to 1973;

7. Opposes attempts to limit access to abortion by:
   A. Denial of funding for abortions to women who receive federal funding for their medical care;
   B. Restriction of coverage by insurance companies for abortion procedures;
   C. The passage of federal, state and local legislation which has the effect of harassing women contemplating abortion;
   D. Restriction of federal funding to medical centers and teaching institutions where abortions are performed;
   E. Passage of a Constitutional Amendment or other legislation which would return control over abortion to individual states or prohibit it as a national policy;
   F. Restriction of the jurisdiction of Federal and Supreme Courts in the area of abortion.

8. Urges the Presbyterian Church through its members, congregations, governing bodies, boards and agencies, including Presbyterian Health, Education and Welfare Association, to model the just and compassionate community by:
   A. Opposing adoption of all measures which would serve to restrict full and equal access to contraception and abortion services to all women, regardless of race, age and economic standing;
   B. Working actively to restore public funding by federal, state, and local governments for the availability of a full range of reproductive health services for the medically indigent;
   C. Supporting funds, such as the Choice Fund of the Synod of the Northeast, for use by women who face abortion decisions but who no longer have access to public funding so they may freely choose an appropriate course of action without coercion or restriction;
   D. Challenging Presbyterian doctors and institutions to provide contra-

ception and abortion services at cost or free-of-charge to those who no longer have access to public funding;

E. Providing openness and hospitality to women who need new structures of support while making an abortion decision or awaiting the delivery of a child;

F. Providing continuing support for women who, having made an abortion decision, may have doubts as to the wisdom of their choice, or having delivered a child are not able to cope with the separation of adoption or the responsibilities of childcare:

G. Opposing efforts to use zoning regulations to preclude the establishment of abortion clinics.

9. Recognizes that the issue of teenage pregnancy and premarital sexual activity is sometimes confused with the abortion issue itself. While time, task and space have not allowed for extensive presentation in this paper, we express our concern by requesting that the General Assembly Council, through the appropriate agency, pursue a study of teenage sexuality and responsibilities in light of the Covenant of Creation.

Appendix 6
THE DISSENTING CHURCH

by James Hitchcock

One of the great ironic injustices of our times is the fact that, despite everything which has happened in the past twenty years, the Catholic Church is still vilified as a monolithic bastion of authoritarianism. Such stereotyping is doubly unjust, in that the Church suffers the obloquy for being dictatorial while enjoying none of the benefits which might accrue if the charge were accurate. The truth of the matter is that, at least in the United States, it would be difficult to find a major institution more internally disorganized, more ideologically divided and less effective in its governing structures than is the Catholic Church.

Although the authoritarianism even of the "old" Church is (and was) exaggerated, most of the present disarray has come about only since about 1965, or the end of the Second Vatican Council. The unravelling of the Catholic system of authority has proceeded with incredible speed, although in retrospect this should perhaps not have been surprising—precisely because in some ways the preconciliar structure was indeed rigid; it was possessed of a brittleness which was bound to crack, and to crack with sudden force. Put another way, the Church now is like a superb athlete who, once he stops training, becomes even flabbier than those who never developed their muscles at all, as his own quickly turn to fat.

Debate will rage for many years over whether the radical changes in the Church since the Council occurred because of, or in spite of, that assembly. A close reading of the conciliar documents dictates the latter conclusion (for example, the uncompromising statements about papal authority in *Lumen Gentium*). However, even if the unravelling occurred despite the Council, it is still an object lesson in the subversion of authority,

172

since it means that the Church's leaders in effect had their council stolen from them almost as soon as it was over. One of the many failures of leadership over the past twenty years has been the failure to articulate, even to the Catholic public, much less to a larger audience, what the Council really said and did. That task has mainly been left to people who have special agendas of their own, and who use the public forum to achieve through propaganda and agitation what they failed to achieve on the floor of the Council. Many bishops, for example, have remained silent as all kinds of tendentious interpretations of the Council have been offered to the public, a silence often suggesting that the bishop himself is confused as to the assembly's true significance.

For almost twenty years "dissent" has been a word to conjure with in American culture, carrying an automatic implication of courageous, principled, lonely defiance of repressive authority. Every historical totem—from the execution of Socrates to the civil rights movement, and including the Crucifixion—has been enlisted to confer automatic moral authenticity on those who reject official doctrine of any kind.

Since the Catholic Church was variously feared, hated, or admired for its seeming ability to exercise unruffled authority prior to the Council, the phenomenon of dissent within the Church has naturally attracted tremendous attention. It is no exaggeration to say that, over the past twenty years, almost any Catholic willing publicly to criticize Catholic teaching or practice has been given a forum, often all out of proportion to the individual's own importance. Endlessly the media have featured nuns who demand to be priests, priests who demand to marry, laymen who demand to be allowed to divorce, their manifestoes now grown so stereotyped that they could literally be composed by computers.

There should be no mistaking the fact that this obsessive interest in Catholic dissenters stems from a deep-seated animosity towards the Church, not, as is routinely claimed, from a mere desire to present "all points of view." It is the spectacle of a great institution apparently coming apart that excites interest, and it is a spectacle in which many viewers take unholy delight. Those willing publicly to criticize their Church may think of themselves as hardy and independent souls, rejecting a social role defined for them by the hierarchy. In fact they are playing the most rigid and stereotyped role of all—that of embittered Catholics confirming all the prejudices of their culture. It is a pathetic role, partly because those who play it do not even realize how they are being used.

The very word "dissenter" implies "outsider," and its positive emotional connotations largely derive from that implication. As now used, it draws on the long American tradition of favoring the "underdog," of asserting individual liberty in the face of tyranny, of risking retaliation in order to speak the truth. This is the way dissenters tend to look at themselves, and it is the way in which the media generally present them as well—as courageous and embattled individuals refusing to bow before a rigid authority.

However, the glamour of American Catholic dissent reveals itself as cosmetic only, once the truth is known—dissent in American Catholicism is no longer the province of courageous outsiders but is itself established. It challenges the Church not from the margins but through the Church's own central organs. Indeed, it is the official institutions of the Church which are now used to propagate dissent and, often enough, to repress orthodoxy. Almost unnoticed, a quiet revolution has occurred. Like all revolutions, it began simply with a demand for tolerance. Like most revolutions it ends in a new orthodoxy which enforces a conformity even more rigid than the old.

Perhaps the easiest way of seeing this is in the Catholic press. For years *Commonweal* magazine prided itself on being an independent, lay-edited journal. During the Council the *National Catholic Reporter* was started for the same purpose—to offer a voice in Catholic matters not controlled by the hierarchy. Both publications have been immensely influential. However, from the standpoint of the early 1980's, it is arguable that both are now redundant, since journals published under official Church auspices are now often just as hostile to authority as the legally-independent entities. The magazine which has most consistently questioned official doctrine, sparing almost nothing, has not been the lay-edited *Commonweal* but *U.S. Catholic,* published by the Claretian fathers. *America,* a Jesuit publication; *The St. Anthony Messenger,* published by the Franciscans; and the Paulists' *New Catholic World* have been only slightly more cautious. *Theological Studies,* also published by the Jesuits, has been the chief organ for advancing dissenting opinion on the scholarly level. As for newspapers, it is a conservative estimate that at least half of the diocesan papers in the country are quite open to dissent, giving it more space than they give to orthodoxy. For all practical purposes there no longer exists an official Catholic press in the sense of publications which faithfully convey only official positions. Catholics are likely to find the Church's teachings questioned not only in the secular press or the independent religious press but in those publications which come to them with the endorsement of their religious leaders (and which those leaders, often enough, require the laity to pay for whether or not they want to).

A representative sampling of dissent in the diocesan press could include the following:

• When the Vatican issued an official declaration reaffirming that women cannot be priests, a columnist for the Rochester diocesan paper, Father Henry Atwell, accused Paul VI of being "still a captive of advisors" and referred to the declaration as "a disastrous 'no.'" He also enjoined the

Vatican "to begin to learn honest and common sense rather than chattering on in its own involuted ecclesiastical and antiquated rhetoric."
• The Davenport (Iowa) *Messenger* strongly criticized the Vatican's investigation of dissenting theologians, claiming that the process is a scandal and that those who pay attention to theologians like Hans Kung, Charles Curran, and Edouard Schillebeeckx cannot understand why their theology should even be suspect.
• In *Westmont World* of the diocese of Helena (Mont.), a priest, Emmett O'Neill, savagely attacked the Vatican's Congregation for the Doctrine of the Faith and defended Hans Kung as one of the greatest men in the Church. (His article brought a brief rejoinder from the bishop of the diocese, an extremely rare occurrence in the diocesan press.)

Probably a majority of diocesan newspapers refrain from publishing explicit rejections of Church teaching. However, the cause of dissent is served—wittingly or unwittingly—with equal effectiveness by the handling of "news." Each weeks hundreds, possibly thousands of speeches are given in the United States under Catholic auspices. Only a handful are ever reported in the press. Those expressing dissenting opinions are by far the most likely to receive such attention.

Perhaps only a minority of Catholics read the religious press with any degree of care. However, this scarcely guarantees that they are immune from being propagandized against the Church's teachings, for with increasing frequency such propaganda is now brought to them by their own priests, those officially commissioned to teach and form them in their faith.
• A Murfreesboro (Tenn.) pastor, Joseph P. Breen, has published numerous attacks on Vatican policy. Insisting that the official teaching on contraception "must" be reversed, he has described the relationship between the American bishops and the Vatican as "similar to a son's relationship to his father—a father who is not very wise and compassionate, a father who does not listen very well and seemingly does not care to understand the needs and pains of the young son."
• A young woman in Los Angeles described pre-Cana conferences sponsored (and required) by the archdiocese, in which the instructor, Father Larry Bartsavich, told engaged couples the encyclical *Humanae Vitae* is a "non-issue" and that, while the Church teaches objectively that contraception is wrong, in fact it wants each couple to be "comfortable" with whatever method of family planning it has chosen. A divorced and remarried couple also spoke to the gathering, providing what was described as a "valuable perspective." The couple revealed, among other things, that they often miss Mass on Sunday because they have other things to do.
• When the Vatican reproved liturgical irregularities in the United States,

the pastor of a Brooklyn parish, Father James E. Goode, told the *New York Times* that he would ignore the document and told his parishioners, "Every one of you do what you want to do."

• Following Pope John Paul's visit to the United States, a Dayton pastor, Father J. W. Goetz, gave a speech at a Protestant seminary in which he warned that Catholics were in danger of betraying the Gospel by their admiration for the Pope. John Paul, he urged, should recognize the "distortions" inherent in his office and foreswear teaching in favor of "listening." (Goetz was also a professor at the Cincinnati archdiocesan seminary.)

• The radical feminist Gloria Steinem, who is militantly pro-abortion, was once invited to give the homily at Mass in a Minneapolis parish where the pastor, Father Harvey Egan, proclaimed to the congregation "Glory Be to God for Gloria" and Steinem smilingly accepted the adulation of the congregation on its way to communion. Egan was reproved by his archbishop but, although he agreed not to repeat the action, used the reproof as an occasion for one more attack on Church authority. He continued in his pastoral office.

• Following the official Vatican declaration that women cannot be priests, the priests' senate of the diocese of Richmond issued a formal challenge to the document, suggesting it was inconsistent with "our growing understanding of personhood in the Church."

• At the chapter meeting of the Immaculate Heart Sisters of Monroe (Mich.), all actions of the "Mass" except the Consecration itself were performed by nuns in liturgical vestments. A priest was kept inconspicuously in the rear and brought to the altar only to utter the actual words of institution.

• When the Benedictine order celebrated its 1500th anniversary with an international gathering in Minnesota, one of the principal speakers was a nun, Sister Joan Chittister, who used the occasion to condemn the Church for "sexism."

These examples convey the flavor of much of contemporary American religious life but scarcely tell the whole story. Even a superficial acquaintance with religious communities reveals that in many of them dissent has in effect become the new orthodoxy. Dissenting theology is taught in the colleges and seminaries operated by these communities, and men and women openly sympathetic to dissent are regularly elected or appointed to governing offices. Community members who speak boldly in favor of orthodox positions not uncommonly find themselves treated as deviants and their beliefs as divisive.

In addition, both individually and collectively, many professionals, who have been given official charge of particular areas of Church life, use their positions not to support official policy but to undermine it, and do so with impunity.

• At a workshop on homosexuality sponsored by the archdiocese of Milwaukee, a parish priest, Father James Arimond, told participants that sexual perversion merely means going against one's own sexual orientation. Thus for homosexuals to act in a heterosexual way would be a perversion, he asserted.

• When the Vatican authorized an official inquiry into American seminaries, the rector of the Cincinnati archdiocesan seminary, Msgr. John Breslin, told the press that "it could get ugly" if attempts were made to inquire into the orthodoxy of seminary faculty.

• A textbook example of the confusing ways in which authority is now exercised in the Church was the handling of a "report" on homosexuality issued by the San Francisco archdiocesan commission on peace and justice. The lengthy report defiantly justified homosexual behavior, bitterly criticized the Church for its past "injustices," and called on the archdiocese to throw its full resources into the struggle for "gay rights."

• Similar confusion occurred in Detroit early in 1983, when a Mercy nun, Sister Agnes Mary Mansour, was appointed to a state government post and announced that she would cooperate in administering state payments for abortions. At first Archbishop Edmund Szoka of Detroit told the press that he recognized her right to accept the office and affirmed that she did indeed have to obey the law relative to the public funding of abortion. He required merely that she publicly affirm her own acceptance of Catholic teaching on the question. He also suggested that those opposing her were exaggerating the importance of the issue. Two months later, however, in a strongly worded statement he told her to resign her position and characterized her stance as incompatible with Catholic doctrine.

Church bureaucrats in the United States now operate effectively under a style of what can be called "horizontal" rather than "vertical" accountability, meaning that they are not chiefly answerable to their nominal superiors (the bishops) nor to those they allegedly serve (the laity) but to each other. A bureaucrat's chief concern is to retain credibility with his peers, namely, other professionals. Whatever misgivings a bishop may have about particular policies are allayed when he is informed that the best current professional opinion favors those policies, even as unhappy lay people are silenced by telling them that they are ignorant and have no right to criticize professionals in the exercise of their duties. Thus the prevalent dissent found in national professional organizations, as well as among academic theologians, quickly communicates itself to diocesan bureaucrats, who are constantly alert for signals as to what current professional wisdom thinks is good or bad.

A key to the professionals' independence is their ability in effect to jam the broadcasts of the hierarchy, a tactic which is employed quite regularly with regard to the teaching of the Pope. When, for example, the

American bishops issued a Catechetical Directory designed to insure authentically Catholic catechisms, religious-education bureaucrats first complained bitterly about the document, then managed to get authorization to publish their own "commentary" on it, which effectively undercut everything in it they did not like. Not surprisingly, the directory was a dead letter from the day of its inception. (Typical of the way religious professionals often operate on the local level was an article by Robert Y. O'Brien, director of religious education for a parish in Rock Island (Ill.) who publicly attacked the Vatican document stipulating that children should go to confession before receiving first communion. O'Brien, a former Jesuit priest who was one of the first American theologians to deny the official teaching on birth control, lambasted the Vatican statement as theologically and psychologically deficient and strongly implied that children are incapable of committing sin.)

There are self-serving aspects to this, since professionals know that the advancement of their own careers depends on their being in harmony with prevailing opinion within the profession. A religious educator known to be "conservative" soon finds many potential jobs closed to him. (It is highly revealing that, week after week, the militantly dissenting *National Catholic Reporter* publishes numerous advertisements for religious-education directors, liturgical coordinators, members of "pastoral teams," etc. Orthodox newspapers like the *National Catholic Register* contain many fewer such notices. Obviously the advertisements are placed specifically in order to attract dissent-minded individuals.)

At least some Church professionals are aware that a power struggle is going on—essentially between themselves and the bishops—which they are winning. Often their strategy has been not to minimize conflict but to exacerbate it, to the point where bishops find themselves so overwhelmed by the magnitude of the problem that they abandon all efforts to control their own bureaucrats and clergy. (Thus a director of religious education in a Minnesota parish, Timothy J. Langley, has called for the systematic use of pressure tactics, such as the withholding of contributions, as a way of forcing the bishops to "share power.")

Despite dissenting opinions on a variety of topics, from birth control to women priests, there is an impression in the United States that there is at least one subject about which the Catholic Church still maintains undeviating solidity—abortion. In fact, however, this impression is mistaken. For if the Church has been in the forefront of the anti-abortion movement, this has been true only selectively. Few religious orders show any collective interest in the subject, for example. When they put forth lists of burning social issues, abortion rarely appears, and only stray individuals from within those communities have involved themselves in the anti-abortion movement or even spoken publicly on the subject. There are numerous parishes where the priests likewise show no interest in the subject and it has never been addressed from the pulpit. Whole dioceses are known for their lack of tangible support for the anti-abortion cause.

As yet, however, it is at least imprudent for clergy openly to support abortion (although women religious who have done so have not been called to account by their superiors). But certain Catholic leaders nonetheless signal their lack of commitment to the cause, signals which can only be interpreted, both by the Catholic laity and the larger public, as indicating that the Church does not take the issue as seriously as its official pronouncements suggest.

• In Utica (N.Y.) Msgr. John R. Madden, an official of the diocese of Syracuse, voted, as a member of a regional health commission, to allocate Federal funds to Planned Parenthood for the performance of abortions. When challenged, Msgr. Madden said that he had voted according to his conscience.

• The Association of Chicago Priests, an unofficial organization which includes many prominent Chicago clergy, gave an award to a notoriously pro-abortion physician. The award was presented at the archdiocesan seminary.

• The official newsletter of the diocese of San Bernardino (Cal.) quoted Bishop Phillip F. Straling as telling high-school students, "There are many shades of gray, things you personally must consider before you can say, 'yes, in God's plan abortion is right or wrong.' That's why it's important to make sure your conscience is giving you correct advice."

• A paid lobbyist for the National Abortion Rights League was invited by the diocese of Sacramento (Cal.) to speak at an officially sponsored conference on disarmament. After much criticism, the speaker voluntarily withdrew from the program. Bishop Francis Quinn then expressed regret over the cancellation because he said it gave the impression that the Church was imposing its views on others. (When asked whether the diocese would invite an official of the Ku Klux Klan to speak, Bishop Quinn said it would not, because the group's goals were clearly opposed to those of the Church.)

• When the Supreme Court issued its sweeping decision legalizing abortion in 1973, it was hailed in the most enthusiastic terms by a priest-lawyer, Father Raymond Decker, who called it "more Christian than its critics." Father Decker was subsequently appointed director of planning for the archdiocese of San Francisco.

For the most part American bishops are personally orthodox. The chief problem in many dioceses over the past ten years has been that the bishop's personal principles do not necessarily govern the policies of his diocese. However, the number of bishops openly at odds with official Church doctrine or policy has also been growing, and becoming more conspicuous.

Even seeming affirmations of authority are often made in so weak and tentative a way as to be scarcely convincing even to those who may already accept that authority. Thus Auxiliary Bishop Norbert Gaughan of Greensburg (Pa.), writing in *Our Sunday Visitor*, told readers that there have always been diverse theological voices in the Church and the present division is consequently nothing to be alarmed over. Asking where a principle of unity might be found, Bishop Gaughan had difficulty finding one but suggested that "Probably if you took a poll among Catholics, they might say John Paul II, seeing him as a unifier; this for the kind of person he is, as well as for the papal office." Although the Second Vatican Council strongly reaffirmed the authority of tradition in the Church, Bishop Gaughan concluded that "the past is only to give light to our vantage point of the present, as we determine where we want to go for the future."

On rare occasions when individual bishops have taken strong stands, the results have not been happy for them. The late Bishop Joseph V. Sullivan of Baton Rouge forbade Charles Curran to speak in his diocese and subsequently removed a Newman Club chaplain who had attempted to sponsor Curran's talk. Bishop Sullivan was met with a storm of criticism and abuse, including demands for his removal. Once he was actually called to Rome for questioning, although apparently exonerated. During his ordeal not a single bishop offered him any public support. A few other bishops have had similar experiences, albeit less severely. The lesson, apparently, has not been lost on others.

Some bishops seem in fact to relish the exercise of their authority almost in proportion to the degree that it offends the sensibilities of traditional Catholics. Thus in dioceses where many kinds of liturgical deviations occur, lay people know that any celebration of the Tridentine Mass is likely to bring the full wrath of the bishop down on the head of the celebrant. When the conservative newspaper *The Wanderer* published an article, with photographs, of a blatantly irregular liturgy, the late Archbishop Leo C. Byren of St. Paul-Minneapolis focused most of his anger on the newspaper, for causing a scandal, not on the offending priest.

Dissent has been a major organized force in American Catholicism at least since the issuance of *Humanae Vitae* in 1968. Yet since its first appearance the strategy of the bishops has been an odd one. It might have been supposed that, faced with a growing assault on major teachings and a measurable falling away of members, Church leaders would have encouraged the "hard core" Catholics—those loyal to the institution and its stated beliefs and prepared to make a stand on their behalf. From this solid base they could then have attempted to deal with the problem of infidelity. Instead the common policy has been to ignore and even to discourage those perceived as "conservative" while making increasingly strenuous (and counter-productive) efforts to woo dissenters. In the process Catholics have gotten used to thinking of the Church as divided into parties or factions, of which "conservatism" is merely one. The so-called conservatives are not, however, for the most part dissenters from the right—those who reject the new liturgy, for example. They are people who precisely affirm every official teaching, as articulated by the Second Vatican Council and by recent popes. By treating such people as merely a faction, and a troublesome one at that, American bishops sometimes give the impression that they regard all doctrine as merely the product of political conflict, their own duty that of splitting the difference between opposing factions.

Many American Catholics regularly experience, from official sources, direct attacks on their faith. Even those who do not have now experienced, for nearly two decades, the gradual erosion of that faith, as a rock is eroded by small but relentless drops of falling water. A tone of voice, a passing comment, a strategically situated smirk, a raised eyebrow are means by which those charged with upholding official teaching in fact contrive to undermine it.

If liturgy is at the heart of the Church's life, then liturgy has been one of the chief means by which this erosion has been accomplished. For liturgical deviation has been endemic to American Catholicism since the Council ended. This is true not only of gross and sensational violations (many of which have been tolerated by the authorities) but even more of small but consistent signs of disregard for official norms. Thus priests routinely make verbal emendations in the text of the Mass, to suit their own purposes. Long before American Catholics were authorized to receive communion in the hand, many did so anyway, often as a conscious act of defiance, one which their priests and sometimes their bishops countenanced. Girls are often used as altar servers despite specific prohibitions of the practice, and "extraordinary" ministers of the Eucharist are employed even when priests are readily available. Communion is routinely distributed in both species even though Vatican directives state that this is to be done only on special occasions.

If all of these matters are relatively small things which the Church could permit if it saw fit, it is also the case that the habitual flouting of law in small matters inculcates a similar disregard for what is important. In liturgy especially, the message American Catholics now receive is that Church laws are to be obeyed only to the extent that the individual sees fit to obey them.

Inevitably dissent tends to focus on a few "bottom line" issues which have immediate practical relevance. In the United States at present these are celibacy for the clergy, ordination for women (especially nuns), divorce and contraception for lay people. Dissent has become organized and entrenched because there are fanatical lobbying groups determined to change Church practice in each of these areas. Every question which arises is immediately evaluated in terms of its likely eventual effect on these issues. Hence a broadly based constituency for dissent has been created, whose various members strategically reinforce one another.

It would be shortsighted, however, to think that dissent focuses only on practical questions. Those who are determined to change the Church on these particular questions instinctively oppose any reaffirmation of teaching authority, in no matter what area, and any attempt to validate the Catholic tradition, since they know that ultimately such reaffirmations will redound against their own favored causes.

In addition, although present dissent tends to focus on questions which have a "bottom line," it would be naive not to realize that virtually all the teachings of the Church are in jeopardy. Among theologians dissent extends to the most profound and central doctrines of the faith. If these are now rarely attacked in public, it is only because they lack the practical dimension likely to attract broad support. Their time will come.

The fact that dissent is now promoted through official Church channels can no longer be doubted. Explanations as to why this is allowed to happen could range from simple confusion and timidity on the part of some Church leaders, through the mistaken idea that the flames should be allowed to burn themselves out, to undeniable active sympathy with dissenting positions on the part of an increasing number of bishops.

Although many surveys have established the growth of dissent among the Catholic laity since the time of the Council, there has been little effort to explain that growth. Dissenters themselves, for obvious propaganda reasons, like to assume that it is a spontaneous flowering, the result of conscientious people communing with their best selves before uttering a courageous *"non serviam."*

In fact dissent, like most attitudes towards life, is usually a learned response, the result of signals conveyed to the individual by the surrounding society.[1] The simple and startling truth is that most Catholics now learn dissent from the Church itself. Moreover, they also perceive, if they look closely, that those who aggressively uphold orthodoxy often find themselves isolated and relegated to the margins of the Church, even as dissenters and those in sympathy with them increasingly exercise the levers of power. Today's ecclesiastical careerists understand well how to cultivate the proper "open" image.

But cynical opportunism is not the main consideration. In most societies the majority of people are not intellectuals and have no principles to which they adhere tenaciously. They are moved essentially to accept the beliefs which the credible leaders of that society seem themselves to accept. In the Catholic Church those leaders increasingly shift the "moderate middle" leftwards, so that the sincere Catholic trying to do what the Church wants may come to think that what the Church now wants is the repudiation of past beliefs.

Most American Catholics are aware that the Pope himself affirms what they have always taken to be Catholic doctrine. If they take the trouble to read the decrees of the Second Vatican Council, they realize that that assembly did not authorize many of the things done in its name and that it even forbade some of them (for example, liturgical experimentation). If they pay little attention to what is happening in the Church in the United States, their own faith may remain relatively untroubled and they may remain in spiritual unity with the Church of the ages.

Paradoxically, those Catholics who do seek to be informed and alert are probably those most likely to be troubled, because they will inevitably become aware of the widening gap which separates the Church's official teachings, as articulated by pope and council, from what is actually being taught in the United States.

Such a dichotomy can only be frustrating, forcing the individual to be simultaneously responsive to two conflicting signals. For many, a rational solution to the dilemma is to assume that, while the Church must still formally reaffirm certain of its classical teachings, it no longer holds them and that this is the real message now being given the laity.

It is surely time for the leaders of American Catholicism to ask if this is really the message they want to send their people.

Notes
1. See for example Hitchcock, "The American Press and Birth Control: Preparing the Ground for Dissent," *Homiletic and Pastoral Review,* July, 1980, pp. 10-26.